Barbarians of Oil

Barbarians of Oil

How the World's Oil Addiction Threatens Global Prosperity and Four Investments to Protect Your Wealth

Sandy Franks
Sara Nunnally

WILEY

John Wiley & Sons, Inc.

Published by John Wiley & Sons, Inc., Hoboken, New Jersey.
Published simultaneously in Canada.

Wiley also publishes its books in a variety of electronic formats. Some content that appears in print may not be available in electronic books. For more information about Wiley products, visit our web site at www.wiley.com.

Library of Congress Cataloging-in-Publication Data:

Franks, Sandy.
    Barbarians of oil : how the world's oil addiction threatens global prosperity and four investments to protect your wealth / Sandy Franks, Sarah Nunnally.
        p.   cm.
    Includes index.
    ISBN 978-1-118-00182-0 (hardback); 978-1-18-08234-8 (ebk); 978-1-118-08273-7 (ebk); 978-1-118-08281-2 (ebk)
        1. Petroleum industry and trade.   2. Petroleum industry and trade—Environmental aspects.   3. Petroleum industry and trade—Political aspects.   4. Petroleum products—Prices.   5. Energy policy.   I. Nunnally, Sarah.   II. Title.
    HD9560.5.F73 2011
    338.2'7282—dc22
                                                                    2011004108

Printed in the United States of America

10 9 8 7 6 5 4 3 2 1

This book is dedicated to all Americans who envision a day when we are no longer the helpless victims of a barbaric oil industry that is blinded by dollar signs and driven by greed. The choices we make now and in the next few years will determine the energy future we hand down to our children and grandchildren. I hope we make the right choices.
—Sandy Franks

■ ■ ■

For my family . . . all of you.
—Sara Nunnally

Contents

Acknowledgments

I would like to thank Sara Nunnally, once again, for her continued hard work on this second book. She has proven herself a valuable researcher and writer. I hope we are able to continue this writing partnership for many more years.

I would like to also thank the many Taipan Publishing Group readers who wrote such wonderful congratulatory notes on our first book, *Barbarians of Wealth*.

I should again acknowledge members of the Taipan Publishing Group who have show their commitment and loyalty daily, including Jeanne Smith, Jeffrey Little, Amy Pflaum, Jen Cappe, Amanda Fowler, Emily Dobash, Adam English, Andy Snyder, Kelly Cunningham, Howie Ng, Joseph Hill, and so many others.

Of course, I want to thank my husband Mark, son Zachary, and daughter Rachael for their continued support. They keep me most grounded.

My list of acknowledgments will fill up several chapters; therefore, it is impossible to acknowledge everyone personally. But I thank everyone who provided tremendous support to me through this wonderful endeavor.

—SANDY FRANKS

■ ■ ■

After writing *Barbarians of Wealth*, I was supremely content with the privilege of seeing my name in print with Sandy Franks, who has offered me countless opportunities and a wealth of encouragement. But when Sandy asked me to write *Barbarians of Oil* with her, I cannot voice how grateful I was to have this second opportunity. It has truly been an honor and a joy, and this achievement is only due to her faith and trust in me. I am thankful for the challenge and the support.

—SARA NUNNALLY

Preface

When Sara Nunnally and I wrote our previous book *Barbarians of Wealth*, we concentrated our research efforts on Wall Street financial institutions, the banking industry, financial political lobbying groups, and the Federal Reserve. Little did we know that our search would lead us to the oil industry and the writing of a second book, *Barbarians of Oil*. Oil is a dirty business, literally and figuratively.

There's not a politician alive who could deal cleanly with the oil industry, and the greasy fingerprints lead all the way to the White House. Oil has created multi-billion dollar businesses—the largest corporations on the planet. Money often changes people's behavior, sometimes for the good, sometimes for the bad. Most often money is the oil industry's only allegiance.

As we looked deeper into industry, we saw how often money influenced the decisions related to this country's energy policies. For example, as secretary of defense in 1991, Cheney gave millions of dollars worth of contracts to Halliburton, and when he left office in 1995, he served as CEO of Halliburton until he was chosen by George Bush to be the vice presidential candidate. Cheney resigned his post, but as vice president, he again gave hundreds of millions of dollars worth of contracts (sometimes illegally) to Halliburton during the Gulf War in 2003. If that wasn't enough, Halliburton was overcharging the government by as much as $61 million for transporting fuel from Kuwait to Iraq. Bunnatine Greenhouse, a whistle-blower in the Army Corps of Engineers brought the incident to the public's attention. She was fired for doing so.

But the dirty deeds continued. For example, in 2005, Bush asked Vice President Cheney to head up a special task force to help develop the country's energy policies. Many of the components in the energy bill Bush signed were recommendations made by the task force. In addition to tax breaks for the industry, the task force did away with exemptions that the industry considered were not beneficial. In reality, the task force was a meeting of the big oil companies including ExxonMobil, ConocoPhillips, Shell, BP, and Chevron to enact regulations that favored their industry.

When information about the task force became public, many of the company officials denied they had attended any type of meetings. However, the *Washington Post* had obtained documents that showed that on April 17, the task force met with Royal Dutch / Shell's chairman, Sir Mark Moody-Stuart and two other oil company executives. The group met again on March 22, this time with BP regional president Bob Malone, chief economist Peter Davies, and company employees Graham Barr and Deb Beaubien.

The truth is, for the past century, oil has ruled the world. It has thrust small, often impoverished countries into the political arena. It has caused wars that cost countries not only millions in dollars but in precious lives. Consider the explosion of the *Deepwater Horizon* drilling rig in the Gulf of Mexico. Eleven people lost their lives, needlessly. Researcher and veteran engineer Dr. Robert Bea, who has a long history of investigating disasters, says the accident was the result of a series of mistakes and flawed decisions, which included safety. Bea writes, "This disaster was preventable, had existing progressive guidelines and practice been followed." Researchers estimate 4.4 million barrels of oil spilled into the Gulf of Mexico. It is considered the worst marine oil spill in history.

But let's not forget previous oil-related tragedies. Consider the 2005 explosion at BP's Texas refinery. In that incident 15 employees died and 170 were seriously injured when the unit responsible for making jet fuel burst into flames. Evidence showed that BP was too focused on reducing costs on maintenance at its refineries. Reduced costs mean higher profits. BP was always chasing a dollar. Brent Coon, the lawyer who sued BP on behalf of the families of the workers who died or were injured, said the company's safety record in the United States was poor.

Speaking of poor safety records, Amnesty International, a leading human rights group, says Shell Oil has been covering up catastrophic oil spills in the Niger Delta by blaming them on sabotage by local people. Shell claims that 98 percent of its oil spills in the area are caused by vandalism. But environmental watchdogs dispute the claims entirely. They say the leaks come from rusted and corroded pipelines and storage tanks, derelict pumping stations, and old wellheads. Environmentalists call the area the global capital of oil pollution. We call the oil companies' actions barbaric.

Our quest for oil has led us on a path of destruction with barbarians leading the charge. Our addiction has started wars that corrupt politicians use to snatch oil reserves and make a handful of oil companies rich. The sad fact is that we could greatly reduce our dependency on oil starting today. There are alternative energy sources available to us right now—viable technologies that have proven themselves to be powerful innovations that could truly break our addiction to oil. Countries like Brazil and the small island of Samsø have shown us what is possible.

Whether we use these technologies to wean ourselves from oil, is simply a matter of choice.

SANDY FRANKS
Baltimore, MD
January 2011

Part One

HISTORY OF OIL

Part One

Chapter 1

Emergence of
Black Gold

O il. No other resource dominates the world economy more than oil. Wars have been fought for control of it. Lives have been lost over it. Fortunes made from it.

Although oil has been around for thousands of years, the industry itself has only existed for 150 years. You can trace the birth of the industry back to when Edwin Drake and William Smith dug the first oil well in the small town of Titusville, Pennsylvania. Their single well produced roughly 15 to 25 barrels of oil a day, enough to meet demand. Today, OPEC estimates worldwide demand for oil at 86.56 million barrels a day.[1]

Although we can give credit to Drake and Smith for setting in motion a California style gold rush for oil, the black substance has seeped from the ground for almost 4,000 years. In fact scientists suggest the earliest evidence of petroleum can be traced back to the ancient city of Nineveh in Iraq, which served as the capital of Assyrian Empire from 705 to 612 B.C.[2] The difference between then and now is that oil wasn't "actively" sought after. In other words, there were no oil wells or drilling equipment to pump massive amounts of it out of holes in the ground.

But this doesn't mean people didn't use oil. They did, but they used what naturally seeped out of the ground. You see, petroleum is a fossil that is found in sediment below the surface. Petroleum means rock oil. The word itself comes from Latin; petra which means rock, and oleum which means oil.[3]

Petroleum is found mainly in fine grain sedimentary rocks such as shale, but not just any type of shale rock. It's found only in rocks that are older than 2 million years. Oil is trapped in tiny holes in the rocks along with gas and water. Depending on how porous the rock is, and if the holes are capped, the oil remains trapped inside the rock. Oil can only seep out of holes in rocks that are not capped. Because of the makeup of gas, it leaks out from the rocks into the atmosphere while the oil seeps to the surface.

The oil that naturally oozes from the ground was used by civilizations from all over the world that date back thousands of years. For example, evidence shows that naturally seeping petroleum was used in the construction of buildings in the ancient city of Babylon, where it was taken from local springs. In ancient Sicily, petroleum was used in lamps, referred to as "Sicilian oil." Petroleum (or pitch) is even found as an ingredient used by Egyptians in the embalming process.[4] Ancient Egyptians used petroleum in the construction of pyramids. Boats that traveled along the Euphrates were constructed with woven reeds and sealed with pitch. Herodotus, the Greek historian, speaks of oil wells found on the ancient island of Zante, 500 years before Christ. In the Old Testament, petroleum is referred to as the slime used in the construction of the Tower of Babel. Christian Crusaders put the liquid into boxes that they set afire and then catapulted at their enemies. To defend castles, boiling oil was poured on soldiers climbing up the castle walls.

References to petroleum in Japan can be found in the ancient Japanese history called Kokushiriyaku that tells of burning water found in ancient Echigo around 615 A.D.[5] Believe it or not, petroleum was used as a medicine before it was used for lighting lamps or powering automobiles. Marco Polo talks about petroleum being used as an ointment applied to camels with mange.

Jonas Hanway in his *Historical Account of the British Trade over the Caspian Sea* describes how Russians drank the thinner petroleum as a medicine and a cordial.[6] In Bavaria, around 1436, petroleum gathered from the Tegera Sea was used as a medical ointment, which locals called St. Quirinus' oil. In the United States, the earliest mention of petroleum was around 1627 by a French missionary who described the substance found in the area later known as New York.[7] American Indians such as the Seneca tribes used petroleum not only for war paint on their faces but for medicinal purposes as well. In 1849, S.M. Kier bottled distilled petroleum and sold it as "American Oil" with instructions to be used for external purposes only.[8] Petroleum was a popular remedy for treating arthritis and rheumatism. William Fowler wrote, oil in the 1860s was hailed as "a disinfectant, a vermin killer, hair oil, boot grease, and a cure for kidney stones."[9]

Oil Domination

Crude oil or petroleum varies from a somewhat colorless liquid to green, brown, and almost black. It also varies in density from water-like to almost solid. Depending on where it is found, petroleum is made up mainly of hydrocarbons with small amounts of oxygen, nitrogen, and sulphur. Refineries convert the crude oil into many substances including petroleum gas used to heat homes, plastics, gasoline, kerosene, gas oil (or diesel), lubricating oil, coke, asphalt, and tar, to name a few.

A survey by the American Petroleum Institute of major refineries showed that refinery plants are capable of refining petroleum into over 2,000 different products.[10] In reality, the refining process isn't complicated. It involves heating the oil to various temperatures and separating the vapors. After it is heated, the oil is sent to a distillation column operating under immense pressure. The columns can separate about 25,000 barrels of oil a day. The temperature the oil is heated to determines the end product. See Table 1.1.

Table 1.1 Crude Oil Refining Temperatures

Product Desired	Boiling Point of Oil (Celsius)
Gases	below 30
Gasoline	30–210
Naphtha	100–200
Kerosene and Jet Fuel	150–250
Diesel	160–400

SOURCE: U.S. Government, U.S. Energy Information.

Today there are 717 refineries in the world. The world's largest refinery is located in Ras Tanura, Saudi Arabia and is owned and operated by Saudi Aramco. The world's first oil refinery was constructed in Ploesti, Romania in 1856.[11]

In the United States, which is the country with the greatest number of refineries, there are 148 oil refinery plants.[12] Compare that to the scant 15 refineries that existed in 1860. Called "tea kettle" stills, they could process roughly up to 100 barrels a day. Refineries today can process as much as 17 million barrels a day.

With the building of refineries came pipelines to carry the oil. Before pipelines, oil was transported in railcars mainly controlled by Standard Oil, which owned the Union Tank Line. In fact, John D. Rockefeller springboarded to wealth and fame by controlling the transportation of oil. In later chapters, you'll discover more about Rockefeller's secret weapon for domination of the oil industry.

Pipelines slowly took over railways as the main vehicle for transporting oil to refineries. In 1942 and 1943, engineers built what was then the world's longest crude oil pipeline dubbed "The Big Inch," which spanned 1,254 miles and moved crude from Texas oil fields to East Coast refineries.[13] Now, well over 180,000 miles of pipeline transport oil all across the United States.[14]

Today more than 40 percent of the world's oil travels through pipelines. Pipelines can be found in the following countries:

- Indonesia
- Thailand
- Singapore
- Afghanistan

- Bangladesh
- India
- Myanmar
- Pakistan
- China
- Japan
- South Korea
- Australia
- New Zealand

Of course, you'll find refineries in the Middle East including the following countries:

- Iran
- Iraq
- Israel
- Jordan
- Kuwait
- Oman
- Qatar
- Saudi Arabia
- Syria
- United Arab Emirates
- Lebanon

The list of countries with refineries goes on and on, including Azerbaijan, Belarus, Estonia, Georgia, Russia, Tajikistan, Turkmenistan, Ukraine, Uzbekistan, Bulgaria, Greece, Hungary, Romania, Serbia, France, Germany, Belgium, Italy, Switzerland, Norway, Denmark, Spain, Portugal, Panama, Ireland, United Kingdom, Argentina, Brazil, Chile, Costa Rica, Colombia, Canada, Mexico and the United States.

The oil we consume doesn't just travel through pipelines; it's also carried across oceans on huge tankers. There are approximately 4,000 tankers equipped for carrying millions of barrels of oil. Experts say more than 100 million tons of oil is shipped each day by tankers.[15] In 1873, the Palmers Shipbuilding & Iron Company assembled the first steam-driven oil tanker, named the Vaderland. The first modern oil tanker, the Zoroaster, was designed and built in 1878 by Ludvig Nobel of Sweden.[16]

Needless to say the oil industry has seen significant growth over the past 150 years. In 1920, 95 million tons of oil was produced annually around the world. The number skyrocketed to 500 million tons by 1950. By 1960, that number had doubled to a billion tons. By the early part of 1990, average annual production reached 3 billion tons.[17] The truth is, the petroleum business has grown to become one of the largest in the world. In the first quarter of 2010, the petroleum business (which includes both oil and natural gas production and petroleum refining and marketing) saw net income increase more than 1,000 percent from the same time period of 2009.[18]

Today, 50 percent of the largest corporations in the world are oil companies.[19] They include the following:

- ExxonMobil
- Royal Dutch Shell
- British Petroleum
- Chevron
- Conoco Phillips

Who are the largest producers of oil? The top 10 aren't U.S. companies and include the following:

- Saudi Arabian Oil Company
- National Iranian Oil Company
- Qatar General Petroleum Corporation
- Iraq National Oil Company
- Petroleos de Venezuela S.A.
- Abu Dhabi National Oil Company
- Kiwait Petroleum Corporation
- Nigerian National Petroleum Corporation
- National Oil Company, Libya
- Sonatrach, Algeria[20]

But it wasn't always this way.

For the first part of the twentieth century, the United States was king of the oil industry. In 1949 to 1950, we were producing about

5.4 million barrels of oil a day and responsible for 52 percent of the world's crude oil production.[21] And our consumption was right in line with what we produced—about 5.6 million barrels a day. We imported about 6 percent of the rest of the oil we needed. As for exporting oil, until the end of the 1940s, the United States and Latin America provided Europe's oil.[22]

We continued on this path of oil domination until about 1970, when the U.S. oil production reached its peak. At the time, the United States produced about 9.6 million barrels a day, which was about 43 percent of all world oil production. We were consuming 13.8 million barrels of oil a day. It's also around this time that petroleum-related imports totaled 6.3 million barrels per day. And that number grew each year until October 1973, when the Arab members of the Organization of Petroleum Exporting Countries (OPEC) embargoed the sale of oil to the United States, and petroleum imports fell for two years. This led to long lines at gas stations, worldwide energy crisis, and elevated oil prices. This is also led to the creation a U.S. Strategic Petroleum Reserve. Today, the U.S. Strategic Petroleum Reserve is the largest stockpile of government-owned emergency crude oil in the world with 727 million barrels.[23] The 1973 oil embargo led to a decline in U.S. consumption of petroleum to16 million barrels per day. By 1975, it slowly began to rise again, until 1979 when the Iranian revolution caused oil prices to rise and consumption to decline.

A marked decline in petroleum consumption in the United States continued into the early 1980s. By 1983, the United States was consuming a low of 15.2 million barrels per day, a decline of almost 20 percent from the record consumption level of 18.9 million barrels per day in 1978. By 1994, the trend of importing more oil continued and has stayed that way ever since. By 2004, the United States was producing only about 13 percent of world oil production. Yet our consumption of oil has grown to 21 million barrels of oil a day or roughly 25 percent of world production.[24] Today, imported oil accounts for 53 percent of all U.S. oil consumption.[25] OPEC now accounts for 43 percent of world oil production.[26] Oddly enough, OPEC consumes very little of its own oil. Most of the oil we consume is used for gasoline. Of every 10 barrels of petroleum consumed in the United States more than 4 barrels are consumed in the form of gasoline. The transportation sector alone accounted for two-thirds of all petroleum used in the United States.[27]

For the Love of Oil

Until the mass production of the automobile, gasoline was considered a wasteful by-product of petroleum refining. Today, the United States uses more than 320 million gallons of gasoline per day, or about 3,700 gallons per second, every single day.[28]

Our thirst for gasoline is greater than South America, Europe, Africa, and Asia combined.[29] You could say our addiction to gasoline is self-induced. After all, we love our cars. But it was a slow burning love until 1908, the year that Henry Ford debuted his Model T. Up until then, cars were bought by rich and wealthy people. And the process took months because each car was built by hand.

The first production Model T Ford was assembled at the Piquette Avenue Plant in Detroit on October 1, 1908. By 1914, the moving assembly line enabled Henry Ford to produce far more cars than any other company.[30] For $825, a customer could buy a Ford Model T, billed as a reliable and easy to drive car. In his first year of production, Henry Ford sold over 10,000 cars. The number of cars on the nation's highways jumped from 8,000 to 125,000.

From 1920 to 1930, the number of cars owned by Americans jumped from 8.1 to 26.7 million.[31] Standard Oil of California opened the first gas filling station in 1907.[32] Today there are 244 million cars on U.S. highways. And there are roughly 93,374 gas stations at which you can stop and "fill'er up."[33]

Over the years, the cost to fill the tank has steady increased. In 1950, the cost of a gallon of regular gasoline was 26.8 cents. Gas prices rose about a cent every year until 1957. From 1957 to 1969, prices went up, but only by a total of 3.8 cents from 31 cents per gallon to 34.8 cents per gallon. However, by 1974, the cost had risen to 53.2 cents per gallon.[34] The cost rose dramatically because of the Clean Air Act, which forced gas stations and automakers to meet an octane standard of 87, which limited lead to 4.0 grams per gallon. But the more significant reason for the price increase was the Oil Embargo by OPEC.

Gas continued to increase slowly but reached a new high in 2004, when it was selling for almost $2 a gallon. Just one year later, in 2005, prices skyrocketed to $3.36 dollars per gallon. The price jumped up and down over the next few years. In 2009, the average price of a gallon of gasoline was $2.83. In 2010, the average price hovered around $2.73.[35]

Although the oil industry was forced to meet certain octane standards, the U.S. auto industry hasn't been as progressive in increasing fuel efficiency as industries in other countries. Did you know that in Europe, the average vehicle gets more than 32 miles to the gallon while in the United States a similar-size car gets only 22 miles to the gallon? European automakers have better fuel efficiency standards. Had we pushed for better standards, even as little as increasing fuel efficiency by 0.4 miles per year, the United States could have saved about 3.3 million barrels of oil a day.[36]

The lack of fuel efficiency is not the only problem; it's also the lack of reliable, dependable public transportation. On average, new highway construction projects receive up to 80 percent of federal funding, whereas new public transportation projects receive just 50 percent. In 2009, the proposed U.S. budget would cut $202 million from transit spending and transfer another $3.2 billion from funds dedicated to transit to other sectors. Our own Treasury Department estimates that the Highway Trust Fund and the Mass Transit Account will both face massive deficits in 2009 and 2010 because of these budget cuts.[37]

Of course, gas isn't the only factor that drives our oil consumption through the roof. Other uses include jet fuel, chemicals to make plastic, lubricants, greases, pharmaceuticals, pesticides, clothing, cosmetics such as lipstick, nylon, agricultural fertilizer, and other household products such as petroleum jelly, shampoos, and even DVDs.

The Rise of OPEC

Unfortunately when the United States moved from being its own supplier of petroleum to being dependent on foreign oil, control of the industry went to OPEC, the Organization for Petroleum Exporting Countries. OPEC was created at the Baghdad Conference in Iraq in

September 1960. The founding members of the organization were Iran, Iraq, Kuwait, Saudi Arabia, and Venezuela. OPEC's share of world production was only 28 percent in 1960. By 1970, this figure would rise to 41 percent. Today, the demand for OPEC crude oil is estimated at 28.7 million barrels per day. OPEC expects that number to reach 28.9 million barrels a day in 2011.[38]

Before OPEC, seven companies, often referred to as the Seven Sisters, dominated the oil industry:[39]

1. Exxon (was Standard Oil of New Jersey, then Esso)
2. Royal Dutch Shell (formerly Royal Dutch Petroleum)
3. British Petroleum (Anglo Iranian)
4. Chevron (formerly Standard Oil of California)
5. Texaco
6. Gulf Oil
7. Mobil (Standard Oil of New York)

Together, they were responsible for 76 percent of the world's oil production. Because the Seven Sisters were made up of American and European companies, they controlled the market. And control it they did. These seven companies controlled every aspect of oil production and distribution including extraction, refining, and transportation. As oil production increased so too did the earnings and profits of the Seven Sisters.

Here's why. Because the Seven Sisters had access to low production costs, they agreed to set the price of a barrel of oil to match the higher prices being sought by other companies. In 1950, a barrel of oil, which by the way holds 42 gallons, sold for $1.75. But costs for the Seven Sisters were extremely low, roughly $.10 for production, on top of their royalty fees of $.50. This left them with a nice profit on each barrel sold. Over time and through mergers and acquisitions the Seven Sisters have become four: ExxonMobil, Chevron-Texaco, BP (acquired Amoco and Arco), and Royal Dutch Shell. Although they are not quite the OPEC cartel, they still are huge players in the domination of the oil industry.

In later chapters of this book, you'll learn more about these companies and how they've hoodwinked us into believing that alternative sources of fuel aren't possible or in our best interest. You'll also learn how they've destroyed the environment and, in some cases, a way of life for those living in oil-rich areas. You'll also learn how OPEC has manipulated oil prices and brainwashed us into thinking oil shortages are imminent. You'll come to understand why we call oil companies and OPEC Barbarians of Oil.

Chapter 2

Drilling for Oil

As a little boy, Abraham Gesner dreamed of becoming a doctor. When he was old enough to attend college, with his parents' blessing, Abraham moved to London to study medicine at St. Bartholomew's hospital. Abraham received his medical degree in 1824, and returned to his home country of Nova Scotia, Canada. For 14 years Abraham practiced his beloved profession. But it turns out medicine alone wasn't enough to satisfy his curious young mind.

Abraham soon turned his attention to scientific studies. And the scientific field that interested him the most was geology.[1] In fact he was appointed by the legislature of British North America to study the area's geological resources. Over time, Dr. Gesner built up quite a collection of the area's mineral resources and began experimenting with them, including illuminants from hydrocarbons. That lead to his discovery of kerosene, the name he gave to the waxy oil-like substance produced from asphalt.

Demand for kerosene grew quickly because using it cost about $10 a year to heat homes versus $120 a year using whale oil.[2] With the popularity of his discovery, Gesner founded the North American Kerosene Gas Company. His company was producing more than 5,000 gallons of kerosene a day. Just five years later, the kerosene industry was in full bloom, generating $5 million a year.

Although kerosene can be extracted from coal, oil shale, and wood, it is primarily derived from refined petroleum. This created a "petroleum gold rush." Many men were eager to make their fortunes with this new commodity that was heating homes across the country. One of those men was Edwin Drake.

Oil Seeps from the Ground

At first, Edwin Drake hadn't thought much about the kerosene business, nor how it might impact his future. At least not until he read an article in a newspaper that told the story of dogs being covered in oil that was seeping out the ground in Titusville, Pennsylvania, a small lumber town of about 150 people.[3]

The story piqued his interest. Drake was curious to see for himself where and how the oil seeped from the ground. So he traveled by train to Titusville, the town mentioned in the article. When Drake arrived in the small town, to his amazement, he found oil did indeed ooze from the ground. The oil seeped out of a small stream the locals referred to as Oil Creek.

Although Drake was not a geologist, scientist, or engineer, he knew immediately the black gold coming out of the ground in Titusville could make him a wealthy man. It would make his partners rich as well. You see, Drake had been hired by the Pennsylvania Rock Oil Company to investigate whether it was possible to get much larger quantities of oil from the Titusville area than the very small amounts that naturally oozed from the ground.

George H. Bissell, a New York attorney, and James Townsend, a businessman from New Haven, had already formed the Pennsylvania Rock Oil Company. Initially the two were hoping to secure enough oil from the Titusville find to sell it to kerosene companies. Bissell asked Drake to join him and Townsend. Drake was eager and determined to dig for oil. But unlike Bissell, Drake didn't share the enthusiasm Bissell had for the amount of money the three could make drilling for oil. But the black substance he found in Titusville fascinated Drake. So he agreed and put up $200 of his own money to buy shares of the Pennsylvania Rock Oil Company.

Drake was also a practical man. He knew he couldn't dig for oil by himself. So he contacted William Smith, a local salt well driver and blacksmith, and asked him to help dig for oil. In 1857, Drake and Smith began digging where oil was oozing out from a freshwater spring. But the water proved more difficult than they imagined, slowing their progress and draining the firm's resource. Bissell and Townsend were losing faith that Drake could succeed. Even the local folks thought the two men were crazy and called the project Drake's Folly.

Smith proposed they switch tactics and drill for the oil by hammering a pipe down into the ground. Drake agreed, and they moved forward on the new plan. They began hammering the pipe down the hole but eventually struck bedrock. Smith, however, was certain his idea would work and modified it slightly by driving a hollow cast-iron pipe into the ground. Then he drilled inside the pipe. At 69 feet, the two struck oil. The well was producing about 40 barrels a day. The firm was selling it for $.50 a gallon or $20 a barrel.[4]

News spread of Drake and Smith's discovery. By late 1859, the Titusville oil boom had begun. Hundreds of wells were being set up in Oil Creek Valley. The small town of Titusville grew into a city of 10,000 people. Machine and boiler shops, barrel factories, and oil refineries sprang up to support the new oil boom.

Of Titusville's 220 square mile area, only about 67 miles contained oil shale.[5] So drillers move out to other areas of Pennsylvania that most thought contained large deposits of oil. By 1884, drilling for oil had become a state-wide obsession. Oil wells could be found throughout Pennsylvania. Oil City, located 20 miles south of Titusville, grew just as quickly. So did other towns including Petroleum Center and Pithole.

Oil was being discovered in other areas of Pennsylvania. For example in 1874, the Bradford oil field, which was roughly 100,000 acres, was open for drilling. Later, the Bradford field would become the largest producing oil fields in Pennsylvania. Unlike the Titusville find, the oil in this area was about 1,000 feet below ground.[6] But that didn't stop the speculators from drilling.

By August of 1875, six wells were up and running which were owned by the Foster Oil Company, Fagundas and Company, Butts and Company, Crooker, Olmstead and Company, and Jackson and Walker. In fact it was the Butts well that proved how much oil was lying dormant under the ground. In 1875, the well was producing about 25,000 barrels of oil a day. However, just one year later, the well was producing as much as 382,000 barrels of oil. In 1876 it skyrocketed to an incredible 1,468,000 barrels of oil a day.[7] In 1881, this field was producing 83 percent of the USA's total oil output. Since its discovery in 1871, Bradford field has produced more than half a billion barrels of oil.[8]

Pennsylvania oil wells dominated the industry. Its naturally oil rich grounds would make the men who hunted it rich. But not everyone enjoyed its spoils. Drake, who was instrumental in igniting the oil rush, didn't believe there was more oil to tap. Instead of staying with Bissell's Pennsylvania Rock Oil Company, he took a position in Titusville as the Justice of Peace.[9] A few years later, he moved to New York. Whatever money he made from oil, he spent. He was penniless and in frail health. A friend ran into Drake and was shocked to see his condition. No one suspected the founding father of the oil industry was so badly off.

A meeting of Titusville oilmen was called. They handed the man who had opened the door to their fortunes $4,300. Later the state of Pennsylvania publicly recognized Drake as the man who spearheaded the industry and passed an act that guaranteed him $1,500 a year.[10] When he died, the money passed on to his widow.

The Great Texas Gusher

The "sour wells" that run through Beaumont Texas were mixed with sulphur and minerals and often served as a medical treatment for local residents. Just south of the town, in Jefferson County, was a huge hill the locals called Round Mound, Big Hill or Spindletop. The mound was about one half mile in diameter and jutted out of the ground to a height of 12 feet. The mound was formed from a giant underground dome of salt. As the salt slowly moved toward the surface, it pushed the surrounding ground upward, into a hill or dome-like shape. For fun, children in Beaumont would wander out to the local mound and set fire to the bubbles that oozed in the surrounding black swamp. Yet it never occurred to the Beaumont residents the hill and nearby swamps contained oil.

But Patillo Higgins knew differently. Patillo, known as Bud, was born in Beaumont on 1863. His parents were on their way to California to join the gold rush. But when Civil War broke out, they decided to wait it out and settled in the small town of Beaumont.

Patillo was no stranger to the black marsh of his hometown. He had played near the mound and marsh as child. As a young adult, Patillo worked in the timber industry as a cutter, and later as a log man on the river. He moved from the timber industry to the brick making business. That's how he became acquainted with oil.

While working for a brick-making firm, Patillo had the opportunity to travel to Titusville, Pennsylvania, where bricks were manufactured. One of the key ingredients was petroleum. As he saw the oil stockpiled in the factory, he realized the black substance in the marsh that surrounded the mound back home was mixed with oil.

Returning back to Beaumont, Patillo was eager to drill for oil. He only needed a few people to back him financially. Unfortunately he found little support. Locals laughed at the notion of drilling for oil. But he wasn't about to give up. After all he had seen the oil in Titusville. He knew it was the centerpiece to a fortune in oil. To his pleasant surprise, Patillo managed to secure a few backers and began drilling for oil in 1893. But his oil fortune wouldn't be so forthcoming. After six months of drilling, Patillo hadn't struck "pay dirt." His wells were dry. But he wasn't going to call it quits, not yet anyway. He did, however, need more financing to continue.

For that, he turned to mineral geologist Anthony F. Lucas who was already in the area. Unlike Patillo, Lucas was on the hunt for sulphur, not oil. Mining and supplying sulphur was already a healthy industry in the early 1890s. And it was mined in much the same way as oil. Holes were drilled to find the sulphur deposits. Then steam was forced down into the deposits to melt the sulphur, which was forced to the surface with air pressure.

Lucas was an Austrian immigrant who had graduated from the mining and engineering school in Graz, Austria. After visiting an uncle who had immigrated to Michigan, Lucas decided to leave the Navy, stay in America, and become a citizen. He changed his name from Luchichs to Lucas.[11] He stayed in the States looking for sulphur deposits. He traveled throughout the lower half of the country and had made his way to the Texas area when he met up with Patillo.

Anthony agreed with Patillo that the area did indeed contain deposits of oil. Furthermore, Anthony agreed to provide the additional financing Patillo needed to continue his operation. But in doing so, Lucas arranged the deal so that he would receive a 90-percent interest in the operation, for funding the search, and Higgins would only be given a 10-percent interest.[12]

Patillo agreed to the terms. The first thing the two men did was sign a lease-purchase agreement for a 663-acre tract on top of the mound. Then they immediately began drilling for oil. However, no luck would come to the two men. Their hard work returned only more dry wells. Patillo couldn't take it any longer. He gave up on the hunt for oil, leaving Lucas on his own. Lucas was still eager to continue, except he had no more money to finance the operation. Before he could hunt for oil, he needed to hunt for financing. He turned to the Pittsburgh wildcatting firm, Guffey and Galey. Both men, James Guffey and John Galey, had worked as agents for the Titusville oil supply firm of Gibbs & Sterrett. The two had been successful backers of several other oil wells in Pennsylvania and Kansas. One of their more successful wells, named the Matthews, produced about 40 to 50 barrels an hour. At its peak, the well produced over 10,000 barrels a day.[13]

Guffey and Galey formed a partnership with Lucas, the J.M. Guffey Co. In 1900, Lucas once again began drilling for oil. On January 10, 1901, his drill had reached a depth of 1,000 feet. This was one of his deepest holes, and Lucas wasn't sure how long the drill could hold out before breaking. As the drill began to sputter, Lucas was certain the bit was ripping apart. Then sludge oozed from the hole. And seconds later, oil was gushing as high as 200 feet in the air.[14] Lucas wasn't prepared for this type of gusher. The oil spewed for 10 full days until Lucas figured out how to cap it. Lucas named his well, Lucas No. 1. The well pumped 70,000 barrels of oil a day.[15]

Lucas No. 1 marked the beginning of the Texas oil boom. Within days, Beaumont's population grew from 9,000 to 15,000. Oil speculators came from everywhere. Suddenly farmers were getting rich as they sold their barren cattle pastures to oilmen. Businesses in the area were blossoming. There weren't enough hotel rooms to house the newcomers. People were sleeping in the streets. It was a mania few had seen or experienced.

Lucas and his backers continued to find oil in Spindletop, drilling two more wells. Both were extremely successful finds. Guffey bought out the interests of both Lucas and Galey in May 1901 for $766,000. The news of gushers in Beaumont infuriated Patillo Higgins. He filed a $4 million lawsuit against Lucas. However, the suit was settled for a lot less money than Patillo had hoped. But Spindletop would prove to be one of American's greatest oil finds. It was producing as much as 340,000 barrels of oil an acre. Unfortunately the fame and fortune found at Spindletop wouldn't last. Within six years, most of the wells would be dry. All the oil that could be pumped from the field was extracted at breakneck speed.

Hollywood Oil Fields

We can't talk about American oil fields without mentioning California. By 1865 oil wells were sprouting up in California's Central Valley area, just east of San Francisco. Locals referred to the area as Mattole because it sat near the Mattole River.

Although the first successful well in the area was drilled by the Union Mattole Company, the first mention of oil seeping from ground is found in a newspaper article in the Humboldt Times in 1859.[16] The article mentions that the nearby petroleum springs were seeping rock oil near Bear River.

Just as in other areas of the country where oil was found naturally seeping from the ground, native Indians of the area were using the seeping oil for medicinal purposes. Then oil mania swept the country. But after oil fever took hold, the land was flush with oilmen seeking

their fortunes. An article from the Pacific Oil Reporter tells the story
of the hunt for oil in California:

> The great oil excitement that followed the discovery at Oil
> City, Pa, and the ones that followed in that Eastern region
> naturally soon drew attention to the many oil indications in
> California, and as naturally set fire to every seepage from Santa
> Barbara to Humboldt.[17]

The initial attempts to find oil in the area weren't successful. More
dry holes were dug than gushers found. The excitement slowly faded.
Then in 1864, attention on oil drilling was reignited when the entire
area was divided into districts. Of those districts, one square mile was
owned by the Union Mattole Company. It later became the most
successful well in that area.

But the big oil producers weren't in the Mattole area at all. The
greatest producing fields could be found in Los Angeles. But they
wouldn't be discovered until 1892. That's when Edward Doheny discovered the black gold that lay beneath the city's streets. Doheny was a
smart man. He had graduated from high school at the top of his class.
As a teenager, Edward secured a job with the U.S. Geological Survey
Department. Most of the time, his job sent him traveling the country
surveying areas. Some say Doheny, who would later become known
as the Emperor of Oil, learned the art of negotiating not from his oil
deals, but in his early years when he bought and sold horses. The story
goes he purchased 92 horses at a government auction for $5.35 each
and sold them later for a $2,000 profit.[18]

At age 18, Doheny quit his job to prospect for gold. He hooked
up with a gold mining expedition that was hunting for gold in the
hills of South Dakota. Having no luck in the area, Doheny traveled to
Arizona, which was part of the New Mexico territory. Not striking
it rich in Arizona, Doheny picked up his belongings once again and
moved to the Black Range mountain area.

Although he didn't exactly strike it rich, he did manage to mine
enough gold to remain in the area, which became known as Kingston.
"Fifty dollars a year saw me through, with game plentiful and salt
cheap," writes Doheny.[19] However, by 1889, Kingston had become

nothing more than hard labor for Doheny. His mine wasn't producing enough gold to properly provide for his family. He was forced to
take a job just to put food on the table. He moved his family to Silver
City, New Mexico, where he received a notary commission and began
processing mining claims.

But Doheny longed to strike the mother lode. Partly because of
his wife's continued ill health, Doheny moved his family to California,
where he would take up prospecting for gold again. But he had also
heard that one of his prospecting friends, Charles Canfield, whom he
had met in Kingston, had also moved to California. Doheny figured
the two might be able to work together.

Doheny had spent 20 years of his life looking for that one vein of
gold that would fulfill his dreams of striking it rich. He never found
it. But you shouldn't feel too badly for Doheny. Instead he found a
"black gold" that would give him the title of one of the richest men
in America. According to legends, Edward was in downtown Los
Angeles when he noticed a cart carrying a black substance. Curious
as to what it was and where it came from, he asked the driver of the
cart to tell him about it. The driver told him it came from an area just
outside the city, known as Westlake Park. In the book, *Dark Side of
Fortune: Triumph and Scandal in the Life of Oil Tycoon Edward L. Doheny*,
author Margaret Davis recounts Doheny's story of his stumble upon
the black substance:

> My heart beat fast. I have found gold and I have found silver
> and I have found lead, but this ugly looking substance . . . was
> the key to something more valuable than any or all of these
> substances.[20]

With $400, Doheny partnered with his friend Canfield and the
two leased a three-lot parcel of land that was already bubbling with
the black ooze. The two men immediately started digging for oil.
With no drilling equipment, they dug the well by hand. On April 20,
1892 at 60 feet down, they uncovered oil soaked shale.

Doheny finally realized his dream of striking the mother lode.
He and Canfield became extremely rich men. They led the development of Southern California's major oil fields. Within two years of

the find, 81 wells were producing oil in the area bounded. By 1897, the number of wells increased to 500. By 1900, the number of wells totaled 1,000. All told, Doheny's wells produced 350,000 barrels of oil.[21]

But Doheny is probably more famous not for his discovery of oil in Los Angeles, but a political scandal known as the Teapot Dome Scandal. Doheny was accused, along with Harry Sinclair, another oilman, of bribing Secretary of the Interior for leasing and drilling rights to public land areas that had been previously designated as the navy's emergency fuel supply reserves. Because of having that special designation, the fields weren't meant for development. The three naval oil fields included Elk Hills and Buena Vista Hills in California and Teapot Dome in Wyoming.

The Teapot Dome oil field received its name because of a rock resembling a teapot that was located above the oil-bearing land. At the time, many politicians and private oil interests had opposed restrictions placed on the oil fields suggesting that the reserves were unnecessary and that American oil companies could provide enough oil for the U.S. Navy. One of those opposed to the restrictions was the Secretary of the Interior, Albert B. Fall. He had managed to convince the Secretary of the Navy, Edwin Denby, to turn the control of the oil fields over to him. Interestingly, the Secretary of the Interior happened to be a very good friend of Doheny, who he had met in his early mining days. Of course, we all know that having friends in high places pays off. And this was the case with Doheny, who managed to convince Interior Secretary Fall to lease two of the reserve areas to his company.

But sometimes these types of "back door" deals can come back to haunt you. And so it did with Fall. Initially Fall had "brushed" the incident off as a matter of national security and kept the details secret. Some say his lavish lifestyle indicated that an investigation should take place. That's exactly what happened. In 1924, a Senate investigation found that Fall had received as much as $400,000 from both men.[22] Fall called the money "gifts." Doheny explained the money was a more like a loan, from one rich man to another.

Nonetheless, the investigation involved countless congressional inquiries, hearings, and testimony. Doheny's son was accused of delivery the bribe money to Fall. Worst of all, that same son was murdered by a family confidant, Hugh Plunkett. In 1927 the Supreme Court ruled that the oil leases had been corruptly obtained and invalidated the Elk Hills lease in February of that year and the Teapot lease in October of the same year. In 1929 Albert Fall was found guilty of bribery and fined $100,000.[23] In 1931, he was sent to prison, the first cabinet official to suffer such fate. Harry Sinclair refused to cooperate with investigators and was charged with contempt. However, he received a short sentence after being found guilty of tampering with the jury.

In 1930, Edward Doheny was acquitted of bribery charges. Although Doheny walked away unscathed, the scandal rocked President Harding's reputation because Albert Fall, a close friend of Doheny's, was also a good friend of President Harding's. David H. Stratton, author of *Tempest Over Teapot Dome: The Story of Albert F. Fall* details the scandal. In his preface Stratton says,

> Drawing on the expansive historical freedom, I have included many events and forces in Fall's life that may seem to have little relevance to his guilt or innocence for his oil sins.[24]

Oil sins. Stratton couldn't have penned better words to describe the corruption you'll discover in later chapters of this book from propaganda oil shortages to price manipulation.

Oil has become a major part of our global economy since it was discovered by Colonel Drake 150 years ago. However, not only has it become a major part of the U.S. economy, it now dominates every aspect of the world economy. Oil is big business. Unfortunately, big business often breeds contempt and fraudulent behavior. The oil industry is not immune. Contempt and fraud have destroyed lives and environments all in the name of oil. And this is the very reason we associate the industry with barbarians.

Chapter 3

The Struggle to Survive

George Bissell didn't intend to become an oilman. He spent most of the early years of his professional career as a teacher. He was a professor of languages at Norwich University in Vermont.

George was lucky enough to be educated in military schools and earned his degree from Dartmouth College. To help pay for his education, George worked as a freelance writer for magazines and other print publications and sometimes managed to travel the country working as a reporter for newspapers.

In 1846, he was elected Superintendent of Public Schools in New Orleans.[1] Unfortunately Bissell's health began to decline, along with his hearing, and in 1853 he moved back north. Upon his return, George decided to visit an old college professor at Dartmouth College. During the visit, George noticed a bottle filled with a dark substance sitting on the professor's desk. As it turned out, the substance was petroleum collected from Oil City, Pennsylvania. The professor had been asked to analyze the petroleum.

Bissell was instantly curious and wanted to know more about the dark, goopy substance. So he asked his friend and business partner J. C. Eveleth to travel to Pennsylvania to see firsthand just how much there was of the black substance. When Eveleth confirmed that petroleum could be found in the area, Bissell's intentions were to mass-produce enough of it to fill the needs of the medical industry. Yes, that's right, the medical industry. As noted in earlier chapters, petroleum was often used as a medicinal treatment long before it was known as an illuminant for lamps or to heat homes.

With confirmation of petroleum in Pennsylvania, Bissell formed the Pennsylvania Rock Oil Company.[2] However, the first few years were less than desirable for Bissell and his new company. He couldn't produce enough of the petroleum to make the venture worthwhile. But he wasn't ready to throw in the towel and shut down his newly formed company. So he sent a sample to a former colleague and chemist at Yale University, Professor Benjamin Silliman, wondering if the petroleum could be used for purposes other than medical.[3] The professor wrote up his findings in a report entitled, "Report on the Rock Oil, or Petroleum, from Venango Co., Pennsylvania."[4] In Silliman's report, he concluded that if the petroleum were refined, it could be used for a wide array of products. That was enough for Bissell. Hoping to mine the oil in larger quantities, Bissell hired Colonel Edwin Drake to be his "man in the field," drilling for oil.

On August 27, 1859, Drake struck oil. Unlike Lucas' oil well in Beaumont Texas, Drake's well didn't gush 200 feet up in the air. But it didn't have to gush high into the air to give birth to the oil industry. Bissell and Drake showed the world that it was the amount of oil and how fast it could be produced that mattered. Their determination to mass-produce oil spurred one of the greatest "gold rushes" this country has ever seen or experienced. Their findings ignited an oil frenzy.

Oil Frenzy

In the infant years of the industry, scientific knowledge of petroleum was limited. Most experts thought that crude oil could only be accessed in the lowlands along riverbeds or mountain range areas, because most of the large deposits of oil were usually located at the base of mountain ranges. That's why the initial hunt for oil took place mainly on the East Coast. During that time, most of the oil discoveries were made near the Allegheany Mountains. However, over time, oil exploration moved to areas such as Kentucky, Ohio, Illinois, and Indiana. These discoveries changed the industry's perspective on where oil could be found, and that change lead to discoveries in Texas and California.

Every time oil was discovered, it ignited an oil mania. Money-hungry oilmen hustled and bustled to drill as much oil as their equipment could handle. Oftentimes the wells came up dry, because no technology existed that could pinpoint where the oil lay underground. So the wells were drilled randomly and oftentimes close to one another. The landscape became littered with oil derricks.

A derrick is an upright stationary platform designed to hold a large pole, which repeatedly beats the earth until a hole is formed in the ground. See Figure 3.1.

In Triumph Hill, an oil rich area in Titusville, Pennsylvania, 100 oil derricks were constructed. From the drilling of the first well in 1859 to 1903, 211,573 wells were drilled in the U.S. Of that number, 69,819 (or one-third) were dry wells.[5] From the wells that were

Figure 3.1 Oil Derricks
SOURCE: www.fotosearch.com.

successful, 1,080,800,000 barrels of oil were produced in the United States. The average price of a barrel of oil during the early years was around $3.00. That puts the value of the early oil industry at around $3.2 billion.[6]

By 1865 the state of Pennsylvania alone was selling $17 million worth of the petroleum. Five years later, of the $19.3 million in total petroleum sales, 94 percent came from Pennsylvania.[7] However, no oil could be drilled until two important items were worked out: the right to extract the oil and ownership.

When Drake or Lucas realized there was oil in a certain area, they first negotiated for the rights to extract the oil with the person who owned the land. Most of the time lease agreements were negotiated where the landowner would agree to lease the land to the oil company for drilling purposes. Those were called mineral leases. A mineral lease is a contractual agreement between the owner of a mineral estate (known as the lessor), and another party such as an oil and gas company (the lessee). The lease gives an oil or gas company the right to explore for and develop the oil and gas deposits in the area described in the lease.

Oil and gas can be leased separately to different parties. Not only that, but different deposits of the same minerals can also be leased or sold separately. In many states the mineral estate may be separate from the surface (real) estate. Many leases were modeled after one of the first oil leases, that of J. D. Angier and Francis Brewer in 1853. Dr. Francis Brewer was a Vermont physician and native of Titusville, Pennsylvania. Like many locals, Dr. Brewer knew oil existed in the area. In anticipation of becoming an oil millionaire, Brewer formed Brewer, Watson and Company.

Dr. Brewer hired J. D. Angier, a local man, to drill for oil. Angier had already been skimming oil from the springs and selling it as medicine. Before any work began, Dr. Brewer drew up a contact that both men signed. In fact, Dr. Brewer is credited with creating the first formal oil contract. The lease designated that J. D. Angier would be responsible for maintaining the oil spring as well as finding other oil springs. In return, Mr. Angier would receive one half of the proceeds. The lease was signed on the Fourth of July between J.D. Angier and Brewer, Watson and Company. The contract spelled out the terms:

Agreed this 4th day of July, 1853, with J.D. Angier of Cherrytree township, Venango county, Pa., that he shall repair up and keep in good order the old oil spring on land in said Cherrytree township, or dig and make new springs, and the expense to be deducted out of the proceeds of the oil, and the balance if any, to be equally divided, the one-half to J.D. Angier. . . .[8]

Unfortunately Mr. Angier's efforts to dig new springs were in vain. The ditches and pits he painstakingly dug by hand never produced enough oil to make the enterprise profitable. After a few months of digging for oil by hand, the efforts were abandoned. But the agreement Angier and Brewer became the industry standard.

From Here to There

As more men rushed in to get a piece of the new American fortune being sought from oil, the industry experienced dramatic periods of boom and bust. Newer discoveries overwhelmed demand. Oil prices fell from $10 a barrel in January 1861 to 10¢ a barrel in December 1861. Prices rose again and were up to $7.25 a barrel by September 1863. However, by 1867, prices dropped to $2.40 a barrel.[9] Some oil experts say that the industry didn't stabilize until more reliable ways of transporting the oil were figured out. Once the oil was pulled from the ground, it had to be transported to the refineries where it was turned into useable products.

Just as Pennsylvania is credited with the country's first oil well, the state also deserves credit for being the first to figure out how to reliably and efficiently transport oil. In many ways, that creation came out of necessity. Railroads hadn't yet reached the small, remote area of Titusville, which was located near Oil Creek. Titusville was so remote that stagecoaches only passed through the area about twice a week.[10]

Using small flatboats was the most common method of transporting oil in those early days. The barrels were loaded onto flatboats and then floated down the creek to a pond freshet.[11] A pond freshet is an artificially created swell of water. At certain points along the creek, manmade dams were built that caused the water to dam up. When the water reached a certain level, the dams were released, and the flatboats floated freely with the rush of the current.

Simple in premise, this method wasn't without disaster. Flatboats often collided with one another because neither their direction nor speed could be controlled. According to one estimate, only three out of five survived the trip down the river.[12] In fact one of the first recorded oil disasters occurred in 1864 when hundreds of flatboats collided. Roughly 20,000 to 30,000 barrels of oil spilled out into the creek.[13] Once the flatboats reached the Alleheany River, the barrels were then loaded onto barges that traveled to the refineries in Pittsburgh.

But floating oil down the river wasn't the only way it was transported. Drillers hired men to haul the barrels from the derricks straight to the refineries or to the barges. These men were known as teamsters. The teamsters stacked the barrels in wagons drawn by horses. It was hard work, and hauling the oil wasn't easy as the terrain encompassed dense forests as well as hills and valleys. When it rained, the dirt paths that served as roads turned to mud, making them almost impassable. Charles Whiteshot, author of *The Oil-Well Driller: A History of the World's Greatest Enterprise, the Oil Industry*, describes the mud as deep and indescribably disgusting. The muddy roads made Oil Creek famous. Whiteshot writes,

> Oil Creek Mud attained a fame in the earlier and subsequent years that will be fresh in the memory of those who saw and were compelled to wade through it. Teamsters and horsemen swore both loud and deep at it.[14]

Initially the teamsters charged $1 a barrel. But as more oil was drilled from the ground, the teamsters upped their price to $5 a barrel.[15] The teamsters charged more to move a barrel of oil five miles by horse than the entire rail freight charge from Pennsylvania to New York City.[16]

Of course, this boom in oil created a boom for the teamsters. At one point there were roughly 6,000 teamsters in the area hauling barrels of oil for the oil drillers.[17] The teamsters had their own oil transportation network, which required that they build barns to buy fresh horses on a regular basis, house the horses, buy feed, and hire blacksmiths. Often their rates were determined by weather, road conditions, and the amount of oil they were asked to carry.

They were a tough group. If the drillers tried to circumvent the teamsters by using other people to haul the oil, they would fight back with a vengeance, often violently. No matter how hard they fought to remain the only source of transportation for the oil producers; technology would eventually emerge as the winner. Railroads and pipelines could transport the oil faster and cheaper.

Big Engines, More Oil

Living in Wales, Samuel Homfray watched in amazement as a horse pulled a wagon along a set of rails. Homray was mesmerized and wanted to imitate what he had just witnessed. So Homfray, already familiar with steam engines, asked his friend Richard Trevithick to build a steam engine that could run on rails.

In 1804, Homfray introduced Europe and the world to the first steam engine capable of carrying passengers.[18] But it could also carry goods, supplies, and merchandise. That's what attracted the attention of a group of American businessmen who went to Europe to learn more about the steam engine they had heard so much about. These men knew that building railroads back home in the United States could transform the country's outdated transportation methods of canals and horse drawn carts.

They were right. Not only did railroads transform traditional transportation methods, but they also helped catapult the oil industry into one of the fastest growing industries. The first railroad to reach Oil Creek was the Oil Creek Railroad in 1862. The railroad was chartered in 1860 and ran until 1868 when it was merged with another line. The railroad was considered a "short line" in that its sole purpose was to transport oil. The line ran seven miles from Corry, Pennsylvania to Petroleum Center.

The first set of rail lines reached Titusville in 1862. From there, lines were laid to other oil-producing fields including Miller's Farm in 1863 and Shaffer Farm in 1864. The railroad cars were capable of hauling hundreds of barrels of oil. Eventually the railroads were able to haul as much as 30,000 barrels of oil in a single month.[19] Although this was much more than the teamsters could haul, the producers soon found limitations to using railroad cars.

The oil was transported in wooden barrels on flats or converted stock cars. The wooden barrels often leaked, and the railroads made the leaks worse as the barrels rocked back and forth on the flatbeds. The railroads had to make frequent stops, which caused the oil to slosh about, often spill out over the edges of the barrels. Even though transporting oil by railroads was cheaper than using teamsters and much more efficient, oil producers soon became wary of using the rails because of the amount of oil that was lost on the lines.

In 1865, two brothers, Amos and James Densmore, invented the Densmore tank car, which were made of pine blanks banded together with iron. The tank could hold as much as 1,700 gallons of oil.[20] The brothers tested their invention in September, and it proved successful with hardly a single drop of oil spilled. One year later, on April 10, 1866 they patented their invention. Now the Densmore tank car was available to all rail lines to haul oil. And haul they did. It cost $170 less to ship 80 barrels of oil from Titusville to New York in a tank car than in individual barrels.[21]

As with most inventions, the Densmore tank was copied and improved upon. Wooden plank tanks were replaced with metal tanks. Boiler type tanks were created that could easily carry 80 to 100 barrels each. As suddenly as it had started, the Densmore's tank car business went bust. A new "kid on the block" would take the industry by storm and build one of the biggest oil empires the country would ever know—John D. Rockefeller and his Standard Oil Company. In fact by 1888, Rockefeller owned or controlled some 5,600 of the 6,100 tank cars in service.[22]

In later chapters of this book, you'll learn more about Rockefeller's billion-dollar monopoly on the oil industry. For now, we'll focus attention on how pipelines further revolutionized the industry.

Built for Oil

In his book, *Growing Up in the Oil Patch*, John Schmidt recalls that the teamsters' lobby group was so powerful that the Pennsylvania

Legislature refused to grant charters to pipeline companies.[23] Two attempts were made and each time refused.

But J. L. Hutchinson wouldn't wait for a charter to test out his idea. Hutchinson, inventor of the rotary pump, deserves full credit for the first attempt to transport oil in pipelines. The line was laid from the Sherman well to the railroad terminal located at Miller's farm. The distance was approximately three miles.[24] The weak point in the pipeline was the joints, where the two lines were joined together. Unfortunately, Hutchinson couldn't figure out how to prevent oil from leaking at the joints. It was such a problem, and so much oil leaked at the joints that the pipeline was deemed a failure.

Of course the teamsters weren't happy with the idea of pipelines transporting oil and taking business away from them. As more and more pipelines were built, they would often resort to sabotage including damaging the pipelines. Sometimes they threatened oil producers with violence. But remember, the oilmen are not only a barbaric group, but ingenious as well. Any interruptions in their operations meant less money to line their pockets. They weren't about to let a group of teamsters stop them from making money.

The man who eventually solved the problem of leakage at the joints was Samuel Van Syckle. Van Syckle had moved from New Jersey to Titusville to become an oilman. The move paid off as he struck oil at the Pithole field. Van Syckle was already paying as much as $1,500 a day to have his barrels of oil hauled out by the teamsters.[25] Somewhat of an inventor and determined to reduce his transportation costs, he spent a good portion of his time experimenting with oil pipelines.

In 1865 he built a pipeline from Pithole to Miller's Farm, a distance of about five miles. To solve the problems of oil leaks, Van Syckle welded the joints together. To overcome the damage that he knew the teamsters would inflict, Van Syckle buried the pipeline underground, about two feet deep. But those weren't the only obstacles his pipeline faced. The rest were geographical. One portion of the pipeline climbed 600 feet up a hill.[26] Most people didn't think the line would work, especially considering the height of the hill. Van Syckle turned the pipeline on and the oil began to flow. To everyone's surprise, but not Van Syckle's, the oil made it the entire distance without leaking.

Naturally, the teamsters were less than thrilled and immediately rallied forces to dig up the pipelines. To protect his line, Van Syckle hired armed men and recruited help from the local sheriff's office to guard the pipeline. The men were positioned at certain points along the five-mile route. When the teamsters converged on the buried pipeline, the sheriff and the armed men were there to defend the lines. The teamsters fought hard but were often arrested and hauled off to jail by the sheriff. It was too much for them. Eventually conflicts with the teamsters ended and the oil producers won out.

Shortly after the success of Van Syckle's pipeline came that of Henry Harley's pipeline. Harley, a civil engineer, constructed a pipeline that ran from Benninghoff run to Shaffer farm. Harley also built the first pipeline that ran straight out to the seaboard. Other companies followed in Van Syckle's and Harley's footsteps. By 1877, 10 different pipelines were constructed. It was almost overwhelming as lines ran in every direction, zigzagging across the landscape.

A pipeline war broke out in which companies began undercutting prices to the point that some companies would lose money on the deals they made with the producers, all in an attempt to control the market. The situation continued to worsen until Captain J. J. Vandergriff formed the United Pipeline Association. The association was incorporated in 1874 and consisted of several local pipelines including Oil City, Karns, Grant, Antwerp, Union, and Clarion.[27] The association worked, and oil flowed from the wells through the pipelines to refineries. The oilmen overcame all the obstacles that held them back, and were now free to dig for oil.

Their quest would take them all over the world. Oil would become a billion-dollar industry. It would create world empires and spur personal fortunes as yet unseen. And oil would become the world's most coveted commodity.

Chapter 4

Birth of an Industry

Samuel Kier was the son of Irish immigrants Thomas and Elizabeth Martin Kier. Samuel was born in the small town of Saltsburg, Pennsylvania. Kier's childhood was ordinary by all accounts, and he attended the local school in Saltsburg with his friends.

At about the age of 21, Kier moved to Pittsburgh where he found a job with a local freight express company. He did quite well with the freight company, working his way up to the much-coveted position of partner. Kier stayed with the company until it went under during the Panic of 1837, which wiped out many businesses. But that failure didn't weaken Kier's budding entrepreneurial spirit.

Kier began to dabble in a variety of business ventures including operating canal boats that carried coal between Pittsburgh and Philadelphia with his partner, James Buchanan, who would later become president of the United States. But once again, Kier's business would encounter difficult times, especially as railroads began transporting good and merchandise, including coal. Suddenly his canal boats became obsolete. So Kier reorganized his company and, yet again, ventured into different industries. He took up brick manufacturing, coal mining, steel making, and even got involved in the lumber business.

One of the businesses he found most interesting was his small, but growing pharmaceutical business. He had one medicine: petroleum, or rock oil. Although Kier was already familiar with rock oil from his father's salt wells in Tarentum, Allegheny County, where oil regularly oozed out of the wells, he had no idea it could be used for medicinal purposes. That's because Kier and his father saw the black substance as a nuisance and dumped much of it into the Allegheny River. What they couldn't dump, they burned. *The Derrick's Handbook of Petroleum: A Complete Chronological and Statistical Review* says Kier dumped as much as two to three barrels of petroleum in the river.[1]

Western Pennsylvania had large underground salt wells, which local people mined for the salt. In fact Pennsylvania had been a major supplier of salt since 1790. The salt well owners would dig holes several hundred feet deep and drop a metal weight down the shaft. The sheer weight of the metal object would crush the rock-like formations, releasing the salt. Along with salt, petroleum would be released and ooze to the surface. Salt well owners often tossed the oozing petroleum in the river. For them, it was simply a by-product of salt wells and served no useful purpose. Kier felt the same way until his wife's doctor prescribed rock oil as a medical treatment for her consumption. He instantly recognized it as the same oil-like substance that he tossed in the river. His entrepreneurial instincts took over and Kier began bottling petroleum as a special medicine to treat various illnesses including gout, coughs, sprains and bruises.[2] Kier put the petroleum into 8-ounce bottles and sold them for 50 cents each.[3] Luckily for Kier, the petroleum that oozed out of the wells on his father's land provided a natural supply of ingredient for his new pharmaceutical business.

Kier sold his rock oil medicine using what was then considered a common method for selling such ointments. He used agents who traveled from town to town in vividly decorated wagons pulled by horses. These traveling medicine men touted the bottled petroleum as a cure-all for all kinds of everyday ailments.

In addition to traveling salesmen, Kier also advertised his medicine local flyers that he circulated in nearby towns. An example of

Kier's sales flyer can be found in the book, *The Derrick's Handbook of Petroleum: A Complete Chronological and Statistical Review*:

Kier's. Petroleum or Rock Oil, Celebrated for Its Wonderful Curative Powers. A Natural Remedy! Procured from a Well in Alleghany County, Pa., Four Hundred Feet Below the Earth's Surface. Put Up and Sold By Samuel M. Kier, 363 Liberty Street, Pittsburg, Pa. The beautiful balm, from Nature's secret spring, the bloom of health and life to man will bring; As from her depths the magic fluid flows; To calm our sufferings and assuage our woes.

Although Kier was able to sell his rock oil in good quantities, many customers often complained of its odor. Kier wondered if the medicine would be more desirable if he could distill the petroleum into a less offensive smelling substance.

Kier sent a sample of his rock oil to James Curtis Booth, Professor of Chemistry Applied to the Arts at the University of Pennsylvania, Philadelphia.[4] Booth recommended Kier find a way to distill the petroleum, and so Kier began experimenting with distillation methods. One method he tried involved filling a large metal kettle with petroleum, closing off the top with a cover, and then boiling it over an open fire. Boiling the petroleum gave Kier the idea that his refined crude could be used in lamps. In addition to selling petroleum as a medicine, Kier now began to sell the petroleum as lamp oil. Kier even invented a lamp that reduced the odor that came from the burning petroleum.

Demand for this new lamp burning oil increased, and Kier built a bigger "refining" kettle that was capable of producing as much as six barrels of refined petroleum a day.[5] Kier's business grew and he set up a refinery known as the Radiant Oil Works, located outside the city of Pittsburg. The refinery continued to operate up to the time of Kier's death in 1874.

Little known to most people, Kier paved the way for the petroleum industry to emerge as a major economic force, not just here in the United States, but the world over. It was Kier's discovery of refining petroleum that gave birth to the industry.

Boom and Bust

The oil refinery industry flourished from 1867 to 1869. Anyone could start an oil business, because the barriers to entry were low. You didn't need much money to get started. In the early days, land leases were cheap and plentiful, and little expertise or labor were needed to dig a well. And while new firms were "digging in," older, more established oil companies were rapidly expanding. But these easy entry and expansion points created one of the biggest problems with the industry: booms and busts. Because so many companies were able to get into an already crowded market place, the industry often experienced rapid and continual periods of booms and busts.

One of the more pivotal moments in this cycle of boom and bust was near the end of 1869, when crude oil prices declined 19 percent, ripping into the profits the refineries were enjoying.[6] To survive, the refineries could do one of three things: (1) remain independent; (2) join an agency; or (3) form a closely held firm that could monopolize the industry. The third option gave rise to the Standard Oil Company of Ohio. That firm would eventually grow to control 90 percent of the oil refinery market. But before Rockefeller monopolized the industry, it continued with its boom and busts periods. In fact after the bust period of 1869, the industry would enjoy an upswing. By the end of the 1880s, the American refining industry, which employed over 11,000 men, was generating over $85 million annually.[7]

The petroleum and refining industry continued to grow. From 1907 to 1910, the U.S. industry experienced exceptional growth as follows: In 1907, U.S. output of petroleum reached 166,000,000 barrels; in 1908, output climbed to 178,000,000; in 1909, output soared to 183,170,974; and by 1910, it was recorded at 209,556,048 barrels.[8]

If you compare these numbers to world output, you get a sense of how important oil was for the United States. For example, in 1900 worldwide crude oil production stood at nearly 150 million barrels. Illuminants served as the primary product of the oil industry. However, by 1925, according to Answers.com, worldwide oil production stood at 1 billion barrels and doubled 15 years later.[9]

Industrialized countries became the largest consumers of oil, and the United States would emerge as the biggest consumer of oil. Even to this day, petroleum is the single largest source of energy used in the United States. We use *two times* more petroleum than either coal or natural gas and *four times* more than nuclear power or renewable energy sources. About 90 percent of the products refined from petroleum are fuels such as gasoline, aviation fuels, distillate and residual oil, liquefied petroleum gas (LPG), coke, and kerosene. In fact two-thirds of all oil use in the United States is for transportation. In most of the rest of the world, oil is more commonly used for space heating and power generation than for transportation. And of our transportation demands, gasoline accounts for two-thirds of total oil used.[10]

A Motor Carriage with a Gasoline Engine

The emergence of the automobile (or horseless carriage) almost immediately revolutionized the petroleum industry. Gasoline, which is a by-product of the petroleum refining process, now had a useful purpose.

Before the automobile, gasoline was allowed to "weather" (evaporate into the atmosphere) naturally. Sometimes the refineries would burn the gasoline in pits or dump it in nearby waterways. Most refining of petroleum was for kerosene, which was used for lighting or heating homes. No one considered that the gasoline by-product of refining could be used to fuel automobiles. But this isn't to say that many centuries before the automobile was actually invented, people hadn't envisioned some form of a horseless carriage. For example, in 1335 Guido da Vigevano drew plans for a wind-driven vehicle.

Nicholas Joseph Cugnot designed the first vehicle to move under its own power. It was powered by steam, which relied on coal that was fed into a furnace that heated water to its boiling point. The steam drove a plunger through a cylinder. The plunger was attached to a rod that was connected to a wheel, which would move with the rod. Cugnot turned his design over to M. Brezin, who built the first model in 1769. It consisted of a carriage with three wheels and the steam engine mounted on the front. Because of its tremendous weight, the steam-powered carriage could only move about 100 feet an hour. A second model was built one year later, which was much lighter, at 8,000 pounds, and had a top speed of two miles per hour.[11]

The earlier models of the automobile were so heavy they were impractical for everyday use. Railroads became the most convenient model of travel. Self-powered vehicles would remain a fantasy until Jean-Joseph Etienne Lenoir invented the internal combustion engine. Between 1838 and 1860 many combustion engines were designed but never built. And the few that were built, failed.[12]

Unlike the steam-powered engine, which relied on boiling water, internal combustion engines used the energy released from high-pressure gases such as hydrogen, gunpowder, stove gas, kerosene, and oxygen. Perhaps Lenoir's experience as an engineer enabled him to finally figure out how to build a reliable internal combustion engine. Lenoir converted a steam engine into one that was fueled by stove gas. He patented his engine in 1860. It was a huge success, and Lenoir sold about 400 engines in five years.[13]

Lenoir tinkered with his engine until he found a way to use a separate mechanism to compress the gas before combustion occurred. The new engine supplied enough power to drive a three-wheeled carriage 12 miles. But it was a slow journey. The trip took a full eleven hours to complete.[14] Encouraged by Lenoir's success, Alphonse Beau de Rocha, a self-taught civil engineer, figured how to compress the gas in the same cylinder in which it was burned. Although he never built his design, he received a patent on January 16, 1862.[15]

Work on self-powered cars continued with Austrian engineer Siegfried Marcus building one that ran on a one-cylinder engine. He named his car the *Strassenwagen*. It had approximately a ¾-horse power engine, with wooden wheels. The car's brake system was made up of wooden blocks, which pressed against its iron rims.[16]

Nikolaus Otto and Eugen Langen improved on Marcus and Lenoir's engines, by creating one that worked off four cylinders. The two founded an engine factory in Germany and built 5,000 engines. They hired Wilhelm Maybach and Gottlieb Daimler to work in the factory as automobile engineers. But it would only be temporary for Maybach and Daimler. Unhappy with Otto's direction for his factory, the two engineers quit and began collaborating on their own engine design. They used Alphonse Beau de Rochas idea of compressing the gas in the same cylinder.

In 1865, the two engineers created a gasoline-powered engine and fit it on a stagecoach, which sat on a frame that had four wheels. Their invention is the basis of today's modern automobile. In 1890 Daimler founded the Daimler Motor Car Company. In 1901, Maybach designed the Mercedes model automobile. But Maybach didn't stay in the automobile business.[17] He chose instead to develop aircraft engines.

In 1926, Daimler merged his automobile company with that of German engineer Karl Benz, who had been independently working on an internal combustion engine of his own. In fact, Benz received the first patent for a fuel-powered car. After the merger, the cars the two produced were branded Mercedes-Benz automobiles. Europe was now the main manufacturer of automobiles. It would take several more years for the automobile to sweep the American market and change the face of the petroleum industry.

The Petroleum Market Advances

The truth is it would take Henry Ford 10 years to revolutionize the automobile industry. On June 4, 1896, Henry Ford built his first prototype automobile. He later sold it for $200. In 1903, Ford formed the Ford Motor Company using start-up funds from coal merchant Alexander Malcomson and a few other outside investors. Ford served as chief engineer.

The Ford Motor Company began producing cars. The first car was the Model A, which sold well and made the company flourish. By 1907 company profits reached $1,100,000.[18] But Ford wasn't happy. He longed to produce a car that was less expensive . . . one that everyone could easily afford. But other members of his company were hesitant to make any changes. After all, cars were selling nicely, the company was profitable, and life was good.

But Ford insisted on his new concept. So he bought enough shares of the company to take control. He immediately went to work on a lighter-weight, less expensive car. In 1906 Ford introduced the world to his Model T, which sold for around $825. Initially it took 14 hours to assemble a Model T car. But Ford continually experimented with assembly process until he figured out how to manufacture more cars in less time.

That experimentation lead to his "moving assembly" method which made it possible to put together a chassis in one hour and 33 minutes. In 1925 the Ford Motor Company was producing 10,000 cars every 24 hours. This represented 60 percent of America's total output of cars. By 1927 Ford had sold over 15,000,000 Model T cars,[19] and by 1931 he had manufactured 20 million cars.

By 1910, over 500,000 cars were traveling the highways of the United States,[20] and refineries could barely keep up with the demand for gasoline.

More Cars, More Gas

Fast forward to the twenty-first century and the number of cars in the United States has grown substantially. At the end of 2009, there were 246 million cars in the United States.[21] Since 1999, the number of automobiles produced in the world has grown by 30.7 percent as indicated by Table 4.1.

Most of the cars are fueled by petroleum. According to the U.S. Energy Information Administration, in 2009, the United States consumed about 137.93 billion gallons of gasoline. In 1998, the United States

Table 4.1 Number of Automobiles Produced Yearly since 1999

Year	Total Cars
2009	51,971,328
2008	52,940,559
2007	54,920,317
2006	49,886,549
2005	46,862,978
2004	44,554,268
2003	41,968,666
2002	41,358,394
2001	39,825,888
2000	41,215,653
1999	39,759,847

SOURCE: www.worldometers.info/cars/.

Table 4.2 Yearly Crude Oil Percentage since 2000

Month / Year	Retail Price	Refining Percentage	Distribution and Marketing Percentage	Taxes Percentage	Crude Oil Percentage
December, 2000	$1.44	8.0	17.9	29.2	44.8
December, 2001	$1.09	11.7	12.7	38.7	36.9
December, 2002	$1.38	11.7	12.3	30.3	45.7
December, 2003	$1.48	11.5	12.6	28.4	47.5
December, 2004	$1.84	8.9	18.1	23.9	49.1
December, 2005	$2.19	13.5	7.9	20.1	58.4
December, 2006	$2.31	12.9	9.4	19.7	58.0
December, 2007	$3.01	8.1	10.5	13.2	68.1
December, 2008	$1.68	0.7	19.5	23.6	56.2
December, 2009	$2.60	6.6	11.2	15.4	66.6
July, 2010	$2.72	9.4	9.5	14.8	66.1

Source: The U.S. Government supplied this information from the U.S. Energy Information Administration.

consumed 126.52 billion gallons. That means our gasoline consumption has increased 9 percent in 11 years. Our peak consumption year was in 2007, with 142.35 billion gallons consumed.

As far as gas prices, the nationwide average for one gallon of regular unleaded gasoline (as of September 2010) was $2.68. The highest price for a gallon of gasoline was $4.14, which was reached in July 17, 2008.[22]

What's the largest component of a gallon of gasoline? If you guessed crude oil, you'd be right. As of July 2010, crude oil accounted for 66 percent of the price of one gallon of gasoline. In fact, if you look at Table 4.2, you'll see that the crude oil component of gasoline has risen 40 percent in the past 10 years.

One of the biggest factors contributing to our need for petroleum to fuel our cars is automobile fuel inefficiency itself. Of the 20 million barrels of oil consumed each day:

- 70 percent is used in transportation (including gasoline, diesel, and jet fuel).
- 24 percent is used by industry and manufacturing.
- 5 percent is used in commercial and residential sectors.
- 1 percent is used to generate electricity.[23]

This isn't to say we haven't tried to make our cars more fuel-efficient. In 1975, Congress passed the Energy Policy and Conservation Act (EPCA), with the goal of saving 2 million barrels per day by doubling the fuel economy of cars and light trucks.[24]

Fuel efficiency standards were set for cars with model years from 1978 to 1985. The 1985 goal of 27.5 mpg for passenger cars was set. This goal was designed to reduce our oil consumption as well as our dependency on foreign oil. Yet, today the United States imports more oil than when the Corporate Automobile Fuel Economy (CAFE) program was enacted. However, the 1985 standard remained unchanged for almost 18 years.

The Heritage Foundation (THF) and the Competitive Enterprise Institute (CEI) say that the fuel efficiency standards failed because of the way in which Congress responded.[25] Congress had put regulations in place to keep the price of oil and gas artificially low. Congress was worried that the reduced prices would signal to the Big Three car makers that they could continue making large-sized, gas guzzling SUVs. The Heritage Foundation says had Congress let the price of oil and gasoline rise to normal market levels, this in itself would have caused the automakers to pull back on their plans for bigger automobiles. The Heritage Foundation might be right. Regardless, we now know that SUVs became the centerpiece of the auto manufacturers' arsenal of cars.

The sad fact is that by 2004, half of all vehicles sold every year in the United States were gas guzzling SUVs.[26] This made it hard to reduce oil consumption and even harder to reduce our dependency on foreign oil. We became puppets not only to the oil industry, but the auto industry as well.

Part Two

OIL DYNASTIES

Part Two

Chapter 5

A Homegrown
U.S. Oil Cartel

B y 1871, the small town of Titusville, Pennsylvania, had grown into a city of 10,000 people. Once nothing more than a few shacks, timber factories and dirt roads, the town now had a school, a church, an opera house, and even its own local newspaper. The oilmen who had made their way to Titusville 10 years earlier could now look back and revel in their achievements. Ida Tarbell, a journalist who grew up in the oil region of Pennsylvania, wrote:

> We have built this business up from nothing to a net product of six millions of barrels per annum. We have invented and devised all the apparatus, the appliances, the forms needed for a new industry.[1]

But soon, their stories, their achievements, even the original oil town of Titusville itself would be overshadowed by an oil company that would come to dominate the industry—a domination that could only be stopped by the U.S. government. And the man behind the company would become one of the wealthiest men in the world.

John D. Rockefeller and the
Standard Oil Company

John Davison Rockefeller was born on a farm in Richford, New York. He was the second of six children born to William and Eliza Rockefeller. At the age of 13, his father moved the family to a farm in Cleveland. John's family was not wealthy, not even middle class. His father was a vagabond. William often undertook ventures that resembled scams more than a good man's honest work. His moneymaking adventures often kept him on the road, and this left John with his mother and siblings struggling to survive. They got by on what little money they could scrape together. It was a meager living at best.

In the spring of 1855, John spent 10 weeks at Folsom's Commercial College studying bookkeeping, commercial history, mercantile customs, and banking. He would have liked to continue his studies at the college but because of his family's financial situation, he was forced to get a job and earn money for the family.

The business environment in Cleveland was quite depressed, so finding work wasn't easy for the young man. But he was persistent in his efforts and eventually found work as a bookkeeper at the firm of Hewitt & Tuttle, a produce shipper and merchant. Bookkeeping proved a good fit for John as many people described him as "a mental math genius."[2] However, the pay was meager. According to records, from September 1855 to January 1856, he earned a grand total of 50 dollars. But he was a good bookkeeper, and that's why the company raised his salary to 25 dollars a month.[3]

Being a man of numbers, John managed to put a small portion of his earnings into a savings account. That money would soon become the basis of his budding oil empire. In 1858, John met Maurice Clark, a young man who had recently emigrated to the United States from England. When Maurice came to America, he landed a job working for the Ohio and Erie Canal. Eventually that led him to a job with the firm of Otis, Brownell & Co., dealers in grain and the owners and operator of a grain-loading elevator on the river.

John and Maurice hit it off quite well and the two went into business together. Each man put up $2,000 and formed the firm of Clark & Rockefeller, merchants in grain, hay, and meats.[4]

Their little business was quite successful. In their first year they managed to gross $450,000.[5] That was enough to earn the two a profit of $4,400. One year later, they saw their profits grow fourfold to $17,000.[6] Their business continued to flourish, even as the Civil War broke out. In fact, because of the war, grain prices skyrocketed, which naturally increased their profits.

However by the early 1860s, the grain business was undergoing changes. For that matter, everything in Cleveland was changing, because for Cleveland, the port at Lake Erie was the most important means of transporting goods. Businesses that found ways to use the port prospered nicely. But as the days of the railroad came thundering in, the prosperity Cleveland business owners enjoyed would soon be challenged.

Seeing the Future

Rockefeller seemed to sense the impending impact railroads would have on the grain business. He knew the railroads would overtake the ports. After all, railroads could offer faster, cheaper means of transporting goods.

And indeed that vision was realized when the long awaited Atlantic & Great Western Railroad was built. The A&GW line traveled east to Meadville, Pennsylvania, then northeast to Corry, Pennsylvania, and then across the border into New York where it connected to the Erie Railroad. Coincidentally, the A&GW also had branches that ran into the heart of the oil regions—Titusville and Franklin.

Most oil refining was concentrated in Cleveland because of its proximity to the oil fields in Western Pennsylvania. It was the natural shipping point for petroleum headed west as well as cities on the eastern seaboard. Besides railroad lines, Cleveland offered the oil industry cheap water transportation (via Lake Erie) and an abundant supply of low-cost immigrant labor.

Rockefeller felt the only way for Clark & Rockefeller to survive was to be involved in some way with raw materials and natural resources. He wasn't sure exactly what raw material, but he was certain that their business would have no option but to abandon agricultural products altogether. Rockefeller only needed to look a few hundred miles to the state of Pennsylvania to find the answer: oil.

It seems Rockefeller instinctively recognized that Clark and Rockefeller's new interests would be oil. Perhaps it was the stories of sudden success and riches from the men who ventured in the oil business that drew Rockefeller's attention. He heard those stories first hand from Samuel Andrews, who suggested that Rockefeller get into the oil business. Andrews was a chemist who already had experience in the oil business and was also considered a mechanical genius.

Andrews had already developed a new refinery process that allowed him to produce not only better quality oil, but also larger quantities. But to continue his work, he needed money. It was a perfect pairing. Rockefeller needed a way into the oil business, and Andrews needed funding. A deal was struck. The firm of Clarke and Rockefeller invested $4,000 in Samuel Andrews' oil refinery business.

With the new money he received, Andrews went to work and built a refinery in Cleveland in an area known as "the flats." Clark, Rockefeller, Andrews, and Clark's two brothers, whom he had brought into the business, owned the new refinery. The refinery did well. And Clark & Rockefeller soon upped their investment to $100,000.[7] At the same time, Cleveland was growing as a major oil refinery area. It had a refining capacity of 12,000 barrels a day compared to other areas such as New York, with 9,000 barrels a day.[8]

As Rockefeller and Clark's new oil refinery grew more successful, Rockefeller was eager to add more capital to the business to expand it beyond their initial projections. But Clark's brothers were hesitant to do so.

Rockefeller didn't bend to their desires but instead followed his instincts. He borrowed money to expand the business. Being able to get banks to lend him money seemed to come naturally to John. His partner Clark said of Rockefeller's ability to get money, "he was the greatest borrower you ever saw."[9] And to boot, he completely bought out Clark's brothers for $72,500. Then he established a new firm,

Rockefeller & Andrews.[10] In the new partnership, Andrews was the manufacturer and Rockefeller the purchaser of raw materials as well as the salesman.

On top of borrowing, Rockefeller plowed all the company profits back into the business in order to expand it further. John was also gifted at cutting expenses. Wherever he could shave a nickel, dime, or penny in costs, he'd do so. For example, John refused to buy insurance on his refineries. To Rockefeller, insurance was an expense the company could afford to do without. And instead of paying the customary $2.50 per barrel in which to store the oil, John bought his own supplies to have barrels made right there at the refinery. John saved the company $1.54 on each barrel.[11] His efforts at cost cutting paid off, and in 1865, the company had enough money to build a second refinery, Standard Works. An office was opened in New York, which sold the oil the refinery produced with John's brother William heading up the new office.

John also took in a new partner, H. M. Flagler, who had previously owned a salt mining company in Michigan. Flagler managed to carve out a nice living for himself mining salt and selling it to the Army. Unfortunately with the outbreak of the Civil War, Mr. Flagler's company went bankrupt as demand for salt dramatically declined. Just like Rockefeller, Flagler had a talent for making money. So he started a grain business in Cleveland, where he met Rockefeller, who was employed at Hewitt and Tuttle. The two remained friends. That friendship proved vital when Rockefeller was ready to open the second oil refinery. Rockefeller turned to Flagler to help him find more funding

Of course, Flagler didn't have to search too far to find the money. That's because Flagler was married to the niece of Stephen Harkness, a distillery owner in Ohio. Harkness had made himself a handsome fortune selling whiskey, mainly to the Union army. Harkness agreed to provide Flagler with $100,000 in funding, on the condition that Rockefeller make Flagler a partner, and Harkness a silent partner. Rockefeller agreed to the terms. But make no mistake. Rockefeller was the head of every company he created. And those companies grew beyond Rockefeller's wildest imagination.

In fact Rockefeller's oil business had grown so big that by 1868 it was the largest oil refinery company in the world. At one point, the business employed 900 workers and could turn out 1,500 barrels a day, or roughly 10 percent of the world's output.[12] The company could afford to hire its own chemists, and that in turn allowed them to turn petroleum into 300 different by-products. Some of those products included paint, varnish, dozens of lubricating oils, and anesthetics.

The main product they produced was kerosene. Rockefeller produced it so cheaply that most of the traditional oils used for illuminating houses such as whale and coal oil became almost nonexistent. This is exactly what John envisioned. He wrote to one of his partners: "Let the good work go on. We must ever remember we are refining oil for the poor man and he must have it cheap and good."[13]

Five years after he entered the oil refining business, John consolidated his companies into one: the Standard Oil Company of which he owned 27 percent.[14] Other members of Standard Oil included Henry M. Flagler, Samuel Andrews, William Rockefeller, and Stephen Harkness. This band of five would transform the oil industry and create one of the largest oil cartels on U.S. soil.

The Center of Control

You could say that Rockefeller found his calling in the oil refinery business. But simply finding his calling wasn't enough; he wanted more . . . much more. And he would stop at nothing to see the next vision of his oil empire come true. That vision would come at the expense of other men with hopes and dreams of finding a fortune in the oil business. Rockefeller was intent on keeping the fortunes for himself, so he devised a plan that would give control of the industry to the Standard Oil Company.

Business historian Matthew Josephson states that Rockefeller developed a plan that was designed to ". . . control and direct the flow of oil into the hands of a narrowed group of refiners."[15] Ida Tarbell, the journalist who wrote extensively on Rockefeller's climb to power—whose work that President Theodore Roosevelt referred to as "muckraker journalism"—saw the impact of Rockefeller's plan first hand.

Her father, Frank Tarbell, started in the oil business by building wooden oil storage tanks and then later became an oil producer and refiner. His business was one of the small businesses crushed by

Rockefeller's giant oil ogre, the Standard Oil Company. Ida writes of the destruction as follows: "Things were going well in father's business. There was ease such as we had never known; luxuries we had never heard of. . . . Then suddenly [our] gay, prosperous town received a blow between the eyes."[16] Rockefeller's plan was simple: Destroy the competition until his company was the last standing. Rockefeller's plan had already been put in motion as he began expanding his oil empire under the Standard Oil banner.

You see, Rockefeller realized that anyone who could secure financing could get into the oil refining business, because start-up costs were low, ranging from $10,000 to $50,000. John wasn't going to let just anyone into the business, however. John knew Standard Oil had to control as much of the business as possible, and this meant Standard Oil had to:

- Own and build the best refineries available
- Make their own storage barrels
- Own their own boats and pipelines to transport the oil
- Own their own holding and storage tanks
- Produce not only the highest-quality petroleum by-products but a huge variety
- Make those products available at cheapest prices possible

Owning every aspect of the business is exactly what John achieved. But there was one element of the business John couldn't control and that was the railroads. While he couldn't control them, he could do the next best thing: He could use the power of his mighty oil business to influence them. Amazingly, John already knew that the railroad companies would be susceptible to his influence, because John understood the business model railroads operated under in order to be successful.

Railroad companies had two business peculiarities to overcome. The first was the high ratio of fixed costs to variable costs. Before a passenger or freight could be carried on the rails, the railroad company had to secure rights-of-way, put down track, build terminals, and buy locomotives. Once these upfront investments have been made, other costs such as labor, fuel, and maintenance decreased as the volume of passengers and freight increased.

The second peculiarity of the railroad business was excessive
demand for railroad lines to be laid. During the late 1800s and early
1900s, the government encouraged people to move westward. And
to entice people to do so, the government offered special land grants
to those Americans willing to populate new areas of the country. But
getting to these remote areas proved difficult as there were no roads or
major highways yet built. The most common method of transportation was the horse-drawn wagon. But this method of travel was slow
and tedious. Horses needed to be refreshed, and wagon wheels needed
regular repairs.

The government wanted to move large numbers of settlers at once
into the new areas. Eager to capitalize on the government's land rush
and need for efficiency, railroads began aggressively laying track to
these new areas. This allowed for masses of people to travel to the new
areas in a single trip. But this also created a problem for the railroads.
Once the settlers who traveled to these remote areas put down roots,
railroad traffic declined. Now the railroads were stuck with rails and
routes and not enough passengers to make the endeavor worthwhile.

Dormant tracks are detrimental to a railroad company's success.
Railroads can only successfully operate when they have a consistent
and large volume of passengers or freight to carry back and forth on
the lines. This keeps costs low. To secure the volume of passengers and
freight needed to survive, railroads began reducing their rates. This
often ignited a rate reduction war. The truth is, rate wars had begun
as early as 1869, when the New York Central and the Pennsylvania
railroads laid lines that connected with Chicago. The battle continued
with the completion of the Erie and Baltimore and Ohio railroads into
the Chicago area around 1874.[17] To prevent rate wars, the agents of the
railroads met annually in New York to agree upon standard rates.[18]
Although attempts were made to develop a set of standard fares, the
truth is, the railroads were free to cut rates from the published price as
long as the reduced price covered their variable costs.

This aggressive reduction in rates often forced smaller railroads out
of business because they reached a point where they could no longer
afford to reduce their rates. Any further reductions in rates meant they
were operating in the red, and too much red ink led to bankruptcy. It
was a common business practice to offer certain customers preferred

rates. It was also common for large shipping companies to shop around for the best "preferred" rate.

In many ways, the early days of the railroads were wild and chaotic and could be characterized as the "Wild West Days" of the railroads. The first attempt to regulate railroads and their rates was in 1887 with the passing of the Act to Regulate Commerce. Even so, the Interstate Commercial Commission could only make determinations as to rates that were just and reasonable. It had no power or authority to set minimum rates. This rate reduction war-like environment and an unregulated industry gave Rockefeller, an astute businessman, the leverage he needed to work out preferred deals with the railroad companies. Those preferred deals would have an immediate impact on Standard Oil's bottom line. Shipping was an important component in calculating an oil refinery's profitability. The lower Rockefeller could reduce shipping expenses, the more profitable his company would become.

Working with Flagler, Rockefeller approached the railroad companies about negotiating exclusive special shipping rates and rebates for Standard Oil. If the railroads would provide special shipping rates, in return, Rockefeller guaranteed the railroads the volume they needed to sustain their business. After all, Rockefeller had already built Standard Oil into the largest shipper. This gave him plenty of firepower to wheel and deal with the railroads. One of those railroads was the Lake Shore and Michigan Southern Railroad Company.

The General Concedes

Like many railroads that battled to survive the chaos of the burgeoning railroad industry, the Lake Shore and Michigan Southern Railroad Company was a merger of several smaller lines. The company was formed in 1869 by the consolidation of The Michigan Southern and Northern Indiana Railroad Company with a line from Chicago to Toledo; The Lake Shore Railway Company with a line from Toledo to Erie; and The Buffalo and Erie Railroad Company with a line from Erie to Buffalo.[19]

About 1877, the New York Central and Hudson River Railroad gained the majority of the stock in the Lake Shore and Michigan

Southern Railroad Company. The line was operated in conjunction with the New York Central line. This lasted until 1914, when the New York Central and Hudson River Railroad merged with the Lake Shore and Michigan Southern Railway, and later formed a new New York Central Railroad Company.

General John H. Devereaux was President of the Lake Shore and Michigan Railroad Company, which would later become one of Rockefeller's preferred railroad companies. The General had spent most of his career in the railroad industry, and his first job was a construction engineer for the Cleveland, Columbus & Cincinnati Railroad.

When the Civil War broke out, Devereaux joined the Union army. Because of his extensive railroad background, he was put in charge of all Union rail lines responsible for moving troops, supplies, artillery, and wounded soldiers. After the war ended, Devereaux returned to his hometown of Cleveland, where he found work on the Cleveland and Pittsburgh Railroad. He later moved over to the Lake Shore Railroad, where he was named vice-president and then later president. That line was consolidated into the Lake Shore and Michigan Southern Railroad Company.

Since the Lake Shore and Michigan Southern had several tracks of lines running in and out of the New York and Chicago area, Rockefeller and Flagler knew this railroad company was a prime target for negotiating special rates. In 1870 Rockefeller approached General Devereaux about reducing shipping rates for Standard Oil. In return for those special rates, Standard Oil would provide the General's railroad company with 60 car tanks a day filled with barrels of oil. The General agreed, and Standard Oil was able to reduce its shipping expenses by as much as 50 percent. Some stories suggest that General Devereaux was blindsided by John's stories of an oil refinery industry in turmoil.

In *John D. Rockefeller and His Career*, author Silas Hubbard tells of the meeting between Rockefeller and Devereaux as Rockefeller "outwitting and bamboozling" Devereaux. Hubbard writes:

Rockefeller had succeeded in outwitting and bamboozling W. H. Vanderbilt and General J. H. Devereaux. And as the Lake Shore's main part of this traffic had to go to Cleveland, Rockefeller persuaded General Devereaux that unless something special was done for Cleveland the oil refiners of that city would have to move their plants to Oil Creek, manufacture there, and ship east over the Pennsylvania.[20]

According to Hubbard, Rockefeller had completely convinced General Devereaux to save Cleveland's share of the oil business and give John D. Rockefeller rebates worth at that time $250,000 a year. To put this dollar amount in perspective, Standard Oil was getting their crude oil carried from Oil Creek to Cleveland for 20 cents a barrel, and all other refiners in Cleveland were paying 40 cents a barrel for transportation.[21] In fact, records show that the Lake Shore Railroad Company hauled Standard Oil's entire crude product. Later Rockefeller would extract this system of rebates and reduce rates from many other railroad companies when he formed the South Improvement Company.

This new company was started with an investment of $200,000, and its main objective was to make special rebates arrangements with railroad companies.[22] Railroads participating in the rebate system were the Erie line, headed by Jay Gould and General McClellan, and the Pennsylvania lines. As the operator of the South Improvement Company, Standard Oil received not only discounts on shipping but also rebates on the fees charged to competitor shippers. The rebates ranged from 40 cents to $1.06 per barrel on crude petroleum and from 50 cents to $1.32 per barrel on refined petroleum.[23] This price reduction and system of rebates gave Standard Oil an unfair competitive advantage and allowed them to control 95 percent of the oil industry. It also helped Rockefeller amass wealth. In 1896 Rockefeller was worth about $200 million.[24]

A Monopoly Is Born

This unfair competitive advantage eventually wreaked havoc on Rockefeller's oil empire. The U.S. government intervened and put an end to business practices it said created an oil monopoly. Those in favor of Rockefeller's business practices say the exponential growth of Standard Oil was due to Rockefeller's savvy businesses expertise and that negotiating special rates and even buying up smaller oil refineries were examples of his remarkable business ability.

Critics argue otherwise. For example, Elizabeth Granitz & Benjamin Klein, co-authors of *Raising Rivals' Costs: The Standard Oil Case,* say the idea that the success of Rockefeller can be attributed to his superior efficiency is contradicted by the timing and behavioral evidence associated with Standard Oil.[25] Silas Hubbard argues that Rockefeller was cunning and devious. While Rockefeller and his associates reaped the rewards of this reduced monopoly and the wealth it brought to them, they did not hesitate to pass the blame on to others. As for the secret reduced rates negotiated with Devereaux, Rockefeller blamed the entire incident on Devereaux. Hubbard writes:

> He [Rockefeller] knew also that the violation of the law would strangle the business of every other oil refiner in Cleveland. He knew it would compel all his business competitors at Cleveland to sell their plants to him at his terms; but yet he would have the world believe that Vanderbilt and Devereaux were alone guilty of legal and moral turpitude, even though that turpitude had been induced by his own cunning and astuteness.[26]

In the end, Rockefeller's Standard Oil Company was declared a monopoly by the U.S. government, and Rockefeller was forced to break the company into separate state companies, each with its own board of directors. Among the various companies were Standard Oil of Ohio, Standard Oil of Indiana, Standard Oil of New York, Standard Oil of New Jersey, Standard Oil of California, Standard Oil of Kentucky, Standard Oil of Iowa, Standard Oil of Minnesota, Standard Oil of Illinois, Standard Oil of Kansas, Standard Oil of Missouri, Standard Oil of Nebraska, and Standard Oil of Louisiana.

Robert "Fighting Bob" LaFollette Sr., a Wisconsin district attorney who constantly battled against corruption—particularly monopolies— reveled in the government's victory of the breakup of the Standard Oil Company's oil monopoly. LaFollette wrote: "So flagrant has been its violation of the anti-trust law that its eminent lawyers were not able to prove it even 'reasonably' innocent. The giant corporation must change its method of doing business."[27]

In the end, how the giant corporation did business didn't really change that much. Standard Oil Company of New Jersey evolved into Exxon, and the Standard Oil Company of New York evolved into Mobil. In 1998, the two merged into ExxonMobil, one of the largest mergers in U.S. history, worth an estimated $83 billion.[28] Although the merger made headlines, the company would soon find itself splattered on the front pages again for creating one of the largest oil disasters—the *Exxon Valdez* oil spill off the coast of Alaska. The *Valdez* oil tanker spilled 10.9 million gallons of the 53 million gallons of oil it was carrying. The oil would eventually impact over 1,100 miles of non-continuous coastline in Alaska.[29] The cleanup of the shoreline began in April of 1989 and continued through 1991. The spill wound up costing Exxon billions and even had a role in the global financial meltdown of 2007, as was later revealed in *Barbarians of Wealth*.

But the price it paid to clean up the spill was almost insignificant to Exxon. The ExxonMobil Corporation became the largest oil company in the world. In 2009, the company reported record profits of $45 billion, which beat its previous record of $40.6 billion in 2007. Its second quarter earnings in 2010 were $7.6 billion. Figure 5.1 shows the continued growth of Exxon's share price.

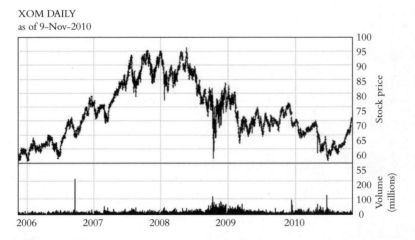

Figure 5.1 Exxon's Dramatic Growth in Share Price
DATA SOURCE: BigCharts.com.

While gas prices at the pump squeeze most Americans for every nickel and dime we can scrape together, the head honchos of ExxonMobil are enjoying generous pay compensations. Take Lee Raymond, the company's former chairman, who received a $400 million retirement package that included pension, stock options, and other perks, such as a $1 million consulting deal, two years of home security, personal security, a car and driver, and use of a corporate jet for professional purposes.[30] Exxon defends the excessive compensation package pointing out that during Mr. Raymond's tenure, Exxon became the largest oil company in the world and the stock price rose 500 percent.

One can only wonder if this reward is really for keeping us addicted to oil.

Chapter 6

From Humble
Beginnings to Oil Giant

T he SS *Murex* was a beautiful ship, the first of her kind. She was
338 feet long, had a beam length of 43 feet, and a draught of
26 feet. She cut through the water powered by a coal-fired
boiler.[1] She had one purpose: to carry kerosene through the waterways
of the Suez Canal. You see, until The SS *Murex* was built, ships carrying
any kind of highly flammable cargo weren't allowed in the Suez Canal
which cut out 4,000 miles off the voyage of maritime shipping merchants,
the distance around the Cape of Good Hope. But Samuel Marcus, a
London merchant was determined to build a ship the authorities would
let pass through the canal. In many ways, Samuel was a much more
aggressive businessman than his father, who made a living selling antiques
and oddly enough, little boxes decorated with seashells imported from
the Far East.

On a family vacation to the beach, Samuel's children were fascinated with the different variety of seashells they found lying on the beach. They liked them so much the children collected the shells and would later use them to decorate the boxes they used to carry their lunches. Samuel figured if his children enjoyed these small, decorated boxes, so would others. So he began selling boxes decorated with seashells. He was right. The seashell boxes became quite popular with the woman of London. Needing more exotic shells, Samuel began importing shells from the Far East.

When Marcus died in 1870, his son Marcus Junior took over the business. His son proved to be a better businessman than his father. Under Marcus Junior's direction, the company expanded from decorated seashell boxes to all kinds of merchandise including textiles and tools, even machinery. He created a thriving import and export business that spanned London and the Far East and also opened branches of the business in different parts of the world. He partnered with his brother Samuel to open the Marcus Samuel & Co. in London, and the Samuel, Samuel & Co. in Japan, which grew into a leading shipping and trading enterprise in the Far East.

During a business trip to the Caspian Sea, Marcus was intrigued with the idea of exporting oil to the Far East. Since he was already doing business in that area, he knew there was a ready-made market. But to make this idea succeed, he had two problems to overcome: (1) transporting the oil in bulk, and (2) going through the Suez Canal to cut 4,000 miles off the trip.

The authorities regularly rejected requests from companies to let oil, kerosene or any other type of flammable cargo through the canal. Canal authorities weren't just worried about explosions and fire; they were also worried that the tankers, weighed down with heavy oil, might become grounded in the canal. Luckily for Marcus, a famous and powerful family had invested large amounts of money into the Baku oil fields in Russia—the Rothschilds. They already had railroads built to carry the oil through the rough terrain to the Black Sea. From there the oil, stored in wooden barrels, was loaded onto ordinary cargo ships.

But the barrels took up considerable space in the ship's cargo hold, and thereby limited how much oil could be transported. On top of this, the barrels often leaked, especially when the ships hit rough seas, which reduced the amount of oil that actually made it to the open market.

It was a natural pairing. Marcus wanted to export oil to the Far East through the Suez Canal; the Rothschilds needed a better type of ship to carry the oil they were extracting from Russian fields. The two agreed to work together. Marcus would transport their oil through the canal and in turn, the Rothschilds would use their influence to secure approval from canal authorities to allow the tankers to pass through. For influence the Rothschild family had only to turn to the British government. The Rothschilds had provided the British government with the money to buy shares in the canal.

Marcus signed a nine-year contract with the Rothschilds to transport their oil. Now he needed an oil tanker that could haul the heavy load as well as please the canal authorities. To help in that endeavor, Marcus turned to Sir James Fortescue Flannery, an English engineer and naval architect. Marcus asked Flannery to design a ship loaded with oil that canal authorities would approve for passage through the canal. Marcus stressed to Flannery that he'd have to take on this challenge without input from canal authorities. It's not that they didn't want to assist, but they had no idea about shipbuilding. They could only express their concerns related to explosions, fire, and ships being grounded.

Flannery was more than up for the challenge. He produced a magnificent ship. It had 10 cargo tanks arranged in a two-by-five pattern placed amid ship, with cofferdams at each end of the cargo tanks which isolated them from the engineering spaces.[2] He added expansion tanks on top of each tank to control expansion of the oil due changes in temperature, and a steam cleaning system for cleaning the tanks.[3] Flannery also designed the ship with water ballast tanks to prevent it from being grounded in the canal. Marcus christened the new ship, the SS *Murex*, named after the murex seashell, a conch-shaped shell which is found most often in tropical environments. But besides being a ship well built to carry oil, the SS *Murex* received the highest safety rating from Lloyd's of London. The Suez Canal authority gave its approval.

Everything was in place, and on May 28, 1892 the SS *Murex* under command of Captain John R. Coundon set sail for Batumi in the Black Sea. At Batumi the ship was loaded with 4,000 tons of Russian kerosene. Once loaded, Captain Coundon and his crew headed south to the Suez Canal. On August 24, 1892 the SS *Murex* became the first ship carrying kerosene to pass through the canal.[4] By 1897, Samuel's business had grown so big, he created a new company specifically for transporting oil. He commissioned several more ships to be built. He named his new company, The Shell Transport and Trading Company. Of the formation of his new company, Marcus said,

This company depends more largely upon its trade as a carrier than as an oil merchant for its earning power.[5]

The design of the SS *Murex* was so revolutionary it's still used as the basis for building modern day oil tankers. Marcus' Shell Transport and Trading Company had a similar impact on the oil industry itself.

At the time, the Standard Oil Company created by John Rockefeller was the major oil company in the world. In fact, Marcus knew that if he was going to enter into the oil business, there was a chance he'd run up against Rockefeller, who ruled the industry (as you learned in Chapter 5). When Rockefeller sensed competition, he put up roadblocks, making it harder for companies to succeed. Those with any chance of success he bought outright.

By the time Marcus entered into the business, Rockefeller had cornered the U.S. oil market and was already exporting oil to the Far East but not in large quantities. The other difficulty Rockefeller faced with his foreign oil exports was that of time. Transporting oil from New York to the Far East took several months. For Rockefeller, the amount of time the oil sat on ships en route was money wasted. He needed a faster way to get the oil to its final destination. But Rockefeller had not figured out how to get ships carrying petroleum through the Suez Canal. He had to use the same routes as everyone else.

Marcus beat him to the punch, and Rockefeller knew it. He saw Shell Transport and Trading Company as a major competitor. S. Goulichambaroff, an authority on petroleum production and transport, and who had studied Marcus' company and tankers, summarized the competition that was brewing between the two entities:

> Sir Marcus Samuel, foreseeing a new way of extending his undertakings with Rothschild to supply him with kerosene. At that time, the Far East was supplied with illuminating oil by the Americans. This market seemed already occupied. Sir Marcus did not hesitate; he decided to enter upon a struggle with American enterprise, and began to export Russian kerosene to places where there was no American competition.[6]

Marcus owned the Far East market, but he wasn't content. He began exporting oil to England, Italy, France, and other European countries. He was going to dominate foreign side of the oil market. But as you'll learn, his dream was bigger than his wallet.

The Dutch Connection

Pull out a map and you'll see that Indonesia is located 15 degrees above and 15 degrees below the equator. More than 17,000 islands make up the country, giving it the title of largest archipelagic state. However, about 6,000 of the islands are inhabitable.[7] The largest islands are Sumatra, Java (the most populated island), Bali, Kalimantan, Sulawesi, the Nusa Tenggara islands, the Moluccas islands, and the western part of New Guinea.[8]

Indonesia is three times the size of Texas, but more impressive than its size is the amount of petroleum hidden underneath its surface. According to the *Oil & Gas Journal*, Indonesia has produced as much as 4.3 billion barrels of oil.[9]

The islanders have had a long history of being ruled by other governments. For example, Muslims once ruled the islands and natives converted to the Islam religion. Later the Dutch invaded the island and set up trading posts. About 1811, the British took control and ousted the Dutch. By 1871, a treaty was signed by the Netherlands and Great Britain, which gave full authority and control of the islands back to the Dutch. Immediately, the Dutch opened up the east coast of Sumatra for private enterprise by Dutch citizens. Most of those private enterprises were plantation owners who were growing tobacco on the islands. But the land was rugged, and plantations had to be carved out of jungle. The men who settled in these areas were hard-working and got by on what little the area had to offer. J.R. Poley, in *Eroica: The Quest for Oil in Indonesia,* describes these men as having wide vision and wills of steel.[10] One of those men was Aeilko Jans Zijlker. Zijlker, a manager working for the East Sumatra Tobacco Company had no idea of the amount of petroleum that lay hidden in Indonesia. But he suspected the black substance could make him rich.[11]

Zijlker had come to the small island of Sumatra to recover from a broken heart. One day while traveling around the tobacco plantation, Zijlker had to take cover under a tobacco shed from a sudden tropical storm that hit the island. Little did he know the storm that forced him to take cover would be a pivotal event in his life in the islands. While waiting out the storm he watched a native islander light a fire using a bamboo torch. Curious about the black substance used to create the fire on the torch, Zijlker asked the native to show him where he found it. The islander took him to a small pond covered with a dark liquid. The islanders had been using the seeping substance not only to light their torches but to caulk their boats.

The odor coming from the pond was overwhelming. Zijlker instantly recognized the substance as petroleum. Anxious to find out the quality of the petroleum, he collected a small sample and sent it on to Batavia for analysis. The results were exactly as Zijlker had hoped. When heated to proper temperatures, the petroleum could yield 21.2 percent of first-rate illuminating kerosene.[12]

Soon after being shown the petroleum filled pond Zijlker started a small scale drilling operation to explore for oil. When that proved successful, Zijlker obtained a concession of 891 acres of land from the Sultan of Langkat. The land Zijlker chose was located on the right bank of the Lepan River because it was already seeping oil.[13]

Zijlker set up his drilling operation and in June 1885 struck oil in the Telaga Said Field. Drilling wasn't easy for Zijlker; the land was harsh and not suitable for drilling equipment. The Telaga field was located in a six-mile stretch of jungle.[14] In addition, Zijlker was always short on funds and had difficulty finding qualified laborers to work the wells. In late 1886, the mining engineer Reinder Fennema was assigned to the Telaga project by the Dutch government. For Zijlker, Fennema was a godsend. He helped Zijlker obtain additional funding from the former head of the central bank of the East Indies, and the former governor general.

Having power players of this caliber helped pave the way for the Royal King, William III, to grant Zijlker a patent to use the word Royal in the name of his company. This was a big deal. Normally, only established and proven companies could carry the title Royal in their name, and Zijlker's enterprise wasn't yet proven, because he was in the early stage of drilling. So receiving a grant from the King was a critical step in Zijlker's enterprise. The new company now known as Royal Dutch Shell was launched in 1890. Of this accomplishment, Zijlker wrote:

> Throughout the entire exploration my motto was: whoever is not with me is against me, and I shall treat him accordingly. I know well enough this motto earns me enemies, but I know also, that had I not acted as I did, I should never have accomplished the business.[15]

Zijlker's quest for oil paid off handsomely. The Telaga field produced 8.4 million barrels of oil.[16] Unfortunately Zijlker didn't live long enough to enjoy the fruits of his hard labor. On his way from Batavia to Deli, he contracted a deadly disease and died on December 27, 1890.

Jean Baptiste Kessler, managing director of the operation was named head of the Royal Dutch enterprise. Kessler was the perfect man to step into Zijlker's shoes. Kessler is described as being high strung, passionate, forceful, and a born leader of men.[17] Under his direction, Royal Dutch opened a second and third well, which were both successful in producing large amounts of oil. Kessler called the company's oil, Crown Oil.

A Competitor Becomes a Partner

Now, Kessler and the members of the Dutch government were a smart group. They had seen the strides Samuel Marcus made in building a fleet of oil tankers to carry petroleum through the Suez Canal, and they figured they could "imitate" his success. Marcus had already proved there was a market for oil in the Far East. They wanted to do the same, but they had an advantage of already being in the area. They knew they could ship their oil for a lot less money than Marcus was spending.

Their location also gave them the advantage of providing a steady and continuous supply of oil to the Far East. They made it their mission to compete head-to-head with Samuel Marcus. However, like Zijlker, Kessler died before he would see Royal Dutch become a threat to Marcus' operation. Royal Dutch needed a new heir, and it found that person in Henri Deterding. In his younger days, Deterding worked in the banking business on the island of Java. He joined Royal Dutch in his early twenties as an assistant to Kessler.

Deterding was an aggressive businessman, who knew how to put together business deals, was keenly aware of his competitor's weaknesses, and was rightly suited for the top spot. So it was no surprise to Deterding that Samuel Marcus was running low on finances. Although Marcus had secured a long-term contract with the Rothschild family to transport their oil to the Far East, he was using much of his own money and capital to expand his business. For example, Marcus bought an oil well in North Borneo, but the oil wasn't good quality, and the odor was nauseating, so his Oriental clients refused to use it. Marcus was stuck with oil he couldn't sell, and without buyers, he couldn't recoup his investment.

Another venture proved just as costly to Marcus. He had managed to secure a contract to transport 100,000 gallons of oil from the Spindletop well in Texas. The rate was fixed and remained so for 21 years.[18] On the surface it seemed like a fantastic deal, but the Spindletop wells ran dry long before Marcus' 21-year contract expired? Short on cash, Marcus needed help to keep his business afloat. In 1902, he visited Deterding who had managed to build Royal Dutch into a thriving business, flush with cash. During the visit, he suggested that the two form a partnership. Marcus would be in charge of transporting the oil, and Deterding would oversee production.

The idea of a partnership roused Deterding's interest, but he asked for a major concession: that he be in complete control of this new venture. Samuel refused. Of the visit, Samuel wrote to his brother:

A Dutchman sits and says nothing till he gets what he wants but of course in this case he won't.[19]

Not long after this meeting Marcus' words would have little meaning. Whatever opinion Samuel formed of Deterding, in the end his need for money won out. The two reached an agreement in which each held a one-third interest in the new firm they would create, Asiatic Petroleum. It would be seen as joint venture. The Rothschild family who interestingly enough had invested money into Royal Dutch held the other one-third interest.

But this agreement wouldn't last. About 1907 another deal was struck. Marcus, still in dire need of money, agreed to a partnership with Deterding, in which Deterding had complete control of the new entity. The new company would be known as Royal Dutch Shell. The partnership with Marcus was just one of many deals that Deterding struck. Through alliances and mergers Deterding built Royal Dutch Shell into one of the largest oil companies in the world. Of course there's no doubt Deterding loved the company he built, but he loved the product he sold even more. He wrote:

> Oil is the most extraordinary article in the commercial world, and the only thing that hampers its sale is its production. There is no other article in the world where you can get the consumption as long as you can make the production. In the case of oil make the production first as the consumption will come. There is no need to look after the consumption, and as a seller you need not make forward contract, as the oil sells itself.[20]

Foul Play

Deterding is right: Oil is the most extraordinary natural resource in the world. For oil companies like Royal Dutch Shell it means billions of dollars in their coffers, not to mention oil executives' bank accounts. Perhaps that's why oil companies have a long list of "dirty deeds," And Royal Dutch Shell isn't immune from foul play.

In 2004, the Securities and Exchange Commission levied a $120 million fine against Royal Dutch Shell for over-inflating its oil and gas reserves.[21] The fine is the third largest by the SEC for accounting fraud. The other notables were WorldCom and Bristol-Myers. In addition to paying the SEC fine, Royal Dutch Shell agreed to pay $30 million to settle related allegations by Britain's Financial Services Authority (FSA).

Reserves are a critical indicator of an oil company's financial health. Investors use the numbers to judge the company's investment worthiness. Having insufficient reserves on hand is seen as a company weakness. Shell agreed to pay the fines, but company officials did not admit blame and instead chose to hang the whole deal on a lone employee. Shell suggested that a company employee responsible for auditing reserve numbers had very little training and no staff and may not have spotted the discrepancy in the numbers.

Although Shell played hide-and-seek by blaming an employee for its problems, the CorpWatch Organization had information indicating that the proved reserves figures reported to the market for at least the previous three years might have been overstated. The company previously announced it had cut its proven reserve estimates by 4.47 billion barrels, or 23 percent, from 1997 through 2002.[22] In addition, a report released by the FSA found that no further steps were taken by Shell to assess the accuracy of its reported proved reserves.

In the wake of the fines and negative publicity, Shell chairman Philip Watts, along with head of exploration and production Walter van de Vijver, and chief financial officer Judy Boynton were forced to resign. In the end, the problems caused the company to reorganize. The Royal Dutch and Shell Transport, who owned 60 percent and 40 percent respectively of Royal Dutch and Shell, were combined into one company with a single board.

But attorney William Lerach, representing shareholders, who filed suit against company executives and board members, said the reorganization was not enough. Lerach said: "It is a timid, inadequate step forward. They are proposing to go from a very bad, very dysfunctional corporate governance structure to a conventionally bad single corporate governance arrangement."[23]

Just when you think things would get better, the oil barbarians do it all over again. In January 2006, the Commodity Futures Trading Commission (CFTC) fined a top oil trader at Royal Dutch Shell PLC and one of the company's trading subsidiaries for a series of bogus oil-futures trades on the New York Mercantile Exchange. The CFTC said it had found that, on at least five occasions from November 2003 to March 2004, traders for Houston-based Shell Trading U.S. Co. and London-based Shell International Trading & Shipping Co. executed prearranged and noncompetitive trades in crude-oil futures contracts, in violation of exchange rules. The CFTC said the mirror-image trades, which were then executed on the exchange via brokers, constituted fictitious sales that eliminated price competition and market risk for the two entities.[24] This was done in an attempt to manipulate the markets. The CFTC claimed to have transcripts of e-mails and recorded phone conversations to outline what it described as highly detailed manipulation efforts.

This isn't the first time the company was fined by the CFTC. In July 2004, the company's Coral Energy Resources had agreed to pay $30 million to settle accusations that it submitted false price data to publishers. The CFTC findings showed that from at least January 2000 through September 2002, Coral reported false, misleading or knowingly inaccurate natural gas trading information, including price and volume information, to price reporting firms such as *Inside FERC's Gas Market Report,* and *Natural Gas Intelligence.* The CFTC also found that Coral attempted to manipulate natural gas prices by delivering trade information to the price-reporting firms with the intent to affect the market price of natural gas.[25]

Let's not be fooled into thinking that Shell's dirty deeds are just about price manipulation or accounting tricks. For environmental misdeeds as bad as or worse then BP's catastrophic oil spill in the Gulf of Mexico, we can point fingers straight at Shell. Environmental writer John Vidal, writing for *The Guardian UK Observer,* says Nigeria's agony dwarfs the Gulf oil spill and that people living in the Niger delta have had to live with environmental catastrophes for decades. In describing a visit to the area, Vidal writes:

> We could smell the oil long before we saw it—the stench of garage forecourts and rotting vegetation hanging thickly in the air.
> The farther we traveled, the more nauseous it became. Soon we were swimming in pools of light Nigerian crude, the

best-quality oil in the world. One of the many hundreds of 40-year-old pipelines that crisscross the Niger delta had corroded and spewed oil for several months.[26]

The country's Niger delta is home to 606 oil fields. According to the U.S. Energy Information Administration, Nigeria is among the top five exporters of crude oil to the U.S. with 1.0 million barrels a day.[27] The Shell Petroleum Development Company of Nigeria is the largest oil producer in the Niger Delta. Shell claims that 98 percent of its oil spills in the area are caused by vandalism.

But environmental watchdogs dispute the claims entirely. They say the leaks come from rusted and corroded pipelines and storage tanks, derelict pumping stations, and old wellheads. Environmentalists call the area the global capital of oil pollution. In fact Amnesty International, a leading human rights group, says Shell has been covering up catastrophic oil spills by blaming them on sabotage by local people. The group prepared a report that says people living in the area are suffering a "human rights tragedy" inflicted by decades of damage caused in large part by Royal Dutch Shell.[28]

Nigeria's national oil spill detection and response agency, known as Nosdra, says that between 1976 and 1996 more than 2.4 million barrels of oil have contaminated the environment. It also suggests that the majority of oil spills come from Shell operations. For example, on May 12, 2009, Shell's Bomo manifold blew up, leaking massive amounts of crude. A second leak, from a derelict oil tap, had already been continuously spilling oil for years. Shell hired a local company to clean up the mess, but the area remains an oil slick.[29]

Shell may have little incentive to fix the problems. The Nigerian oil field helps make the company a profit juggernaut. In 2009, Shell reported record profits of $31 billion, and the stock has been climbing. See Figure 6.1.

Now Shell is targeting the Arctic Ocean for drilling. Shell spokesperson, Curtis Smith says, "We are five years and 3.5 billion dollars into this project. We feel like we have put together a very robust program."[30]

But the freezing conditions and high seas could turn out to be a recipe for disaster. The Pew Environment Group has issued a report that advises oil companies and the government to take a more

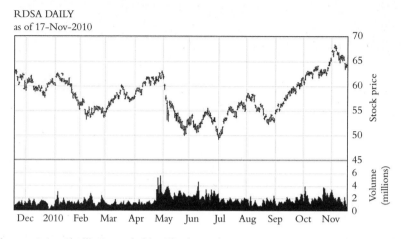

RDSA DAILY
as of 17-Nov-2010

Figure 6.1   Shell's Remarkable Climb in Share Price
DATA SOURCE: © BigCharts.com.

cautionary approach. In their report, they say drillers are unprepared for near-hurricane force winds, 20–30 foot seas, massive blocks of ice, total darkness for parts of the year, and hundreds of miles between drilling sites in northern Alaska. The report also says that skimmers, used to lift oil from the water's surface, won't work in the icy Arctic waters.

It's highly unlikely Shell will heed these warnings. After all, according to a U.S. Geological Survey in 2008, within the Arctic Circle there are 90 billion barrels of oil and vast quantities of natural gas waiting to be tapped.[31] We can only hope that when drilling begins, catastrophes like what happened in the Gulf of Mexico can be avoided in the Arctic, but it could turn out to be another "Niger Delta disaster."

Chapter 7

Cutthroat British Oil Empire

H e was known as the "Great Caruso." As a young boy, Enrico Caruso, who was born in 1873, enjoyed singing in the church choir in his hometown of Naples, Italy. As he grew up, he often sang in local restaurants for what little change the patrons could spare. One day, a young baritone Eduardo Missiano heard Caruso singing and thought he had a wonderful voice. Missiano pleaded with the young boy to see his own voice teacher, Guglielmo Vergine,[1] and Caruso agreed.

That marked the start of Caruso's opera career. His fame and notoriety would take him all over the world as wealthy people sought private performances by the rising star. Among this wealthy clan was notable English businessman William Knox D'Arcy, who was throwing his wife, Elena D'Arcy, a birthday party. D'Arcy made arrangements for the "Great Caruso" to sing at her party.

The couple was well known for throwing lavish parties at their mansion in Grosvenor Square. In fact the D'Arcy family was well known throughout London for its wealth. Mr. D'Arcy had made his fortune in the gold mining business. In 1882, he had invested money in the famous Mount Morgan Mine, which proved to be one of the richest gold mines in Australia.[2] But it would be D'Arcy's next investment that would make him wealthy beyond imagination and turn his company, British Petroleum, into a household name.

It all began in 1900, when Sir Henry Drummond Wolff, who had been a British Ambassador in Tehran, approached D'Arcy with the idea of providing the financing for an oil exploration adventure in Persia (Iran). Wolff was certain there was oil in this barren desert country, because he had seen the attempts to find it made by Baron Julius de Reuter, founder of Reuter's News Agency.

Although the Baron never succeeded in discovering oil, Wolff knew the land contained oil. You see Wolff had read a scientific paper written by a French geologist, DeMorgan, who suggested there were vast oil reserves in Persia. D'Arcy was intrigued. He was used to hunting for gold, so hunting for oil couldn't be that much different. Besides, oil, like gold, could enhance his wealth. This was an offer D'Arcy couldn't turn down; he was in on the deal.

In 1901 he sent Alfred Marriot to Tehran to secure a concession of land from the Shah to explore for oil in Persia. But Persia's neighbor, Russia, didn't want the British entering into the Middle East. Russia's rulers had long sought to control the Middle East countries that touched its borders. The Russian government caused quite a fuss over Marriot coming to visit the Shah. However, Marriot offered the Shah $10,000 in sterling silver (the British currency at the time) for a 60-year contract that gave D'Arcy and his group the right to explore for oil throughout 490,000 square miles of the Persian Empire.[3]

But they were forbidden to go anywhere near the five provinces of Persia that bordered Russia. The agreement read:

The Governor of His Imperial Majesty the Shah grants to the concessionaire by these presents a special and exclusive privilege to search for, obtain, exploit, develop, render suitable for trade, carry away and sell natural gas petroleum, asphalt, and ozokerite throughout the whole extent of the Persian Empire for a term of sixty years as from the date of these presents.[4]

Additional terms of the concession required that D'Arcy form an oil company within two years of signing the agreement. D'Arcy would have to foot the bill for the start-up funds. In addition, D'Arcy would have to pay the Persian Government $20,000 sterling silver along with 20,000 in shares of the newly formed company.[5] That was quite a lot of money back then, but D'Arcy was used to these kinds of deals. Before making his fortune in gold mining, D'Arcy had managed to make a comfortable living speculating on land. So speculating on oil wasn't much of a stretch. But the area of land he negotiated from the Shah, known as Chiah Surkh,[6] in the northwest part of the country, and had no passable roads or cities within hundreds of miles. This put the exploration in a barren output environment. Finding oil would be difficult enough, but how would he transport it?

D'Arcy hired George Reynolds, an engineer with experience drilling for oil in Sumatra to head the project. Finding oil in Sumatra wasn't an easy task, because it too meant the oilmen had to navigate rough terrains, uncovering hidden oil fields buried deep in tropical jungles. So Reynolds was more than capable of leading the exploration in Persia.

The exploration for oil began in September, but it would take much longer than either D'Arcy or Reynolds imagined to find oil in sufficient enough commercial quantities. Reynolds ran into many problems in his search for oil, including finding skilled laborers, encountering local tribes who rejected rule by the Persian government, and hauling equipment as many as 300 miles to the drilling sites. By 1905, no large quantity of oil reserves had been found. D'Arcy was running low on financial resources. He had already bankrolled the operation with his own money, which was about $600,000 sterling silver. He needed to find additional funding or risk shutting the operation down completely.

He found the help he was looking for from the Burmah Oil Company, a British oil company operating in India. The company was founded in 1886, and its main business was drilling, refining, and selling Burmese oil. The Burmah Oil Company agreed to back D'Arcy's venture in the Middle East, and the two parties formed a new company, the Concessions Syndicate. The Burmah Oil Company provided D'Arcy with an additional $50,000 sterling silver for exploration, along with another $20,000 to be held in reserves, if more money was needed. They also gave D'Arcy $25,000 to cover the amount he was overdrawn in his bank account.[7]

Now that D'Arcy had secured additional funding, Reynolds began drilling again. Realizing the site he had been drilling wasn't going to yield large oil reserves, Reynolds moved the operation to a new location in the southwestern part of Iran, known as Shardin. Reynolds stayed in the area for two years, drilling nothing more than dry holes. The Burmah Oil Company was signaling it had had enough. With no source of funding and almost out of money himself, D'Arcy sent a wire message to Reynolds to halt all drilling operations.

But Reynolds wasn't about to give up, because he had spent almost seven years of his life in this forsaken landmass hunting for oil. So once again, he moved the operation to a new site, Masjid i-Suleiman near the province of Khuzistan, about 200 kilometers from the Persian Gulf coast. It turned out to be the wisest decision he ever made. On May 26, 1908 Reynolds struck oil at 1,180 feet.[8] Immediately a new oil production company was formed to develop the oil field. That company, the Anglo-Persian Oil Company, was majority-owned (97 percent) by the Burmah Oil Company. However, now the Burmah Oil Company would have to negotiate a new deal with the Persian government, and that's exactly what they did.

In order to continue to drill for oil, the Anglo-Persian Oil Company agreed to pay a royalty to the Persian government on any oil it extracted from the site. It also had to pay taxes to the British government on any profits it made from the oil it produced from the Middle East. Unfortunately, D'Arcy's role in the new company was minimal. He was appointed as a director, but had little input on how the new company would operate. Sir Charles Greenway was appointed as head of the Anglo-Persian Oil Company. The discovery made by D'Arcy and Reynolds was the first commercial reserve of oil found in the Middle East.

The British Government Steps In

Drilling continued for four years, and in that time, a pipeline 145 miles long was built to carry the oil from the drilling site to the Persian Gulf, where a refinery was built. But as happened in the firm's past, its funds were running low. Sir Greenway needed a new source of funding if the Anglo-Persian Oil Company were to continue oil developments in the Persia, so he turned to Lord Southborough. Southborough, also known as Francis John Hopwood, held several prominent positions in London including Permanent Under-Secretary of State for the Colonies and Civil Lord of the Admiralty.[9]

Being appointed Civil Lord of the Admiralty put Lord Southborough in contact with important people in the British government, including Winston Churchill, who was serving as First Lord of the Admiralty, was part of the Ministry of Defense, and was in charge of the Royal Navy.

Churchill was intrigued by the idea of the British government having a stake in an oil company and immediately recognized the benefits the British government would gain working with an oil company. The most important one was that the British Navy would have access to a steady and permanent supply of oil. So, acting on behalf of the British Navy, Churchill agreed to back the operation. In 1914 the British government invested $2,200,000 British pounds in the Anglo-Persian Oil Company.[10] The arrangement meant the British government had a direct financial interest in the production of oil in the Middle East.

In exchange for its substantial investment, the British government could appoint two company directors and veto decisions that directly threatened or had a major impact on the strategic interests of Britain. In addition, the company would always be bound to help British citizens, home and abroad. But the British government's control didn't stop there. The Anglo-Persian Oil Company had to concentrate on developing products and technology that benefited the British government, such as producing and refining the oil for use as fuel in its fleets of ships and airplanes.[11] The British Admiralty, led by Winston Churchill, signed a 30-year contract with the Anglo-Persian Oil Company to provide fuel for the Navy. However, over time, through separate capital funding issues, the British government eventually came to own two-thirds of the voting stock of the Anglo-Persian Oil Company. The deal later proved to be a godsend for both the company and the British government when World War I broke out. The British government got exactly what it had bargained for—a continual and steady supply of oil to fuel its ships.

The Anglo-Persian Oil Company made out well too. During the war, its oil output climbed from 274,000 to 1,385,000 tons gaining a hefty profit of $200 million.

As mentioned previously, in the original agreement between the Persian government and the Anglo-Persian Oil Company, the company had to pay money to the Persian government for any oil it extracted. The agreement stipulated that the Anglo-Persian Oil Company would pay the government a 16 percent royalty on the net profits it made from the oil it took from the wells. Not realizing how much oil lay hidden in Persia when the agreement was made, it became clear to the Persian government that the amount of money it would receive would be small compared to the amount of oil the company could extract. For example, when the company made $200 million in profits, the Persian government received just $10 million, much less than what it was contractually obligated to pay,[12] because the Anglo-Persian Oil Company could exempt profits it made on refining and distribution of the oil it took from Persia. One Persian economist put it this way:

> In practice with great flexibility in accounting procedures which an integrated company such as APOC enjoyed, the company was able to allocate the largest portion of its profits to downstream activities and the balance to the production end of the operations.[13]

Naturally this kind of flexibility in accounting created discontent between the two parties, particularly the Persian government. Over the years, the Persian government came to resent the Anglo-Persian Oil Company, and tensions were high. Those tensions came to a head when in 1921 a coup to overthrow the ruling dynasty of the Persian government was headed by Sayyid Tabatabai, a popular Iranian journalist. and Colonel Reza Khan, member of the military. They won and

Reza Khan became Prime Minister. In 1925, the Majlis (parliament) voted to depose Ahmed Shah Qajar, whose family had ruled over Persia since 1779. That made Reza Khan, the new ruler of the Iranian empire. In fact by 1926, he became Shah of Iran. The British government had supported Khan in his quest to overthrow the government, and years earlier, they had hired him to protect their oil fields.

Now that he was in power, Shah Pahlavi pressured the Anglo-Persian Oil Company to come up with a new agreement. He insisted that the D'Arcy agreement was no longer in effect since the previous government, which now had no claims over the land, had written it. In 1928, the new president of the Anglo-Persian Oil Company, Sir John Cadman, outlined what he considered one of the most revolutionary proposals in the oil industry, one that would give the government of Iran both 25 percent of the company's shares and a shareholder interest in the company.

But the Shah and his cabinet members rejected the proposal. In a bold move, Shah Pahlavi cancelled the D'Arcy agreement completely. This forced Sir Cadman to come up with an entirely new proposal with dramatically changed terms. Under this new agreement, the amount of land the company could explore for oil was reduced to 100,000 acres. In addition, the Iranian government would receive a large share of the oil profits. The Iranian government also insisted that "no flexible accounting" be used to calculate the numbers. And last, after 60 years, all oil fields and refineries would become the property of the Iranian government.[14]

In 1935 the company changed its name to the Anglo-Iranian Oil Company. Its refinery in Abadan was the largest in the world. The company expanded its reach, with refineries built in Africa, Papua New Guinea, Australia, Canada, and South America, and even discovered oil in Scotland. Eager to capitalize on this newest discovery, the company built refineries in Scotland and also in South Wales. But no matter how much it expanded its oil empire outside the Middle East, it would always be plagued by Iran's political struggles. So once again, political unrest in the area led to another overthrow of the Iranian government. Dr. Mohammad Mossadegh, who held various cabinet positions in the Iranian government including Minister of Finance and Minister of Foreign Affairs, headed the coup.

Dr. Mossadegh was elected to the new parliament along with a group of Iranian nationalists and became Prime Minister in 1951. Mossadegh nationalized all oil from Iran. In another sweeping and dramatic change, The National Iranian Oil Company took ownership of three-fourths of the reserves that belonged to The Anglo-Iranian Oil Company.[15] This forced the Anglo-Iranian Oil Company into negotiating a new agreement with the Iranian government that resulted in a company that was part of a consortium of oil companies. It would rename itself the British Petroleum Company, which would control 40 percent of the consortium.[16]

BP continued expanding its oil exploration and production activities outside of Iran. In fact its reach was wide and far with wells in Libya and Nigeria and the North Sea. It secured leases in Alaska's Prudhoe Bay and even bought a huge stake in Standard Oil of Ohio. Just as it had used "flexible accounting" practices in calculating its royalty payments to the government of Iran, BP applied them in the deal it stuck with Standard Oil.

In exchange for its stake in the company, BP offered up 600,000 barrels of oil per day that it produced from Prudhoe Bay fields. By 1984 BP's stock holdings in Standard Oil of Ohio had grown to 55 percent, and in 1987 it purchased the remaining 45 percent, merging its North American holdings to form BP America, Inc.[17] Eventually British Petroleum shortened its name to BP, and in just over 100 years, it had grown into one of the world's largest oil empires.

Concern for the Environment

Over the past few years, BP has made a conscious effort to market itself as a company concerned about the environment, but considering their track record for oil spills, that marketing pitch doesn't make much sense. The Gulf of Mexico oil spill, which made headlines for months, now takes the title as the worst oil spill in history with roughly 4.4 million barrels of oil spilled into the Gulf waters.[18] Eleven men lost their lives when the *Deepwater Horizon* oil rig exploded into flames.

But that's not the only oil-related tragedy in the company's history. Let's not forget the lives lost in the explosion at the company's Texas refinery. In that 2005 incident, 15 employees died and 170 were seriously injured when the unit responsible for making jet fuel burst into flames. At the time, BP prided itself on its safety record. But a report prepared by James Baker III, who headed a panel appointed to investigate the explosion, said the company had a "false sense of confidence."[19] Other evidence showed that BP was too focused on reducing maintenance costs at its refineries. Brent Coon, the lawyer who sued BP on behalf of the families of the workers who died or were injured, said the company's safety record in the United States was poor: "The reality is that BP has a long history of under-investing and reinvesting in their infrastructure."[20]

It seems the barbarians of oil all think alike. Although BP bears blame for the incident, it passed the *real* blame on to a low-level worker, claiming the employee didn't do his job well. That's the same "pass the buck" mentality that Royal Dutch Shell used when it overstated its reserves, hoodwinking investors into thinking the company had more oil on hand than it did.

Putting its employees in danger and spilling oil seems to come easily to BP. In 2006, about 212,000 gallons of oil spilled onto the cold landscape of Alaska near the company's North Slope drilling operation. The cause was corroded pipelines. During hearings in September 2006, Republican representative Joe Barton of Texas, said, "BP's policies are as rusty as its pipelines." He added, "I'm even more concerned about BP's corporate culture of seeming indifference to safety and environmental issues. And this comes from a company that prides itself in their ads on protecting the environment. Shame. Shame. Shame."[21]

BP pleaded guilty of violating the Clean Water Act and was penalized with a $20 million fine and a three-year probation. But it only gets worse for the environment. The EPA, in an independent investigation, found numerous problems with BP's operations in Prudhoe Bay. The investigation found that in addition to leaking oil into the environment, the company has not implemented an acceptable spill-prevention and control plan and was delinquent in repairing pipelines it was under orders to fix.

Naturally BP disagrees. The company suggests that *only* some of its spill and prevention controls were not up to par. Of the Alaska spills, BP Alaska spokesman Steve Rinehart says, "We are a responsible,

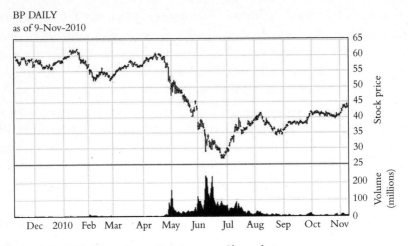

BP DAILY
as of 9-Nov-2010

Figure 7.1   BP's Share Price Continues to Skyrocket
DATA SOURCE: © BigCharts.com.

professional operator. We work to high standards. Safety is our highest priority."[22]

It certainly doesn't seem as if safety is the company's highest priority, perhaps because it is too busy focusing on profits. Although it has been asked to set aside $20 billion for claims related to the Gulf of Mexico spill, the company continues to make monster profits. BP has a market value of $152 billion, and in the first quarter of 2010, the company made about $8 billion.[23] See Figure 7.1 on BP's stock chart.

BP certainly has enough profits on hand to settle the claims related to the spill. But just as BP seems to take its time putting proper safety procedures in place to prevent future spills, it's also taking its time doling out money to those filing claims. Of the 4,700 claims received, only 295 have been paid out for a total of $3.5 million. Fadel Gheit, an oil analyst at Oppenheimer, says the spill was "a major disaster with catastrophic implications not only for the companies involved, but also for the offshore oil industry and the economies of the Gulf Coast."[24] Now you can see why we put BP on our list of cutthroat barbarians.

Chapter 8

Budding Oil Empires

I n Bunwell England, in a small churchyard, stands a statue of John Blake. Several generations of the Blake family lived in the town of Bunwell, a parish of Norfolk that stretches across five miles of agricultural countryside.

The Blake family was a prominent part of the town of Bunwell, so when John died, the town erected a statue in his honor. Unknown to most people, the Blake family has a long and prestigious history. Genealogy records indicate that the family came to England under William the Conqueror, and in fact in 1185, Richard Blake was a Norman knight who fought under Prince John during the invasion of Ireland.[1] In return for his duty, he was given grants to land, which were passed on to his family heirs.

One of those heirs, William, was the first to travel to the new colonies. William married and had several children, and the new lineage of the Blake family was living in America. Part of the new lineage was Isaac Blake, a reverend for the Methodist church in Vermont. The area was barely settled, and the land was harsh. Isaac owned a small farm and sawmill, which produced a small amount of money he used to supplement his income. Although older than most soldiers, Isaac joined the Union Army, where he was made Chaplain, but his time as an Army Chaplain was short lived. He left his wife and children to fend for themselves.

His son, Isaac Elder Blake was a smart boy, who read a good deal and could memorize almost anything he read or saw. It's no wonder that schoolwork came easy to him, so much so that he advanced to the head of his class and graduated from school before his classmates. At age 16, he was granted a certificate to teach school. Certificates were normally issued only to people 18 or older, but because of Isaac's extraordinary learning abilities, he was allowed to receive a teaching certificate at such a young age. After serving as a schoolteacher for several years, Blake took a job with a mercantile firm in a small town located just outside Boston, and it was there that Blake decided he'd like to practice law. But of course, to do so, he'd have to attend college. He began saving money so he could attend Harvard University.

But as happened with many men, Blake got caught up in the oil frenzy that was sweeping the nation. It seemed anyone willing to dig for oil could become a millionaire. Blake was faced with a most important decision—abandon his dreams of becoming a lawyer or try his hand in the oil industry.

He chose the oil industry but wasn't about to dig for oil; instead he considered buying shares of oil companies. He heard the stories of investors who had made small fortunes investing in emerging oil production companies. If they could get rich in that way, Blake figured he could, too. So he took a few hundred dollars of the money he had saved for college and put it into two different oil companies. Unfortunately, Blake's investment didn't pan out, and he was not to become a rich man by investing in oil companies. Although he lost money on the investment, he still believed the oil business could make him rich. In fact, he went to Oil City to see firsthand how people were making their fortunes drilling for oil.

During that visit Blake got the idea that shipping oil from the area might be a better path to his future fortune. As oil was often shipped to refineries on flat-bottom boats on the nearby rivers, Blake saw an opportunity to make money transporting oil in this manner. So he bought a flat-bottom boat for $230.[2] Blake asked his brother-in-law to join him in Oil City, and the two began transporting oil on their boat. But Blake would not see his oil fortune yet. The river water receded so low that the boats could barely float, especially when they were loaded down with heavy barrels of oil, so Blake sold his boat. Now he needed a job, and as much as he didn't want to dig for oil, that's exactly what he wound up doing. He took a job with a drilling company already operating the area.

Blake had no experience handling drilling equipment and knew little about the machinery. But because he could memorize almost anything he saw or read, he learned what to do by watching other men perform the same tasks. Although he earned the company's respect, Blake had no intentions of making his long-term career as a hands-on driller. He was in it to get rich. So from his drilling job, he moved on to another large oil firm. But this time, he held a more responsible desk position. While at the firm, he secured the rights to piece of land that showed the promise of oil. Soon after acquiring the land, he struck oil at 1,000 feet.[3] The well produced as much as 12,000 barrels a month, the largest amount of oil in the region.[4]

Going West

Isaac Elder Blake found his fortune in oil, but this fortune didn't last. The more money Blake made, the more chances he took. Sometimes instead of opening more wells, he speculated on oil itself. Around 1872, Blake agreed to purchase 1,000,000 barrels of oil at about $2.5 per barrel for delivery in the summer months. It was around this time that experts believed that large amounts of oil could no longer be produced from certain areas. Because of the mass drilling that had occurred, with derricks only hundreds of feet apart, experts said that continued drilling for oil would yield minimal quantities.

Yet the population's desire for oil was still strong. Blake figured with a strong demand and fewer reserves available, he could make a fortune speculating on oil. However, what Blake didn't count on was that the experts were wrong. New reserves would be found, some yielding as much as 1,700 barrels a day. Suddenly there was a glut of oil on the market, which caused a dramatic drop in the price of oil to 40 cents a barrel, far below the $2.50 a barrel that Blake agreed to purchase the oil.[5]

Payment for the future shipments was due, and Blake was paying for oil that he couldn't sell for more than 40 cents a barrel. He was now in debt and needed a way to make a fast fortune, so he turned his attention to Ogden, Utah. Ogden was unique because it was still using candles and whale oil to light homes. Kerosene was available to the town people, but at a steep price because the source of the kerosene was an oil refinery located in Colorado. Rather than pay for costly kerosene, the townspeople opted to use whale oil, which was much cheaper. The oil was shipped in wooden barrels, but because of the dry climate, the wood would shrink causing oil to leak from the barrels in large quantities. Having spent a good amount of time in Oil City, and seeing the oil was shipped in specially made oil tankers, Blake knew the same could be done in this area. Before the end of the year, Blake invented and patented his own oil-tank car that allowed him to ship bulk amounts of oil to Utah and surrounding areas at low prices, which made it more affordable.

On November 25, 1875 the Continental Oil and Transportation Company was born.[6] Blake had progressed to building a budding oil empire swiftly. He was transporting oil from the East Coast to Utah, Idaho, Montana, and Nevada. When oil was discovered in California, he built a pipeline, which ran from Pico to Ventura. Naturally, Blake's oil empire caught the attention of John D. Rockefeller. Because Rockefeller couldn't stand competition, he found ways to sideline Blake's success, and when he could no longer succeed at that, he simply bought Blake's company. No burgeoning oil empire was going to get in his way, certainly not The Continental Oil Company. Ten years after Blake started the Continental Oil and Transportation Company, it became part of Standard Oil. It was renamed the Continental Oil Company, and Blake was appointed president and manager.

But Blake's speculative ways would catch up with him yet again. He invested much of his money in railroads, which proved disastrous. In 1893, he resigned his post as president of Continental Oil, and Henry Tilford took over and built the Continental Oil Company into a huge oil enterprise. It gained control of 98 percent of the Western U.S. oil market.

Not Environmentally Friendly

In 2002, Continental merged with Phillips Petroleum and was renamed ConocoPhillips. ConocoPhillips enjoys the title of the nation's third largest energy producer. In the fourth quarter of 2009, it posted $1.2 billion in profits.[7]

Known almost everywhere, the company sells gasoline at 11,800 service stations. But that isn't its only claim to fame. In 2002, the Political Economy Research rated ConocoPhillips the third-worst polluter in the U.S.[8] Like its barbarian counterparts, ConocoPhillips has been the culprit behind huge oil spills. In 2004, 21 miles of land was contaminated from oil that spewed out of the *Polar Texas*, an oil tanker owned by the company. Of course, ConocoPhillips did not admit guilt even though lab tests linked the oil directly from the tanker. Investigations showed that between 1,000 and 7,200 gallons of oil came from the tanker.[9] That same year, the Alaska Department of Environmental Conservation fined the company for violating the Clean Air Act. High carbon monoxide emissions from turbine engines had exceeded posted and approved air-quality limits.[10]

If that wasn't bad enough, the company is still dealing with a spill that occurred in 2003 at Nipomo Creek in California. The oil came from a leaky pipeline. Officials say the contamination area could run as deep as two to three feet below the surface. Although the spill happened in 2003, the clean-up is not slated to begin until 2011 or the summer of 2012.[11]

After the *Deepwater Horizon* oil disaster, President Obama formed an oil catastrophe commission to investigate the implications on future offshore drilling activities. To head the commission, he appointed William K. Reilly and Bob Graham as co-chairs. Reilly has some experience with the oil industry, as he served as EPA Chief for President George H. Bush. However, he also happens to sit on the board of ConocoPhillips. ConocoPhillips has a joint venture in the works with BP to drill for oil in the Gulf's Tiber field. Executives at ConocoPhillips are worried that the *Deepwater Horizon* spill might hold back drilling operations in Tiber Field. But if Reilly sits on their board, is it possible he could report back to the President that things look just fine for drilling?

West Coast Oil

Shortly after oil was discovered in Pennsylvania, California became the center of attention. Isaac Blake made a hefty fortune transporting oil through pipelines he built that ran from the Pico Canyon oil field to Ventura. Charles Mentry, an experienced Pennsylvania oilman, first discovered oil in Pico Canyon, and Mentry commenced drilling on August 22, 1975. He drilled to a depth of about 120 feet, and at that level the well produced about 10 to 12 barrels of oil per day.[12]

Menty continued drilling in the area for several more years and dug a total of three wells. About 1876, Mentry sold out to Demetrius Scofield and Frederick Taylor who had formed the California Star Oil Works Company. However, Mentry was kept on as the superintendent of the drilling operations. Most of the equipment the men had on hand, they got from junk piles left behind from previous oil drilling operations. It was hard drilling for oil in the area, and earlier attempts produced oil, but not in large enough commercial quantities to make the ventures worthwhile. That is until 1877, when Mentry's decided to drill to a depth of 617 feet where he struck a gusher of oil. Mentry called his field, Pico Number 4.[13] It became the first commercially successful oil drilling operation west of Pennsylvania. On top of this, the oil was often of good grade. Initially the wells pumped about 200 barrels of oil a day, and over time, the amount increased to 300 barrels.[14]

However, Scofield, being the numbers man in the group, decided the men needed more money to continue their drilling operations. He managed to convince some high profile businessman and Senator Charles Felton to provide additional funding. A new company was formed, the Pacific Coast Oil Company, and in its first year of operation, the company built the largest and most modern refinery in California. The refinery could produce as much as 600 barrels of oil a day.

Another refinery was built at Lyons Station in Ventura, California, but it was later moved to Andrew's Station to be closer to the Southern Pacific Railroad stop.

In 1895, the company launched its own tanker, the *George Loomis*, which could carry 6,500 barrels of oil between Ventura and San Francisco.

But with the company's fate resembled that of The Continental Oil Company; the Pacific Coast Oil Company became part of Rockefeller's Standard Oil.

Standard Oil had already opened offices in the San Francisco area. Whereas Pacific Coast Oil was exceptional at finding oil, Standard was gifted at refining oil and selling it. The Pacific Coast Oil Company couldn't compete with Standard Oil, and Rockefeller would have it no other way. In 1900, Standard Oil bought out Pacific Coast Oil. However, Pacific Oil was allowed to operate under that name. As Standard Oil strengthened its operations in California from laying pipelines to buying several oil tankers, the company decided to consolidate Pacific Coast Oil and Standard Oil into one firm: Standard Oil Company of California. Gasoline sales nearly doubled between 1906 and 1910, and because of its growing gasoline sales, Standard Oil of California created the world's first "service station."[15]

Standard Oil steadily expanded its service station network, and by the end of 1919, it had a total of 218 stations, more than the next three rivals combined. The growth of its service stations was spectacular. By 1926, the number of service stations in the company's five-state marketing area more than tripled, to 735 units.[16] Standard maintained its position as the number one producer in California. When the United States went war in December 1941, Standard became a key supplier of crude oil and refined products for the Allies in the Pacific. After the war, Standard continued its growth, reaching tremendous revenue milestones. For example, in 1951 revenues surpassed $1 billion for the first time. Their growth never slowed, and by 1961, revenues hit the $2 billion mark and topped $6 billion by 1969.[17]

Just as service stations had become a major component of the company's growth, it focused attention on developing new types of gasoline including Chevron and Chevron Supreme. Those products became two of its most recognizable brands. In 1977, the company made a major organizational change when it formed Chevron U.S.A. Inc., merging six domestic oil and gas operations into one. Chevron now holds the title of the second largest energy company in the U.S. Its third quarter profits for 2010 were $3.77 billion,[18] and its share price sits at $82. See Figure 8.1.

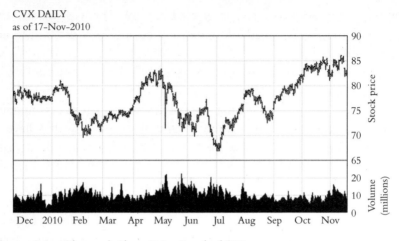

CVX DAILY
as of 17-Nov-2010

Figure 8.1   Chevron's Share Price Reached $82
DATA SOURCE: © BigCharts.com

Chevron's growth story is incredible. But just like its oil counter-parts, it also has its share of oil tragedies. The company is fighting a $27 billion environmental lawsuit in Ecuador stemming from environmental damages. The lawsuit dates back to 1964, when Texaco began drilling for oil in the Ecuadoran Amazon. Chevron bought Texaco in 2001 when Texaco was working in partnership with Ecuador's local oil company Petroecuador. As part of normal operating procedure, Texaco dumped a mix of petroleum and water into open pits near the oil wells. When Texaco pulled out of the country in 1992, it agreed to clean up a portion of the area while Petroecuador continued to operate the wells. But plaintiffs say the cleanup was a sham, and the area's soil and water are contaminated. Residents of Ecuador's oil producing area are seeking damages for environmental contamination caused by Texaco, which operated in the area from 1964 to 1990. Chevron insists that any remaining pollution in the area is Petroecuador's problem. The company insists that Texaco operated under local and international standards.

What's more disturbing is that the *Wall Street Journal* reported that Chevron told shareholders that it would not pay Ecuador if it lost the suit. The $27 billion recommended as judgment for the plaintiffs would be the biggest environmental judgment against an oil company.

If Chevron, which expects to lose the case, does not pay, the Ecuador government won't be able to seize any assets, because Chevron never operated in Ecuador.[19] Chevron won't be able to get out of paying the judgment free and clear, because the matter would be turned over to the U.S. courts.

Of the matter, Chevron spokesman Don Campbell says, "We're not paying and we're going to fight this for years if not decades into the future."[20] Just the kind of statement you'd expect an oil barbarian to make.

Part Three

DANGEROUS LIAISONS

Chapter 9

The Birth of OPEC

sk any energy analyst to describe the Organization of the Petroleum Exporting Countries (OPEC) in one word and you'll invariably get "cartel," which is defined as "a combination of independent commercial or industrial enterprises designed to limit competition or fix prices."[1]

We'd like to add "barbarian" to that description. From its birth, OPEC has ruthlessly hoarded its black gold, and used the world's addiction as a crude weapon in wars of politics. Remember the mile-long lines at filling stations, the ply board signs hastily scrawled with "No Gas" in the early 1970s? We have OPEC to thank for that . . . and we dedicate much of Chapter 11 to their oil embargoes. But what most people don't realize is that OPEC's very nature is an American creation that was originally designed to protect American oil interests from Arab nationalists.

This is important to remember, as it has shaped policy and perceptions of OPEC and the West for the past hundred years. Let's go back to just after World War II. Great Britain (the former imperial powerhouse of the world and long-time Gulf-nations partner) had lost much of its international clout, and its currency was floundering in the post-war years. Europe was in shambles and desperately needed to rebuild. No, wait. Let's go back even further, to the Great Depression when an American oil company called Standard Oil was granted an exclusive agreement with the King of Saudi Arabia to produce his kingdom's oil.[2] This unusual move by King 'Abd al-'Azīz ibn Sa'ūd was the beginning of all Arab-American policy, and the start of what is now the state-controlled oil behemoth, Saudi Aramco, probably the biggest state-owned oil barbarian on the planet.

In 1938, Well #7 in the Dammam field hit paydirt[3] with a massive gusher, and Saudi Arabia went from being an inhospitable desert to one of the most strategic oil producers in the world. During World War II, the United States cemented its ties with Saudi Arabia in order to keep oil flowing to the Allies. The United States even built its first airbase on Saudi soil in 1945 at Dharhan.

As World War II ended, American prominence in the region was assured, and so was a cheap oil supply for rebuilding European nations. In the years that followed it was American capitalism, not British imperialism that ruled the roost. However, America's stronghold was tested before too long, and this testing brought about one of the most self-serving organizations in oil history.

This way of thinking was new to the Arab nations, whose nationalist uprisings were aimed at taking over the oil fields and distributing their wealth to all citizens, not just the royal families and the upper echelons of society. But it wasn't new to U.S. capitalists. In fact, Harold Ickes, the U.S. Secretary of the Interior in the late 1930s and early 1940s, tried to push through legislation that would take over parts of the dismantled Standard Oil Company so that the government could secure a stake in Saudi crude reserve, exclusively for its own use.[4] This was oil-based colonialism, plain and simple . . . and where the government didn't succeed, giant oil barbarians did.

The Seven Sisters

As mentioned in Chapter 1, during the 1940s and 1950s, oil-producing countries in the Middle East, along with Venezuela and Indonesia, were essentially carved up by a small number of barbaric oil companies dubbed "The Seven Sisters."[5] This group included Standard Oil of New Jersey; Standard Oil Company of New York; Standard Oil of California; Gulf Oil; Texaco; Royal Dutch Shell; and the Anglo-Persian Oil Company.

You may recognize some famous names in this group, as Standard Oil Company of New York is now ExxonMobil, Standard Oil of California and Texaco have become Chevron, and the Anglo-Persian Oil Company is now British Petroleum. In effect, this was a pre-OPEC cartel formed by corporations instead of countries. It was called the International Petroleum Cartel (IPC). . . . The cartel decided who was in their elite group and who wasn't, and they set oil prices and determined how much was pumped from where.

The nations under which these oil reserves were sitting had no say or control over oil operations . . . but they did get paid. This "tyranny" was the basis for the formation of OPEC. To be sure, the oil-producing nations where the Seven Sisters held sway began to get rich. The international companies had to pay their host governments signature bonuses, royalties, certain taxes, and other payments.[6] And this gave them economic power that they had not previously seen. In fact, prior to the massive production of oil in the Middle East, these producing countries were under the thumb of colonial rule. It was only after World War II that these countries became successful at seeking independence. But it was only after the presence of the Seven Sisters on their soil, drilling for their oil, that these countries had the means to seek economic independence.

In 1959 and 1960, the Seven Sisters gave oil-producing nations a reason to steal back their oil wealth. The discovery of major oil fields in Libya by the Continental Oil Company (Conoco) led to a massive surplus of oil, even with the burgeoning demand in the United States. The surplus was so great that the Seven Sisters, who had been excluded from the exploration and production process in Libya, got together and unilaterally cut their prices in August 1960. This change meant that payments to their oil host nations were slashed by 7 percent.[7] Douglas Little, author of *American Orientalism: The United States and the Middle East Since 1945,* writes, "Outraged by such high-handedness, oil ministers from Saudi Arabia, Iran, Iraq, and Venezuela gathered hastily in Baghdad, where on 14 September 1960 they founded OPEC."[8]

This was a barbaric move disguised by nationalist trappings. Arab nations had begun to speak out for control over their own resources. As they gained more independence from their former colonial rulers, and more cash from their lucrative oil industries, oil-producing nations gained a significant bargaining chip, because global demand was becoming more and more dependent on Arab oil. And as the Seven Sisters had done most of the heavy lifting in the exploration and production industry, it was easy for some governments to sweep in and nationalize their oil reserves, taking over the entire energy industry. This trend was backed by some United Nations resolutions, such as the 1962 passing of Resolution 1803 that recognized "permanent sovereignty of states over their natural resources."[9]

But these nationalistic moves weren't necessarily made to uplift the dregs of society, even though OPEC structures its policies around "the inalienable right of all countries to exercise permanent sovereignty over their natural resources in the interest of their national development."[10] These moves were made to increase oil-producing nations' wealth. Indeed, OPEC had far less of an Arab-nationalist aim than an oil-barbarian aim. Not all founding OPEC nations were of Arab origin, and that's become even truer as the organization has grown in membership.

The only thing these nations have in common is oil and the desire to make as much money as possible from it. And that makes OPEC no different from the greedy Seven Sisters who had originally colonized Arab oil.

World Response

At first, the formation of OPEC didn't make much of a splash in the international world. The industry had always relied on private businesses to produce the oil for these nations,[11] and many were skeptical that OPEC would change this status quo. Indeed, a year before, Arab oil producers met with Iran, and Venezuela to form a group that preceded OPEC. It was called the Oil Consultation Commission, and it failed because of ideological differences within the Arab oil-producing countries.[12]

Who was to say that this group would fare any better? Ian Skeet, author of *OPEC: Twenty-Five Years of Prices and Politics*, writes:

Those who understood what was intended [by OPEC], and that was a small number of oil company officials, a few members of the specialist oil press and a scattering of diplomats, were interested but for the most part sceptical [sic] of what had been achieved in Baghdad.[13]

News coverage ranged from the mundane to the slightly perceptive, but none guessed the sweeping powers this group would eventually hold. They could have taken note of some of the issues the original Oil Consultation Commission met to discuss in April 1959 in Cairo:[14]

- Improvement of contractual terms and the requirement for consultation on price change
- Integrated approach to oil industry operations
- Increasing refinery capacity in their countries
- Establishment of national oil companies
- National coordination of the conservation, production, and exploitation of oil resources

At first, in an interview with the *London Times*, Juan Pablo Perez Alfonzo, Minister of Mines in Venezuela and arguably the main push behind the formation of OPEC, inferred that oil companies were the "natural allies"[15] of OPEC nations. But clearly these fledgling barbarians were focused on some level of nationalization. Indeed, one of the resolutions passed by OPEC in its first year of existence renationalized all non-producing acreage contracted to international oil companies within the IPC.[16] And beyond that, there needed to be coordination that could keep prices high and all oil producing nations on the same level. This was important for Venezuela in particular, as it had been producing oil since 1917, and costs were much higher there than for other producers.[17]

The key was to introduce quotas, thereby restricting production. It's a simple idea: Restrict access to a product for which there is a growing demand and you can charge more for said product. This was Perez Alfonzo's game-changing idea that he brought to the OPEC table, and one that has served these barbarians well in the first couple of decades of its existence. Production quotas are also serving OPEC well now. As Margaret McQuaile, reporter for Platts.com, explains:

In the world of OPEC, the word production can mean different things. There is official production, whereby OPEC sets
quotas for individual members under an overall volume, and
there is actual production, which can bear little resemblance to
official levels.

And there is a further complication. OPEC, although it
has given out the overall target number for the current output agreement, has not published the individual quotas under
that target. Which means that people like my colleagues and
myself have had to work out those quotas by ourselves, sometimes with a bit of help from delegates or ministers who may
confirm figures or indicate that our calculations are close to
the mark.[18]

This is helpful to OPEC because by not publishing actual production by country, some are secretly over-producing, even as oil prices
climb. In fact, in November 2009, as oil prices climbed above $80 a
barrel from their devastating fall down to $30 earlier in the year, a sur-
vey showed OPEC production to be at 28.89 billion barrels a day, while
the cartel's production quotas only totaled 24.845 million barrels a day.[19]
These barbarians of crude are creating a false supply scenario. They are
trying to convince the oil market that their production is far less than it
actually is. This acts to buoy prices, even in one of the worst recessions
the global economy has ever seen.

Sometimes, though, they get it wrong. For all their production
manipulation with the "Supply Shell Game," they made a huge mistake
in the late 1990s. Specifically, let's look at Jakarta in November of
1997. OPEC members voted to raise quotas in an uncertain market. In
the previous 10 months, oil prices dropped 28 percent as the "Asian
Contagion" began. In one of their most costly mistakes, OPEC
nations raised production quotas to try to recoup their losses by selling more of their product. They were wrong in the worst way. As the
Asian financial crisis deepened, oil prices fell another 44 percent, and
in December 1998, a barrel of crude traded for below $11.[20] But we're
getting a bit ahead of ourselves here. The beginning years of OPEC
were a test of sorts for its members. What would the countries do with
their oil wealth? How powerful would they become?

How Could We Have Known?

OPEC got off to a bit of a slow start. Most of its member nations' oil industries were built by international oil companies, and it took time for countries to build up a skilled population. Take Saudi Arabia and oil behemoth Aramco (before it was nationalized). According to Helen Chapin Metz, editor of *Saudi Arabia: A Country Study*:

> [Aramco] company presidents were virtually United States ambassadors in Saudi Arabia and played a significant role in shaping United States-Saudi relations in the early days of the oil company. Moreover, the undeveloped infrastructure and facilities demanded that Aramco construct virtually everything it needed.
>
> A port to bring in equipment had to be built; water had to be found and delivered to work areas; and housing, hospitals, and offices had to be constructed to launch development. Few Saudis were familiar with machinery, local construction firms hardly existed, and the unavailability of most materials locally necessitated long supply lines.[21]

Aside from the lack of experience in the oil industry, OPEC's young tyrants also had to prove they could work together, and history had shown this to be a difficult prospect. It made some potential members think twice about joining the group. Even though after its inception, several nations rushed to join OPEC out of a sense of Arab nationalism, there were some that didn't think it worthwhile. Qatar became a member in 1961, and Indonesia and Libya joined by 1962. But at the sixth OPEC conference in 1964, Nigeria, Algeria, Trinidad, and Colombia were in attendance. They were largely unimpressed: Algeria didn't become a member until 1969, Nigeria waited until 1971, and Trinidad and Colombia never joined the group.[22]

Truth be told, this first decade was all about how much power OPEC could grab, and if it could survive obstacles that included internal struggles with the Saudi royal family, Iraq's invasion of Kuwait, and the price and production battle with the International Petroleum Cartel.

How could we have known how much power OPEC would wield from this juvenile squabbling? OPEC's very existence butted up against an already powerful group of international oil companies that had brought millions of barrels of Middle Eastern oil to market.

The Seven Sisters were, of course, fundamentally opposed to OPEC, since nationalization of oil reserves meant they were booted out of extremely lucrative production contracts. In late 1961, the Iraqi government passed Law No. 80, which meant that Iraq could take back all the land concessions that were not already producing oil.[23] That was about 99 percent of all the Iraq Petroleum Company hold-ings at the time.[24] No wonder this move sparked a decade of power struggle between the two cartels. But even this move didn't clue in the world into just how much control OPEC would eventually yield with Saudi Arabia at the helm. The internal struggle in Saudi Arabia threat-ened the hard-won accords the country made with the international oil market.

In 1953, Prince Saud succeeded his father, Abd al Aziz. As prince, he was known to squander vast amounts of money, and as king, this behavior was amplified. He spent lavish sums to outfit his "White Army," and to keep the country's tribes favorably disposed to him. By 1958, he was outspending oil revenues that totaled $300 million per year, and the country's currency, the riyal, was devalued by 80 percent.[25] This spendthrift was so unpopular in the country that even his own family called for him to transfer power to his brother Faisal.

Under increasing pressure, which included a strike by Saudi Aramco workers in 1956, Saud signed over executive powers in for-eign and internal affairs (read, fiscal planning) on March 24, 1958,[26] appointing Faisal to the post of Prime Minister. The two brothers continued to struggle, though Faisal's fiscal policies were credited with bringing the nation back from the brink of bankruptcy. Hard to imagine Saudi Arabia, the world's largest oil producer, with money problems, isn't it?

Saud's interference made Faisal decide to relinquish his post of Prime Minister in January 1961. Saud was more than happy to see him go, but the struggles didn't end there. Saudi-controlled Yemen rose up against the Saudis, sparking a "civil war," and aided by Egypt they nearly succeeded in overthrowing the Saudi royal family.[27] With the country's power changing hands, the government was weak and a target for rebellion, and Saud ignored his family's calls for reform, and was outraged when—in order to put down the rebellion in Yemen—the family cut his personal spending while he was on an extravagant tour of Europe in March 1964.[28]

It wasn't long before the royal family forced Saud out of power, and on November 3, 1964, Saud abdicated the throne, and his brother Faisal was installed as king.[29] With Faisal's conservative spending and a threefold increase in oil production in the 1970s, Saudi Arabia's Aramco skyrocketed to become the largest oil company in the world.[30] And oil demand popped right alongside production, which set the scene for a massive energy crisis. Oil has always been tied to politics, particularly as nationalism swept through countries rich in natural resources. And this meant power.

No one could have guessed just how much power OPEC had in its hands, but just a few years into the 1970s, OPEC's hold over oil would send shockwaves through the United States and the world.

Chapter 10

The Arab-Israeli Oil Wars

The Organization of the Petroleum Exporting Countries (OPEC) was still coming into its own when an old conflict broke out anew. Israel and the Arab nations had been fighting, some might argue, since biblical times. But since the creation of Israel as a state after the Second World War through the early years of OPEC, there had been three major conflicts. The fourth would hand OPEC power that seemed unfathomable in the group's infancy.

Oil, OPEC would find, is a powerful weapon.

The Second Sinai Conflict

The major players of the era—the United States, Britain, and Russia—were being forced to share the spotlight with up-and-coming OPEC nations, m ore specifically, Arab members of OPEC.

Everyone knew that Russia still pulled the strings in Syria,[1] that Britain had only recently relinquished its authority in Kuwait, and that the United States was a staunch advocate for the new nation of Israel, even after the Six-Day War in 1967 pushed Israel's borders into Egypt, Jordan, and Syria.[2] But as OPEC nations forced international oil companies out of long-standing contracts, their hold over oil reserves translated to greater political sway, particularly as it related to the Arab-Israeli conflict.

In fact, Saudi Arabia's oil revenues provided a steady stream of financial support to Egypt and Syria who battled against an Israeli state.[3] Consider this from *New York Magazine* in June 1975:

> In addition to helping pay for the 22,000 troops in Lebanon, the Saudis three years ago pledged to give Syria $1.8 billion a year because of its status as a "confrontation state" in relation to Israel.[4]

But let's go back to the Six-Day War, to see the setup for how OPEC would come to dominate the oil market. For that we have to go back to the events leading up to June 5, 1967. And even the histories of these events date back to the formation of Israel back in 1948. The tangled conflict seemingly has no true beginning. But let's focus on the Second Sinai Conflict as a starting point. On July 26, 1956, Egypt nationalized the Suez Canal, a desperate move of retaliation against the West for reneging on promises of financial aid for a $1.3 billion project to dam the Nile.[5]

The Suez Canal was raking in nearly $100 billion,[6] and Egypt's president, Gamal Abd el Nasser took control of it in order to finance the dam. France and Britain operated the Suez Canal jointly, and these two countries received the bulk of the profits. Needless to say, they took offense to the nationalization of this huge moneymaker, and started to plan military action against Egypt. Their next move was to invite Israel to participate.

Israel was more than willing to join in, because Egypt had been intercepting and sometimes destroying ships with cargo to and from Israel attempting to use the Suez Canal.[7] Indeed, Israel was already planning military reactions to Egypt's continued conflicts on the border.[8]

And it was Israel who invaded the Sinai Peninsula, while France and Britain were to play the roles of restraining superpowers; the calm voice of reason in the Middle East, one hand offering an olive branch while the other was brandishing a hot poker. In short order, things got out of hand.

On October 29, 1956, Israel implemented Operation Kadesh,[9] deploying a battalion into the Sinai. It was part of a four-pronged attack, whereby Israel would invade the Gaza Strip, Sharm el-Sheikh, al-Arish, and Abu Uwayulah. By winning these positions, Israel would have access to the Red Sea, remove key Egyptian command centers, and destroy enemy training grounds. In just over a week, Israel had accomplished its objectives, and occupied the Sinai Peninsula. Israel declared victory on November 7, 1956, and sought to claim the entire Peninsula as new territory.[10]

The world objected, including the United States, and forced Israel to back out of most of the territory it had just won. By January 13, half of the Sinai was back under Egyptian rule.[11] Israel's continued occupation of Gaza forced Saudi Arabia to warn that the West's interests in the Middle East would suffer so long as Israeli troops were still beyond the armistice lines established a decade before.[12] This was a huge problem with global ramifications. Isaac Alteras, author of *Eisenhower and Israel: U.S.-Israeli Relations, 1953–1960*, wrote:

> The longer Israeli troops remained in the Sinai, the more influence the Soviet Union gained in the Arab world by blaming the United States for not exerting sufficient pressure on Israel to withdraw. Moreover, Nasser would obstruct the clearance of the Suez Canal until Israeli troops withdrew from Egyptian territory, thus depriving Western Europe of oil from the Persian Gulf.[13]

This is a key observation, as the Six-Day War in 1967 was provoked by Soviet lies about amassing troops on the border between Syria and Israel,[14] and one of the first ways oil became a bargaining chip between the Middle East and the West. We'll get to these lies in just a minute. But first, let's get through the years leading up to that Six-Day War.

Russia Steps In

Throughout this time, Arab nations were rallying around anti-Israeli sentiments. The Palestinians were being pushed out of their own homelands, and they were beginning to fight back. But that wasn't the only fight. Israel and Syria to its north were in constant struggles against each other. Syria even wanted to divert the River Jordan, leaving Israel literally in the dust.

In November 1964, Israeli and Syrian forces clashed on Israel's northern border after Syria attempted to divert the Jordan's headwaters. Israel had been holding certain lands from the Armistice Agreement out of reach of Syrian farmers, and using waters from the Jordan River to support new Israeli settlements. In retaliation, Syria decided not to let the land be cultivated by anyone, and began firing on Israeli farmers.[15]

The West tried to implement compromise over the Jordan River, but that didn't stop the frequent violations of borders from both parties, and tensions continued to climb. Egypt, in the meantime, fortified its position in the Sinai, and rebuilt roads and infrastructure. Chaim Herzog and Shlomo Gazit wrote in their book, *The Arab-Israeli Wars: War and Peace in the Middle East*, "Giant strongpoints [sic] had been established, including air bases, training camps, storage depots—all combining to form one solid fortified framework, stretching back from the border with Israel deep into the heart of the central Sinai."[16]

Through the help of the Soviets, the Gaza Strip was also turned into a military stronghold. In the decade leading up to the Six-Day War, the Russians had supplied $1.5 billion in military equipment to Egypt. Syria also benefited from Russian aid. The Soviet Union shelled out $327 million in weapons and financed the Euphrates Dam.[17] This relationship would continue even through the 1970s when OPEC's new power would manifest itself in a truly barbaric way.

But tensions among Israel and Egypt and Syria (along with Jordan and Palestine) were finally brought to a head by none other than the Soviet Union on May 13, 1967. A delegation of Soviets arrived in Cairo with dire news: Israel had amassed 11 brigades along the Syrian border. This news, which was completely false, would be the catalyst for the Six-Day War. Herzog and Gazit write:

The Soviet Ambassador to Israel was invited by the Prime Minister of Israel, Levi Eshkol, to accompany him to the area bordering the Syrian frontier so that he would convince himself that the information about the concentration of Israeli forces was totally untrue. Indeed, instead of eleven brigades being concentrated there, there were hardly eleven companies in the area.

The Soviet Ambassador, however, declined the invitation. The Russians were interested in pressing Syria's case for political reasons of their own, and had no intention of helping Israel to deny their allegations.[18]

Those political reasons were part of the larger East-West conflict: the Cold War. Russia saw the Middle East as a way to expand its influence, but this conflict was also a way to capture and control oil reserves,[19] and even the movement of oil. As the initial clash of the Six-Day War approached, Egypt initiated a blockade of the Gulf of Aqaba, and did not let any ships flying Israeli flags or ships carrying strategic goods—including oil—bound for Israel pass.[20] It was said that this would not affect shipments of oil to Western Europe, but the blockade was sufficient cause for the U.S. to announce that is was committed to helping Israel if threatened by aggression. In response, Arab leaders went to Cairo in support of Egypt against Israel.

Indar Jit Rikhye, UN Emergency Force Commander in Egypt and author of *The Sinai Blunder: Withdrawal of the United Nations Emergency Force Leading to the Six-Day War of June 1967,* noted: "Among these visitors, the Chief of Staff of the armed forces of the Hashemite Kingdom of Jordan had arrived, and so had the Defense Minister of Saudi Arabia."[21] And we know that Saudi Arabia had financially backed opposition countries like Egypt and Syria against Israel with billions in oil money. Thus on May 13, 1967, when the Soviet Union unleashed its lie to Egypt about Israeli troops amassing on the Syrian border, it did so to gain more control over the Middle East and its oil reserves.

The Six-Day War was messy, and ultimately bad for Arab unity in the Middle East. Most of the war took place on the Sinai Peninsula, where a huge amount of trade normally flows. Bordering the western part of the peninsula is the Suez Canal, so on May 22, 1967, Nasser closed the Strait of Tiran by blockading the Gulf of Aqaba. From this point, war was inevitable. To this day, both sides claim the other side fired first. And trying to unravel this Gordian Knot would diverge too far from the purpose of this book.

We do know that the Soviet Union's assertion that Israel had moved eleven brigades to its northern border with Syria was false. We know that Egypt and Syria armed themselves for war despite Israeli insistence that the U.S.S.R. was lying, and despite an invitation to the Soviet Ambassador to the border to prove the falsehood. Israel deemed Egypt's move to block the Strait of Tiran as aggression, and we know that Israel's best defense was its offense. It responded to Arab troop movements with a preemptive attack on Egyptian and Syrian airbases.[22] But this move too was the result of a build up behind the scenes.

"While Soviet deliveries to Egypt, Syria and Iraq," wrote Raymond A. Hinnebush, author of *The International Politics of the Middle East*, "were quantitatively greater they were mostly defensive in nature while Israel received weapons giving it an offensive capability."[23] This threw another kink in determining who the aggressor was and who was defending their sovereign rights. To add fuel to the fire, Egypt had a reputation of being the Pan-Arab leader. The situation was highly combustible, and on June 5, 1967, Israel struck.

Indar Jit Rikhye wrote of that first day:

> Balwant Singh Garcha, my Public Information Officer, reported from the Headquarters Mess on the beach that two Israeli jet aircraft had attacked the U.A.R. positions in the area. One Israeli aircraft had been shot down, and its pilot had bailed out and dropped down a few hundred yards out in the sea. A U.A.R. [Egypt] motor launch was on its way to pick him up.
>
> Within minutes reports of widespread firing across the Armistice Demarcation Line came in from all the battalions and from Rafah Camp.[24]

Egypt, Syria, and Jordan countered with their own strikes and shot down a number of Israeli airplanes. Within minutes, both sides had claimed they had been attacked first. The fight resembles two fencers in a duel parrying and both claiming victory of the first touch. While both countries claimed to be the victims, their preparations for war leading up to the first strike were aggressive, deliberate, and strategic. In other words, both sides did nothing to stop war from coming, while simultaneously claiming the need for defense.

The war quickly disintegrated into a rout. Within hours of the first air strike, the Israeli army wiped out Egypt's 20th and 7th divisions stationed in Rafah in the Sinai. The same was happening across the Sinai. Israel's air force had destroyed Egypt's air bases, too.

Chaim Herzog and Shlomo Gazit reported, "By the end of the second day's fighting, the main Egyptian defences [sic] manned by elements of three divisions had been overrun, and the Israeli forces were advancing in the depths of the Sinai. . . ."[25] Israel was pushing forward to the Suez Canal.

Indeed, before war broke out, Moshe Dayan, Israel's Minister of Defense, said: "In one or two hours the air force will have achieved its major objectives, as will the land forces on the first day. By the second day we'll be on our way to the Canal. Egypt won't have an air force for at least a half a year."[26] But the battling was brutal for both sides in the land war in the Sinai. During the second day, in one battle for Umm Qatef—a major Egyptian fort—40 Egyptian tanks and 19 Israeli tanks were reduced to burnt-out carcasses. The Israelis lost 14 men with 41 more wounded, while the Egyptians lost 300 men, and 100 were taken prisoner.[27]

The brutality continued, though it became even more severely one-sided. Herzog and Gazit note that Egyptian armored forces were destroyed in many confrontations, and that Israeli maneuvering was funneling Egypt's army into a narrow pass where other Israeli battalions and the air force were lying in wait.[28] By the fourth day, Israeli troops occupied the banks of the Suez Canal.

And let's not forget the Syrians and the Jordanians, Israel's neighbors to the north. The impetus for the war, in fact, originated in Syria, as the Russian's lie supposedly came from Syrian sources.[29] And Jordan and Egypt signed a mutual defense agreement on May 30.[30]

Fighting in Jordan's West Bank commenced with a phone call from Nasser who jubilantly assured King Hussein that Egyptian forces were overrunning the Israelis.[31] These reports, of course, were untrue, and in fact, hundreds of Egyptian planes were burning and in ruins. But King Hussein was forced to initiate the conflict because of that signed agreement, just seven days old.

Jordanian airplanes attacked Israeli targets in the West Bank and the Jewish half of Jerusalem at just before noon on June 5. Less than an hour later, the Israeli air force struck. Twenty-three Jordanian warplanes—the entire air force—was destroyed.[32]

The ground fighting in the West Bank and East Jerusalem was grittier. At first, Israel was outnumbered nearly 2-to-1 on the battlefield, but then Israel dominated the air and supported its ground initiatives. By early morning on June 7, Israel took the Arab half of Jerusalem, and the next day, Israeli tanks rolled through Bethlehem, Hebron, and Jericho.[33] The West Bank and East Jerusalem belonged to Israel.

It was also false news reports from the Egyptians that drew the Syrians into battle.[34] Both state-run media reports and official announcements reported that the Egyptian military were making their way easily to Tel Aviv. Winston Burdette, CBS correspondent in Cairo reported: "There was no sign of panic. On the contrary there was jubilation in the streets. Wild cheers and chanting when the radio claimed: a first indication of victory, 23 Israeli planes shot down. Later a second alert and a second official claim. The total of Israeli planes destroyed had jumped to 70."[35] But none of it was true, and the Syrians blundered into a swarming Israeli air force. In an attempt to bomb the oil refineries in Haifa, the Syrian air force ran right into the Israelis who promptly destroyed the Syrian aircraft.[36] Within minutes of fighting on the first day, Syria was done. An official ceasefire was called on June 9 at 3:00 A.M. but that didn't stop Defense Minister Dayan from sending four brigades against the Golan Heights at 7:00 A.M. that morning.[37]

Israel Gains the Upper Hand

The Israelis had a tougher time in Gaza. According to Michael Oren, author of *Six Days of War: June 1967 and the Making of the Modern Middle East*: "Much as Dayan had feared, the fighting in the area, from Khan Yunis to 'Ali Muntar ridge, was brutal, accounting for nearly half of all Israel [sic] casualties on the southern front."[38] But once Gaza was cut off from Egyptian reinforcement from the Sinai, Israel was able to gain the upper hand.

In Indar Jit Rikhye's first-hand account of the Six-Day War from UNEF headquarters in Gaza, the shelling of the city started at dawn, and by 3:00 P.M. Israeli tanks were advancing along the beach road, and firing had died down.[39] The next day Israeli Minister of Defense Dayan met Jit Rikhye and several other commanding officers and told Colonel Wilhelm van Heuvan, chairman of the Egyptian-Israel Mixed Armistice Commission that the General Armistice Agreement was dead.[40] This meant that Israel controlled the Sinai Peninsula, the Gaza Strip, the West Bank, and the Golan Heights.

For the second time in 11 years, the Arabs were handed a resounding defeat at the hands of Israel. The Sinai Peninsula—that ever-important slice of land through which so much trade flowed—was conquered. Israel had its defensive buffer zone between its lands and Egypt. With the West Bank and the Golan Heights, Israel also secured space between its borders and those of Jordan, and Syria. And Egypt. . . .

Egypt lost its place as Pan-Arab leader. That slot was being filled by oil monarchies.[41] And these monarchies were organizing themselves into an elite group, separate from OPEC.

Now, more than four decades later, Egypt is leading a charge of sorts. . . . At least, its people are. Poverty, high food prices, and accusations of corruption in the Egyptian government sparked an unprecedented revolution.

January 25, 2011, tens of thousands of people marched in Cairo, Alexandria, Ishmalia, and Suez. It was called the Day of Revolt, and 45,000 people flocked to Tahrir Square alone.[42]

By Friday, January 29, hundreds of thousands of Egyptians flooded into Tahrir Square calling for the resignation of President Hosni Mubarak who had ruled Egypt for some 30 years.

He took to power after the assassination of President Anwar el-Sadat in 1981, who we'll talk more about in Chapter 11.

For another two weeks, Egyptians protested, even against armed Mubarak supporters, as the army stood by and did not interfere. The rest of the world watched on Thursday, February 10, as President

Mubarak came to make concessions to the people—that he would hand power to Vice President Omar Suleiman, and oversee the election of a new government.[43]

Day after day, protesters had filled Tahrir Square and marched against government buildings in other cities, demanding nothing less than a full and immediate resignation. This "delegation of authority" was not good enough.

On February 11, 2011, they got what they demanded.

Eighteen days after the "Day of Revolt," Vice President Suleiman announced:

> In the name of God the merciful, the compassionate, citizens, during these very difficult circumstances Egypt is going through, President Hosni Mubarak has decided to step down from the office of president of the republic and has charged the high council of the armed forces to administer the affairs of the country. May God help everybody.[44]

The people were victorious, and this victory has emboldened a number of other uprisings throughout the Middle East that continued as of writing this book.

And they could have dire consequences.

Here's why Egypt is important . . . and it's not because it's a major oil producer. It produces less than 681,000 barrels a day—less than India or Azerbaijan.[45] And it's not that the U.S. is a major importer of that oil either.

Indeed, the United States receives less than 3 percent of Egypt's oil production.[46]

After the Six-Day War, Egypt became a less hostile voice in the Middle East. While other Arab nations continued with anti-Israel rhetoric and actions, Egypt stepped into the role of peacemaker. Now, we don't know what kind of voice Egypt will have . . . and the threat of uprisings spreading throughout the Middle East leaves a lot of uncertainty. In fact, Jordan's King Abdullah II fired his government after small protests, and elections in Palestine's West Bank are now promised.[47]

There have even been protests in Iran, Iraq, Libya, and even Saudi Arabia—all of which are major oil producing countries.

Could oil be used as a pressure point against protesters and those that support them? Could OPEC nations, particularly Arab producers, break out the oil weapon, like they did 35 years ago? And could it have the same global consequences?

The Middle East is on a big stage here . . . bigger than they've ever had before. After the Six-Day War, Saudi Arabia, Kuwait, and Libya met in Beirut on January 9, 1968 to discuss forming an all-Arab oil cartel.[48] It would be known as OAPEC—the Organization of Arab Petroleum Exporting Countries. Quickly, this cartel swelled to include other Arab nations. Egypt, Syria, Iraq, Qatar, Bahrain, Tunisia, and the U.A.E. It was from this close-knit group of oil producers that those involved in the First Oil Shock came.[49]

Needless to say, tensions in the Middle East did not evaporate with the end of the Six-Day War. And these frictions were a natural boost to the build-up of militant nations, all funded by crude oil money. Oil itself would prove to be these nations' greatest weapon as the West weighed in on the age-old Middle East conflict.

Its use would nearly bring the U.S. economy to a standstill.

Chapter 11

The OPEC Oil Weapon

After the Six-Day War, the Egyptians and Syrians wanted their land back including the Golan Heights, the Sinai Peninsula, and the Gaza Strip. Invasion and war plans weren't shelved just because of a cease-fire.

Indeed, Israeli Prime Minister Golda Meir refused to return captured Arab land as part of any peace agreement for fear that any agreed-upon terms would not be kept.[1] Though this was probably a self-fulfilling prophecy, she was right. Egypt deployed two armies along the Suez Canal in autumn 1968. These armies were supported with tanks, air-defense systems and warplanes provided by Egypt's long-time partner, the Soviet Union.[2] President Gamal Abd el Nasser said, "What was taken by force must be restored by force."[3] Of course, pride also had something to do with it.

The Six-Day War was the second time in just over a decade that Israel trounced the Arabs; most notably, the Egyptians. The Israeli performance in the Sinai was definitive and exacting. The air strikes on the Egyptian air bases were perfectly timed and coordinated. In fact,

Israel's air force had been planning such an attack for five years,[4] and they executed the devastating attacks with precision. It was this embarrassing defeat that the Arabs felt compelled to rail against.

Egypt Regains Lost Territories

In the years following the Six-Day War, Egypt was "reloading," fortifying their positions along the Suez Canal, and stocking up on everything from surface-to-air missiles[5] to Soviet military advisors.[6] And these weren't just for show. Egypt and Israel engaged in numerous skirmishes and localized hostility around the Canal. These didn't serve much purpose except to keep tensions high and test out Israeli defenses across the Canal.

President Nasser was determined to force the issue, and the back and forth was not unlike a game of chess. Egypt struck first with an artillery attack on September 8, 1968 and a second one in late October. Israel countered with an airstrike that destroyed a bridge at Kina and a power-producing dam, both in the Nile Valley.[7] Both sides traded attacks in what has become known as the War of Attrition. The War of Attrition was not an official war, but an intermittent, limited war;[8] one that used artillery and air strikes, rather than invading ground forces. In fact, both sides were busier digging in on either side of the Suez Canal than gaining purchase across it.

Eventually, these conflicts would lead to the October War, also called the Yom Kippur War, when the OPEC oil weapon was first used to devastating effect, but President Nasser would not see this day. On September 28, 1970, Nasser suffered a heart attack and was rushed to his home where he was pronounced dead. In attendance were his wife, a close friend and Egyptian journalist, and Vice President Anwar el-Sadat.[9] Seven days later, Sadat was named president of Egypt.

Nasser's death meant a major shift in how Egypt interacted both with the Arab world and with the idea of an Israeli state. Focus shifted to regaining lost territories rather than the destruction of Israel. Three years later, the October War put Egypt's resolve to the test. In preparations for war, Sadat wanted to secure the help of neighboring Arab countries, like Syria and Jordan, the other major players in the Six-Day

War. He did so by arguing for limited involvement by all parties—enough to regain the Golan Heights and the Suez Canal, which would show the world Arab "restraint" in dealing with Israel and the return of all occupied lands taken in the Six-Day War.[10] This strategy won over Syria, and also convinced other Arab nations to pledge troops and other military aid should Egypt go to war with Israel. Saudi Arabia, Algeria, Morocco, Libya, Sudan, and Iraq lined up with military arms, and Saudi Arabia and Qatar got out their oil checkbooks.[11] Oil-rich nations pledged hundreds of millions of dollars to the Arab cause[12] on the eve of war.

Meanwhile, Egypt was on a misinformation campaign. Sadat would not give his Arab allies (aside from Syria) a timeframe for help. He feared that troops would arrive too early and reveal Egypt's only trump card—surprise. In their book, *The Arab Israeli Wars: War and Peace in the Middle East*, Chaim Herzog and Shlomo Gazit explain:

> It was based on a careful analysis of the preconceived ideas obtaining in Israel and expressed from time to time by Israeli military leaders. Thus, statements by General Dayan about the lack of preparedness of the Egyptians and an analysis by General Rabin belittling the prospects of war were highlighted in the media coupled with evaluations emphasizing the lack of preparedness of the Egyptian Army.
>
> Clare Hollingworth, the defence [sic] correspondent of the *London Daily Telegraph*, published an article with a Cairo dateline describing the poor maintenance of equipment in the Egyptian Army and the resultant lack of preparedness. A special staff, which had been assembled for this purpose, monitored the operation and guided it in such a way as to confirm those preconceived concepts, not only in Israel but also in Washington and elsewhere.
>
> There were many impressive aspects to the Egyptian preparations for the assault, but none as original in concept and in execution as the misinformation plan.[13]

It was as though Egypt had taken a page out of Israel's book. Even high-ranking Egyptian officers had no pre-knowledge of the impeding attack until the very last minute[14]—very much like the Israeli air force the morning of June 5, 1967. And it was from the center of this misinformation plan that Egypt attacked.

The U.S.–Israel Partnership

On October 6, 1973, Egypt and Syria crossed simultaneously into the Sinai Peninsula and the Golan Heights. They struck at two o'clock in the afternoon,[15] as many of Israel's citizens were at prayer. It was Yom Kippur, the Jewish Day of Attonement.

Egypt's misinformation plan allowed for the amassing of nearly 1.2 million soldiers and the purchase of two water cannons[16] to attack the embankments on the east side of the canal, right under Israel's nose. Israel was far outmanned. Egypt's surprise attack comprised the first invading troops numbering 100,000 with 1,350 tanks. Israel's forces numbered only 450 men and 44 artillery pieces stretched out in 16 forts along the hundred-mile canal.[17] The same was true on the northern border with Syria. Abraham Rabinovich, author of *The Yom Kippur War: The Epic Encounter That Transformed the Middle East*, wrote: "The disparity in tanks was almost 8 to 1 in Syria's favor; in infantry and artillery, far greater."[18] The opening foray was nearly a knockout.

One hundred thousand artillery shells slammed into the Israeli line across the Canal, followed by 8,000 soldiers who crossed on rafts.[19] In the first few hours, the Egyptians took the east bank of the Suez Canal.[20] Syria opened with a 50-minute barrage of shells into the Golan Heights. In short order, the Syrians had captured Mount Hermon, an important military outpost for Israel.[21]

Though this war was intended to win back the Arab lands taken in the Six-Day War, the success of the first few hours on October 6, 1973, begged the question of the very survival of Israel as a state. The Egyptian air strikes, though not as devastating as Israel's air strikes six years before, inflicted serious damage. Eight different airfields were hit, radar installations destroyed, and missile sites bombed.[22] When the Israeli air force retaliated, sending bombers against the hordes of Egyptians pouring across the Canal, their campaign was relatively ineffective, and Egypt shot down 27 Israeli warplanes.[23] Even Israel's air strikes against Syria were met with a nearly impenetrable wall of surface to air missiles.[24] Syria had nearly won the Golan Heights.

Israel was now talking about using nuclear warheads. Defense Minister Moshe Dayan told Prime Minister Golda Meir, "This is the end of the third temple."[25] "Temple" was a code word for nuclear weapons,[26] and Dayan clearly saw the end of an Israeli state as the Syrians pressed ever further into the Golan Heights. The country held off just long enough for a sudden retreat of the Syrian army at the sight of a fresh contingent of Israeli tanks.[27]

From this point on, Israel regained its footing, and fighting intensified on both fronts. This would not be another six-day war, but by October 12, Israel was in need of help, and the United States came to its aid.

Oil Becomes a Weapon of War

After news of the nuclear threat made its way to the United States, President Nixon ordered the implementation of Operation Nickel Grass, which sought to replace all of Israel's material losses. The airlift, which started on October 14, brought 22,000 tons of supplies to Israel.[28] This operation was worth $2.2 billion. . . .[29]

In response, OAPEC decided to raise oil prices by 70 percent on October 16, 1973, to $5.11 a barrel,[30] and Libya and Saudi Arabia halted all oil exports to the United States and Western Europe.[31] The rest of the OAPEC cartel soon followed: "For the first time in more than 1000 years, the Arabs were united," wrote Arshad Khan in his book, *Islam, Muslims, and America: Understanding the Basis of Their Conflict*. He goes on to note, "The temporary success of the embargo, which disrupted day-to-day life in the West, gave Arabs and Muslims their first sense of power in modern times."[32]

In fact, Herzog and Gazit argue that this was the main goal of OAPEC:

> President Sadat furthermore convinced King Feisal of Saudi Arabia that war was essential in order to activate the oil weapon. In other words, contrary to popular opinion, the oil weapon was not used because of the war. One of the reasons for the war was that it would guarantee the measure of unity in the Arab world necessary in order to activate the oil weapon.[33]

No doubt this was one of the aims of the all-Arab oil cartel, but you can bet that money was another motivator. Indeed, non-Arab members of OPEC were taking advantage of this supply squeeze by raising their own prices as OAPEC effectively slashed oil supplies to international markets by 15 percent. This had a massive effect on the global economy. Without supplies from the Middle East, countries had to focus on oil from other places, like Venezuela, where prices were also being raised.

Major oil companies also had to raise prices as access to cheaper oil was cut off. For more than five months, the Middle East shuttered their taps to the West, and in that time, oil prices climbed from $3.00 a barrel to $12.00 a barrel![34] This was unheard off. Middle East Studies Association of North America's vice president, Dankwart Rustow, famously called the crisis, "a $100 billion tax on the global economy— the most gigantic reallocation of income in history."[35] Economist Thomas Schelling wrote in 1979 that this cost was "equivalent to a deadweight tax of up to 5 percent on our GNP in perpetuity."[36]

The use of this oil weapon would vault OPEC to the top of the world's oil powers. No longer could international oil companies ignore OPEC and force these new oil tyrants into low-cost, high-profit deals beneficial to only the foreign oil companies. And there was an even bigger shift, too. Power within OPEC was becoming more centralized in the Middle East. And this power was growing with every passing month of the embargo. With prices rising so quickly, these oil barbarians could cut back on their export throughout the embargo and still get rich.[37]

The cuts in supplies manifested in panic in some countries. In the United States, the American Automobile Association reported that in the last week of February, 1974, 20 percent of all gas stations had no gasoline at all.[38] Just a few weeks into the embargo, President Nixon signed the Emergency Petroleum Act that instituted price restrictions on oil . . . but this scheme backfired and only made oil prices higher. The Act placed a ceiling on only certain oil—"old" oil. This was oil produced from wells already in production in 1972. "New" oil prices were allowed to fluctuate higher to meet market prices. As a result, "old" oil was not brought to market because producers could get more money for their "new" oil, and this created an artificial scarcity that caused prices to go even higher.[39]

But what could the United States do? Demand for oil was sky-rocketing. In the three years leading up to the oil embargo, the U.S.'s oil imports nearly doubled, climbing from 3.2 million barrels a day in

1970 to 6.2 million barrels a day in summer 1973.[40] With U.S. production beginning to fall off a cliff, the United States was becoming ever more reliant on international oil production. Increasingly, that oil had come from the Middle East and its erstwhile friend, Saudi Arabia—financial backer of Egypt and Syria in the war against Israel.

But it wasn't just the United States that was affected by this embargo. Western European nations like Germany were concerned well before the October War that their dependence on foreign oil would hamstring their economies. German State Secretary Ulf Lantzke said that he started becoming nervous about an energy crisis back in 1968 after America warned that its spare production capacity was decreasing.[41]

Japan, too, was feeling the oil squeeze before the embargo. Having no real resources of its own, Japan relied on international resources for its energy needs. Oil became a major component of its foreign policy. It was called "resource diplomacy."[42] In a cruel way, it was "resource diplomacy" at work in deploying the oil weapon. Toyin Falola and Ann Genova, authors of *The Politics of the Global Oil Industry: An Introduction*, assert:

> The objective of the embargo was twofold: impact both Israel directly and its largest supporters in the Western states. First, the Arab states planned to prevent oil from reaching Israel as a way of creating dissatisfaction among the Israeli people who, in turn, would challenge their government.
>
> Second, the Arab states planned to force the countries of the West, primarily the United States, to choose between their ties to Israel and their need for oil. The Arab states assumed that the countries' economic needs would outweigh their emotional attachment to Israel.[43]

It worked. President Nixon himself blamed both the Arab states and Israel for the conflict. He said, "Israel simply can't wait for the dust to settle and the Arabs can't wait for the dust to settle in the Mid-East. Both sides are at fault. Both sides need to start negotiating."[44] Indeed, some European nations seemed to support the Arab cause. Great Britain called for Israel to withdraw back to its borders before the Six-Day War. The Netherlands and some other countries even made pro-Arab statements.[45]

Nine countries of the European Economic Community met in Brussels to discuss how to approach the oil-producing Arab nations involved in the embargo, and in the war against Israel. On November 6, 1973, roughly three weeks into the embargo, these countries issued a joint resolution declaring that Israel must withdraw to the armistice lines of 1949 and recognize the rights of Palestinians in any peace treaties in the Middle East.[46]

But affecting world policy towards Israel wasn't the only use of the oil weapon. The oil weapon was in play even after the October war ended on the 25th—for nearly five months. Keeping the weapon aimed particularly at the United States meant that OPEC nations could quickly nationalize their oil industries.

OPEC Rises to Power

In the meantime, OPEC leader Ahmed Zaki Yamani had instituted a plan to nationalize oil industries on a gradual scale in order to keep international oil companies happy. The original plan was to assume 25 percent ownership of oil operations, slowly increasing ownership to 51 percent by 1983.[47] The embargo gave OPEC countries—particularly OAPEC countries—the perfect reason to fully nationalize their oil industries. Most OPEC members accomplished this between 1973 and 1975 (the exception being Saudi Arabia, the United States' closest OPEC friend in the Middle East).[48]

No one could have predicted just how devastating an oil embargo would be to the U.S. economy—and to the United States' ego. "The embargo and the shortage it caused were an abrupt break with America's past, and the experience would severely undermine Americans' confidence in the future," wrote Daniel Yergin in *The Prize: The Epic Quest for Oil, Money & Power*.[49]

At this point things became difficult for the United States. The country saw this problem as a political issue stemming from the Arab-Israeli dispute. In the short term, some people believed that if the United States could restrain Israel, things would go back to normal, and the United States would enjoy cheap and plentiful oil. Europe, on the other hand, believed the problem was one of over-consumption and insecure energy supplies. "The industrial world had become over dependent [sic] on a volatile part of the world," wrote Yergin, "and thus was vulnerable to it."[50] This difference would shape how these global powers in the West would address problems in the Middle East in the future, too, as we discuss in Chapter 12.

Meanwhile, oil-producing countries were climbing in global power. "People now knew where Saudi Arabia was," wrote Stewart Ross, author of *The Arab-Israeli Conflict*, "which they didn't when I first went there. What's more, they took the Arabs seriously. They were people who mattered—they could hurt us."[51]

Without aiming a single missile at the West, OPEC turned the tables on both governments and international oil companies. Now, 10 state-controlled oil companies hold 75 percent of the world's oil reserves.[52] And the U.S. economy was now in the hands of rising oil tyrants in the Middle East.

Chapter 12

Political Dangers to the U.S. Oil Addiction

How do you measure the political weight of an oil addiction? Is it by how much force a global superpower is willing to use to control crucial resources? Is it by how handicapped an economy becomes when oil prices hit the roof? Is it by how central energy policies are shaped to keep crude cheap and plentiful?

The United States is an oil addict—as hooked on black gold as an addict to heroin. Our economy needs crude oil to keep growing, and cheap crude at that. It's like the rush of a fiery drug through our veins, the absence of which causes severe withdraw: industrial shutdowns, countrywide blackouts, inflation, and unemployment—in short, economic meltdown.

The United States has done everything in its power to avoid withdrawal, including invading another country to secure oil supplies. Now, in the twenty-first century, the United States is still nothing more than an oil addict, dependent on oil barbarians—crude dealers—for a steady stream of fuel, and the stakes couldn't be higher. Tensions between us and our main international dealer were souring. Saudi Arabia said we'd overstayed our welcome, and U.S. troops began clearing out.[1] We turned over Iraq to the Iraqis, and their oil development is open to the world. In fact, as of December 14, 2009, most of the Iraqi oil concessions were not awarded to the United States. Rather, companies from countries like China, Malaysia, Russia, and Angola (along with several European oil companies) have soaked up the crude opportunities in Iraq.[2]

But the oil embargo was just the beginning of the oil price wars that shook the foundation of the United States economy. In 1974, OPEC raised oil prices from $4.31 to $10.11, but by the end of the decade, a barrel of oil cost $32.50—an increase of more than 800 percent from the start of the 1970s.[3]

One of the reasons OPEC gained so much power so quickly was the nosedive of the U.S. dollar. The United States' break from the Bretton Wood's gold standard on August 15, 1970 allowed the dollar to move without being backed up by physical gold. When you combine a dollar that was rapidly inflating to the size of a Macy's parade float with the costly war in Vietnam and climbing unemployment, you have created a situation in which the United States handed over its economic power to a handful of Middle Eastern oil barbarians.

OPEC could boost oil prices to nearly whatever it wanted, claiming to hold the West in the palm of its hand and brandishing the oil weapon at the head of floundering economies, when in fact, oil prices were just trying to keep up with the falling dollar.[4] The political situation, however, allowed OPEC to profess control over oil markets and jack up prices to absurd levels. The United States could not help but continue to pay, no matter what price a barrel of oil fetched. We were addicted.

"It's incredible," a Swiss oil trader told Anthony Sampson for *New York Magazine* in 1979. "We keep on asking for a higher price and they keep on accepting it. . . . Everyone is just scrambling for what he can get."[5] But it wasn't just the ballooning price for oil that was becoming a big problem for Western countries—particularly the United States. In fact, oil demand dropped 20 percent as a result of the oil embargo and sky-high oil prices.[6] It was growing reliance on foreign oil that was the problem.

Oil Barbarians Pinch U.S. Supply

This issue has steadily been growing in importance since the Eisenhower administration. In 1950, the United States provided 52 percent of the world's oil production,[7] but by the late 1960s and early 1970s, it was more profitable for U.S. oil companies to import oil than to produce it at home.

President Nixon launched a plan called "Project Independence,"[8] in which the United States was to develop domestic resources to meet the nation's energy needs rather than relying on foreign importers. That, of course, didn't work. Indeed, U.S. gasoline consumption equated to 11 percent of world oil production as late as June 2004.[9] The United States didn't have the reserves to meet rising demand, didn't have the money to develop domestic reserves, or couldn't profit from doing so—a deadly combination that has had devastating and far reaching political ramifications still in play today.

After the first oil shock and OPEC's first show of power, member nations were openly courted, and their leaders sought out and flattered by global powers. Everyone needed oil, and OPEC was the only way to get it with U.S. production starting to dwindle and Russia becoming more and more unstable. Daniel Yergin, author of *The Prize: The Epic Quest for Oil, Money & Power*, wrote: "Oil prices were at the heart of world commerce, and those who seemed to control oil prices were regarded as the new masters of the global economy."[10] The United States courted Saudi Arabia, a relationship long in the making.

When the full figure of Saudi Arabia's oil reserves became known in the 1940s, it was U.S. oil companies (like Standard Oil, who owned major concessions in Saudi Arabia) that started urging the U.S. government to take on some responsibility for security in the region.[11] Helen Chapin Metz, editor of *Saudi Arabia: A Country Study*, wrote, "In 1943 the administration of Franklin D. Roosevelt declared that the defense of Saudi Arabia was a vital interest to the United States and dispatched the first United States military mission to the kingdom."[12] This relationship was mutually beneficial. The U.S. presence in the kingdom meant military equipment and training, defense agreements, and arms sales.

Of course, other Arab nations, such as Egypt and Syria, were jealous and suspicious of this bond. According to Robert Vitalis, author of *America's Kingdom: Mythmaking on the Saudi Oil Frontier*, radio broadcasts from Cairo described the Saudi king's harem as laden with "Jewesses from Israel, Yemen and Europe. . . . Has your false faith crumbled before glittering dollars and your American Lords?"[13] The prime directive from the United States was to secure Saudi oil, and other Arab nations knew it. That's how the Soviet Union got its foothold in the Middle East. Western nations were covered with the blood of imperialism in the Middle East, particularly during the World Wars, whereas Russian imperialism penetrated only as far south and west as Iran and Turkey.[14] But the relationship went both ways.

The United States threatened to stop sending air support to protect the Saudi monarchy unless it stopped shipping arms to Yemeni royalists during the 1960s civil war.[15] So let's get things straight, here: The United States and Saudi Arabia were on opposite sides, ideologically, but the United States needed oil, and the Saudis needed U.S. military aid. It was a business deal, pure and simple, and if the United States had thought then that it could just take the entire area by force, it would have. Consider this quote, uttered by former U.S. Ambassador to Saudi Arabia Chris Akins: "We could solve all our economic and political problems by taking over the Arab oil fields [and] bringing in Texans and Oklahomans to operate them."[16]

This echoes Harold Ickes, the U.S. Secretary of the Interior in the late 1930s and early 1940s. He wanted to pass legislation that would allow the government to take over parts of the dismantled Standard Oil Company so that it could secure itself a stake in Saudi crude reserve, exclusively for its own use.[17]

U.S. Oil Addiction Sparks War

By this time, it was clear that both the United States and Saudi Arabia were becoming more and more dependent on each other. By the 1980s, Saudi Arabia was the largest oil supplier to the United States,[18] and the United States was Saudi Arabia's closest ally.[19] Who else would Saudi Arabia call on in the middle of 1990 when Saddam Hussein sent 100,000 troops to invade Kuwait? But it was U.S. oil interests that President George Bush sought to protect by entering the Gulf War.

Saudi Arabia shares a border with Iraq that stretches 506 miles and a border with Kuwait that measures 138 miles. The United States had limited of numbers of troops that were in Saudi Arabia to train Saudi troops, and Saudi Arabia only had 65,000 troops on its own. But after Iraq invaded Kuwait, the number of "coalition" troops jumped to 550,000[20] by the height of the 1991 Gulf War. Why? During its invasion of Kuwait, Iraqi forces crossed into Saudi territory, and Saddam Hussein was sending more and more troops into the captured Kuwait. What else were these amassing Iraqi troops for other than to invade Saudi Arabia?

"Satellite photographs showed that the Iraqi army was massed just north of the border, posing a possible threat to Saudi Arabian oil fields in the very near future," wrote Kathlyn and Martin Gay in their book *Persian Gulf War*. "[King] Fahd asked the representatives of the United States government to send troops and supplies to help defend his land."[21] The United States couldn't say no, and the West had no idea whether Saddam Hussein would stop at Kuwait. Saudi oil fields were awfully tempting, as were the country's access to the Red Sea and the Persian Gulf.

Just south of the Kuwaiti border are numerous Saudi oil fields. The largest, Ghawar, is the world's largest oil field, and represents 50 percent of Saudi Arabia's oil production. Ghawar is so huge that it produces more oil than any other country, save Russia.[22] This field is located about 313 miles from the border with Kuwait, and there were no less than 18 other oil fields between it and the amassing Iraqi troops that had just swarmed Kuwait and taken Kuwait City in less than a day on August 2, 1990.[23]

The United States had a plan that had been drawn up before Iraq invaded Kuwait. In the plan, which was called "Internal Look," General Schwartzkopf detailed a military strategy that would combat "an unnamed dictator attempting to seize the oil resources of the Persian Gulf."[24] Oil resources were critical to the growing global economy, and the United States was willing to go to war over them. It turned out that the rest of the world agreed. Nobody wanted an unstable empire in the Middle East, and Saddam's belligerent invasion created just that.

On November 29, 1990, the United Nations, chaired by the United States, passed Resolution #678, which authorized the use of force against Iraq should the country not withdraw by January 15, 1991. There were no votes against the resolution, even from other Arab states and the Soviet Union. Only Cuba and Yemen abstained.[25] On January 17, 1991, the U.S. launched an all-out air war against Iraq, and did so from Saudi soil. Screeching Tomahawk missiles launched from ships in the Persian Gulf were timed perfectly with F-117 stealth bombers, and lit up the pitch-black skies over Baghdad. In the first day, 2,000 flights were made into Iraqi airspace, and 100 Tomahawk missiles found their targets.[26] They were targeting airports, missile sites, and, yes, oil refineries. Oil is the lifeblood of any military force. Knock out the ability to make fuel, and you win.

Operation Desert Storm was off to a good start, and it was soon clear that the United States wouldn't be content with just pushing Iraq out of Kuwait, which was the express reason why the United Nations approved Resolution #678. The U.S. and coalition forces were targeting things like nuclear research facilities, chemical weapons factories, and other appropriate military installations, but they were also targeting certain government buildings in downtown Baghdad. The Baathist party, the ruling party to which Saddam Hussein ascribed, was being shelled.[27]

Perhaps the United States wanted a regime change. Hussein had spent eight years of the previous decade in a war with Iran.

Regime Change: Dollars to Euros

Of course, it wouldn't be the last time regime change was considered. The second President Bush was responsible for bringing Iraq down, and the eventual execution of Saddam Hussein. There was no doubt in the minds of Congress that Hussein had stockpiled weapons of mass destruction and was possibly seeking a nuclear weapon before the U.S. preemptive strike on March 20, 2003. But there's also no doubt that one of the goals of Iraqi Freedom was to control Iraq's oil.

Remember the break from the Bretton Woods gold standard and the subsequent 800 percent rise in the price of oil we talked about earlier in this chapter? And how a huge chunk of that came from the falling dollar? Well there was an OPEC push to start trading oil in euros rather than in dollars. In the year leading up to Operation Iraqi

Freedom, the U.S. dollar had been falling. On March 20, 2003, the U.S. dollar bought 1.1341 euros, but on March 20, 2003, the dollar bought only 0.9471 euros, a fall of 16.5 percent.[28]

Richard Benson in his August 8, 2003 article, "Oil, the Dollar, and U.S. Prosperity," said:

> In the real world . . . the one factor underpinning American prosperity is keeping the dollar the World Reserve Currency. This can only be done if the oil producing states keep oil priced in dollars, and all their currency reserves in dollar assets. If anything put the final nail in Saddam Hussein's coffin, it was his move to start selling oil for euros.[29]

And this isn't some liberal conspiracy theorist. Richard Benson is president of Specialty Finance Group, LLC, a financial broker and dealer, and supported this war, if not the way it was conducted. He said, "I, for one, would not want to bring back an Arab oil embargo and long lines at the gas pump."[30] That's how addicted the United States has become, and how reliant on Middle Eastern oil.

Just before the mid-term elections in the United States, when Republicans took back control over the House of Representatives, the U.S. dollar bought only 0.7208 euros.[31] If we take the OPEC average price of oil for October 29, 2010,[32] at $80.90 and imagine that price as euros instead of dollars, a barrel of oil would cost $112.50! Now imagine the political consequences of sustained oil prices above $100 a barrel. It's no wonder the United States had a hair-trigger with Iraq. At the rate the United States was consuming crude, it couldn't survive without cheap oil, and it wouldn't suffer anyone else to have control over its share. Robert Dreyfuss noted in his March 2003 article, "The Thirty-Year Itch":

> To the hawks who now set the tone at the White House and the Pentagon, the region is crucial not simply for its share of the U.S. oil supply . . . but because it would allow the united States to maintain a lock on the world's energy lifeline and potentially deny access to its global competitors.[33]

The wars that have been fought over oil, particularly Middle Eastern oil, have created massive geopolitical problems. The underhanded deals and secret ties to oil tyrants have complicated things even further. The business connections between the Bush family and Saudi Arabia raised a number of questions after September 11, 2001. For example, why were two Saudi families allowed to charter a flight out of the country when all other air-travel was grounded? Those two families were the royal Sauds and their long-time friends, the bin Ladens.

You read that correctly. In *House of Bush, House of Saud*, author Craig Unger wrote, "Prince Bandar bin Sultan bin Abdul Aziz, the Saudi Arabian ambassador to the United States, was orchestrating the exodus of more than 140 Saudis scattered throughout the country."[34] Prince Bandar was very close with the Bush family, taking hunting trips and vacations with the first President Bush. And he was very capable of pulling strings with the second President Bush. He met with the president on September 13, 2001, and later that day a group of Saudis were flown from Tampa, Florida, to Lexington, Kentucky. The flight was not logged with the Federal Aviation Administration, and the White House has not acknowledged the flight occurred.[35]

The White House did not want to be seen spiriting away Saudi families after the worst terrorist attack on American soil, but because of the intense connection between political families and oil economies, both the Saudi royal family and the bin Laden family were helped out of the country. As shocking as this story is, it proves that oil is thicker than blood—that even in the worst times in our history, the country will work to secure its oil interests.

Unfortunately, oil companies themselves may be even worse. There were times when U.S. oil companies trampled over the backs of the United States itself in favor of control over oil markets through price and supply manipulation. Consider this excerpt from Leonardo Maugeri's *The Age of Oil: The Mythology, History, and Future of the World's Most Controversial Resource*:

> Oil prices of the largest companies were excessively high in certain markets and inexplicably lower in others; in addition, some buyers were overcharged while others received significant discounts. All of this called attention to the opaque pricing mechanisms of the oil giants.
>
> Public outcry exploded in 1947 when it surfaced that Chevron and Texaco had sold oil to the U.S. Navy at $1.23 per

barrel, well above the $0.95 it charged to French buyers and $1.00 to Uruguay. Even worse, a U.S. Senate committee discovered that the overcharging of the Navy occurred even during World War II, a shocking betrayal of U.S. national interests.[36]

This wasn't the only time that U.S. companies put profits above patriotism. In December 2003, the Pentagon reported that Halliburton, the company whose former CEO was then–Vice President Dick Cheney, may have overcharged the U.S. Army by $1.09 per gallon for almost 57 million gallons.[37] And in mid-March 2005, this same company faced another Pentagon inquiry about overcharging the U.S. government by $100 million for supplying fuel to the military as it rebuilt Iraq's oil infrastructure.[38] We talk more about this particular company, and its relationship to the Bush administration in Chapter 13.

Part Four

OIL'S POLITICAL ALLIES

Chapter 13

The Bush-
Halliburton Era

The idea that a government could collude with a corrupt business is not a new one. Several key industries have always been useful to the government, and the glove-in-hand cooperation intensified with President Bush during the first Gulf War, and has been carried through his son's presidency. "Chevron, Halliburton, Lockheed Martin, and Bechtel represent three key pillars of the Bush Agenda: oil, war, and building the infrastructure of corporate globalization," wrote Antonia Juhasz in *The Bush Agenda: Invading the World, One Economy at a Time.*[1]

Of all the favoritism, the most obvious comes from the connection between Halliburton and the U.S. government. In fact, Halliburton has always had an inside man. In 1969, former Texas Governor John Connally joined the Halliburton board. It wasn't long before President Nixon appointed him to the President's Foreign Intelligence Advisory

Board, which Robert Bryce, author of *Cronies: Oil, the Bushes, and the Rise of Texas, America's Superstate,* called "the super-secret entity that monitors all of America's intelligence operations."[2] But the evolution of Halliburton's relationship to the government has become so obvious that the lines between the two have nearly disappeared.

For example, as Secretary of Defense in 1991, Dick Cheney gave millions of dollars worth of contracts to Halliburton, and when he left office in 1995, he served as CEO of Halliburton until he was chosen by George Bush as the vice presidential candidate. Cheney resigned his post as CEO, of course, but as vice president, he again gave hundreds of millions of dollars worth of contracts to Halliburton during the Gulf War in 2003. We later learned that at least some of these contracts were noncompetitive. And we also learned the Halliburton was accused of overcharging the government, thanks to Bunnatine Greenhouse, a whistle-blower in the Army Corps of Engineers who was, as a result, demoted.

A *New York Times* article by Erik Eckholm back in late August 2005 reported:

> Ms. Greenhouse's lawyer, Michael Kohn, called the action an "obvious reprisal" for the strong objections she raised in 2003 to a series of corps decisions involving the Halliburton subsidiary Kellogg Brown & Root, which has garnered more than $10 billion for work in Iraq.[3]

The issue was a noncompetitive contract worth up to $7 billion for the reconstruction of Iraq's oil operations. . . . But Halliburton was also accused in 2003 of overcharging the government by $61 million for transporting fuel from Kuwait to Iraq. *The New Yorker* reported, "Halliburton charged the United States as much as $2.38 per gallon, an amount that a Pentagon audit determined to be about a dollar per gallon too high."[4]

This reminds us of another scandal that we wrote about in *Barbarians of Wealth: Protecting Yourself from Today's Financial Attilas.* The mid-nineteenth century saw one of the most pervasive government scandals rock the United States. In particular, the Credit Mobilier scandal included highly ranked members of government. It has become one of the best-known scandals of collusion between government and big business.

First exposed by the *New York Sun* in 1872, this scheme was the result of an ambitious plan for a transcontinental railroad, the construction of which was backed by Congress with the Pacific Railroad Acts of 1862 and 1864. It was wildly popular and a mint for certain investors, as the plan was also backed by 30-year government bonds, massive land grants, and the creation of the Union Pacific Railroad company, the first corporation chartered by the government since the Second Bank of the United States nearly 50 years before.[5] That should've told you something about the plan, as national banks were always surrounded with suspicion of fraud. The next section describes the scheme.

Government-Backed Fraud

The government-sponsored company (the Union Pacific Railroad company) issued 100,000 shares at $1,000 a piece, raising $100 million, an immense sum of money, but not nearly enough to fund the project. To subsidize costs, the company would receive $16,000 to $48,000 in government bonds, and 6,400 acres of land for every mile of track built. But that's not all. In 1864, the government said that Union Pacific Railroad (along with Central Pacific) was allowed to sell mortgage bonds on that land, and increased the land allotment to 12,800 acres per mile.[6] You'd think these subsidies would be enough, but these guys were greedy—both the corporate bosses and the Congressmen.

And here's where the scandal comes in. Thomas Clark Durant was the controlling partner and president of the Union Pacific, and under his direction, a construction company called Credit Mobilier was created. This company received top dollar for the construction project of laying the thousands of miles of line. John Steele Gordon, author of *An Empire of Wealth: The Epic History of American Economic Power*, explains:

> They set up a construction company, owned by themselves, with a fancy French name, Credit Mobilier, and hired it to build the railroad. Needless to say, they charged the railroad top dollar, and often then some, for their services. Although the

chief engineer, Peter Dey, had estimated that the initial section, west of Omaha, could be built for an average of $30,000 a mile, when Credit Mobilier asked for $60,000, the president of the line, Thomas C. Durant, ordered Dey to resubmit his proposal, making the sum needed $60,000 a mile.[7]

In other words, it was like a no-bid contract with the government—very similar to what's been happening in the oil world, as we'll get to in just a moment—overcharging and all.

Gordon reports that Peter Dey resigned. But that didn't stop Credit Mobilier and Union Pacific from milking as much money from the government—and from Wall Street—as it could. Remember, the Union Pacific was created by the U.S. government, and many investors were U.S. Congressmen. Credit Mobilier needed some help from Congress, and Congressman Oakes Ames, from Massachusetts, was a stockholder of Credit Mobilier. In order to push through helpful legislation, Ames bought off other Congressmen to grease the wheels. In 1867, he came to Washington with 343 shares of the company that were trading at a 100 percent premium, and sold them at par in order to keep things on the right track.[8]

Ames had many big names involved in his bribery scandal: folks like Schuyler Colfax and Henry Wilson, who would both become vice presidents; James Garfield, who would become president; and James G. Blaine, who would be the Republican nominee for president in 1884.[9] Why do we bring this up? What does a railroad company have to do with the oil industry? The connection is in the players—the government "shareholders," their lack of accountability and their overt greed. Not a single one of the Credit Mobilier scam artists was kicked out of Congress for his behavior. Ames himself was only censured.[10] And though the press may have connected some of the dots on the Halliburton-Bush-Cheney secret deals, the United States government has been deathly silent on the matter, except perhaps in political campaigning. Heaven forbid we actually see any government officials go to jail for fleecing the American taxpayer.

Now, let's fast-forward into the late twentieth century and talk about Halliburton, George W. Bush, and Dick Cheney. We'll start with the former Secretary of Defense at the time of the first Gulf War.

It was, of course, Cheney at the helm when the United States rushed to the aid of the oil-swollen kingdom of Saudi Arabia.

Oil Nepotism

The proliferation of what amounts to oil nepotism has fused government and corporations so completely that it's hard to tell where one ends and the other begins. In "Contract Sport: What Did the Vice-President do for Halliburton?," an article for *The New Yorker*, Jane Mayer wrote:

> Sam Gardiner, a retired Air Force colonel who has taught at the National War College, told me that so many of the contracts in Iraq are going to companies with personal connections with the Bush Administration that the procurement process has essentially become a "patronage system."[11]

Now let's go back to the time when Cheney was Secretary of Defense for the first President Bush. Cheney was pretty much in the right place at the right time. He had no military experience and in fact had deferred his Vietnam War-era draft five times.[12] But President Bush needed someone who was a leader, and Cheney had served as the House Minority Whip during his time in Congress. He was unanimously confirmed, and immediately set to work, forming a cadre of trusted people around him, not hesitating to cut personnel and programs that weren't working.

At the same time, Cheney sought out and received a steadily increasing of the defense budget even after the Cold War had ended and military analysts were calling for massive cuts in the hundreds of billions.[13] Cheney had consolidated power in his position as Secretary of Defense, and cut his teeth on a regime change in Panama by ousting the thuggish president Manuel Noriega. The military action was a success for the United States and solidified Cheney as a leader in President Bush's cabinet.[14]

A year later, the U.S. was on the verge of war in the Middle East. Oil, of course, was at the heart of the matter. Iraq had just spent eight years and more than $40 billion on a war with Iran,[15] and it had a large debt with Kuwait, which Kuwait refused to forgive. Kuwait came to exist because the British drew a line on a map, disregarding old tribal alliances and territories. Unfortunately that line crossed the Rumaila oil field, bisecting the 50-mile wide, 30-billion-barrel reserves. Ninety percent of the oil field is in Iraq, and the remaining 10 percent in Kuwait. For years, Iraq had been accusing Kuwait of stealing billions of dollars' worth of oil from the Iraqi side of the Rumaila oil field.[16] The line also blocked Iraq from the Persian Gulf, leaving only a 36-mile swampy strip with a single harbor.[17]

The United States saw this as conflict as an ideological battle—the Good versus Evil that the second President Bush would bring up in his war on terrorism. Listen to this rhetoric from President Bush in his address to Congress in 1990 in his push for war:

> Out of these troubled times, our fifth objective—a new world order—can emerge: a new era—freer from the threat of terror, stronger in the pursuit of justice, and more secure in the quest for peace. An era in which the nations of the world, East and West, North and South, can prosper and live in harmony. A hundred generations have searched for this elusive path to peace, while a thousand wars raged across the span of human endeavor. Today that new world is struggling to be born, a world quite different from the one we've known. A world where the rule of law supplants the rule of the jungle. A world in which nations recognize the shared responsibility for freedom and justice. A world where the strong respect the rights of the weak.[18]

Few people would remember another line from the same speech. The President said, "An Iraq permitted to swallow Kuwait would have the economic and military power, as well as the arrogance, to intimidate and coerce its neighbors—neighbors who control the lion's share of the world's remaining oil reserves. We cannot permit a resource so vital to be dominated by one so ruthless."[19] Unless of course it's the United States. According to Queen Noor of Jordan, President Bush told King Hussein, "I will not allow this little dictator to control 25 percent of the civilized world's oil."[20]

The Most Cunning Oil Barbarian

Enter Cheney. It was pressure from the Secretary of Defense that forced Arab leaders to allow U.S. troops on Arab soil.[21] Cheney needed to get his foot in the door. He needed an in for his future company, Halliburton, and this was how he got it. President Bush's drive for war in the oil-filled Persian Gulf prompted Cheney to direct the Pentagon to request a report in 1992 on how private companies could provide logistical support for U.S. troops in potential war zones. This report cost the Pentagon $9 million, and the company that was awarded this money was Brown & Root, a wholly-owned subsidiary of Halliburton.[22] It was the first of the sweetheart deals that the U.S. government awarded this company. After reviewing the report Cheney awarded the Halliburton subsidiary a $2 billion contract to support troops in the Balkans. The contract was not bid out to any other companies.[23]

Homer Duncan, author of *Bush and Cheney's War: A War Without Justification,* wrote, "Without any previous business experience, Cheney leaves the Department of Defense to become the CEO of Halliburton Co., one of the biggest oil-services companies in the world."[24] Cheney used his connections in government to secure even more contracts from the Pentagon. Duncan reports that while Cheney was CEO, Halliburton jumped from 73rd to 18th on the Pentagon's top list of contractors.[25]

The money poured in—lucrative government contracts, favorable loan guarantees, and massive overseas operations—all thanks to Dick Cheney, former Secretary of Defense, soon-to-be vice president of the United States.

Then in 1997, Cheney became a contributor to the Project for the New American Century, a conservative group that started advocating for the removal of none other than Saddam Hussein as early as 1998.[26] Of course, regime change means war, and war means even more lucrative contracts.

Consider this statement by Antonia Juhasz:

From this position, [Cheney] advocated for war against Iraq while his company simultaneously conducted at least $73 million of work for Hussein. As vice president, he has ushered the country into war against Iraq, while Halliburton has received

U.S. government contracts in Iraq worth nearly $11 billion to perform services privatized under Cheney's watch.[27]

These companies will always go after profits, even if it's against the government's official voice—and even against the law. But it's certainly much easier when the government's in bed with you, forking over billions in no-bid contracts, and never glancing at the bill.

At the same time, during Cheney's stint as CEO, Halliburton doubled its political contributions and its lobbying budget. It's clear that Halliburton was buying its way into government.[28] When Cheney left the company, he took a massive retirement package worth $30 million in cash, stock, and options. He still gets hundreds of thousands of dollars a year in deferred compensation.[29] He also shed the stain of a damaging SEC investigation into Halliburton's accounting practices.[30] Not two months after he left, an insider charged that the company had overbilled the government by $6 million for decommissioning the Ford Ord military base in California.[31] It wouldn't be the last time.

In fact, Dan Briody, author of *The Halliburton Agenda: The Politics of Oil and Money*, reported, "The cost overruns that Halliburton was booking as revenue accounted for 50 percent of the company's operating profit in the fourth quarter of 1998."[32]

But by the time all of this came to light, Cheney was back in the White House as vice president to a man who would be one of the biggest boons for Halliburton: George W. Bush.

Brown & Root (now known as Kellogg Brown & Root, or KBR, as Halliburton and KBR split into two arms of the same company) was contracted to build the detention facility at Guantanamo Bay, Cuba. It also built and staffed bases in Bagram and Kandahar, Afghanistan, and "won" a no-bid contract with Halliburton to rebuild Iraq's oil infrastructure.[33] Halliburton CEO John Gibson in 2003 was looking forward to war. He said, "We hope Iraq will be the first domino and that Libya and Iran will follow. We don't like being kept out of markets because it gives our competitors an unfair advantage."[34] What a telling statement! Business is business, no matter the collateral damage, and these companies have so much influence in government it's scary. To walk blithely into war for the sake of lower oil prices and plentiful supplies is beyond disturbing. But think about the U.S. position now.

A weak Iraq dependent on the United States makes the oil-rich country a huge staging point for control over other Middle Eastern countries. Think Iran, folks. Had the invasion and occupation of Iraq gone more smoothly, with strong support from the citizens of Iraq (which is what the administration expected), the U.S. government might be looking at Iran in a very different light. And oil companies might already be drooling.

The most damning piece of evidence may be the fact that Halliburton has already been doing business in Iran. On June 23, 1998, Cheney as CEO of Halliburton said the following at the Cato Institute's Collateral Damage Conference:

> There are numerous oil and gas development companies from other countries that are now aggressively pursuing opportunities to develop [Iran's] resources. That development will proceed, but it will happen without American participation. The most striking result of the government's use of unilateral sanctions in the region is that only American companies are prohibited from operating there.[35]

What Cheney didn't tell the conference attendees was that Halliburton had been working in Iran since 1975 when it received an $800 million contract from the Iranian Imperial Army to build a naval base.[36] But business continued even after the U.S. imposed sanctions in 1979 after the hostage crisis. In fact, the company paid the Department of Commerce $15,000 in 1997 to settle allegations that it broke the U.S. Export Administration Act boycotting Iran.[37]

The company never admitted any wrongdoing. And Cheney actually defended Halliburton's business with Iran, saying that the work was done through foreign subsidiaries, and even argued for relaxing sanctions there so that U.S. companies could get in on the oil action.[38] Halliburton's only focus is profits, and the U.S. government's only purpose in its wars has been to secure oil supplies. This was a match made in heaven, and Dick Cheney drove the Halliburton machine right into the Oval Office.

But the United States and Iran weren't the only places that profited from oil hegemony and the Halliburton machine. The company has four offices in Venezuela, an office in Nigeria, and nine offices in Russia[39]—all countries where oil has played a major role in creating relations with the global economy. And they are also all countries where oil gave government more power than it had ever had.

Chapter 14

Petrodollars

The Rise of Venezuela, Iran, and Russia

O il companies hate nationalization. There's no money in it, and most often, international companies are forced to give up their rights to hundreds of millions of dollars when a country sweeps in and takes over the oil industry. But it's good business for the nation's bottom line.

Whenever a country has a substantial amount of crude oil reserves and an authoritarian government, there's trouble brewing. In Chapter 9, The Birth of OPEC, and Chapter 11, The OPEC Oil Weapon, we talked about the power that nationalization can give a country with vast oil resources. We saw how countries could band together and usurp the oil supremacy of the Seven Sisters, the International Petroleum Cartel whose members accounted for the majority of oil production in the mid-twentieth century, and who were making money hand over fist by exploiting their host nations' oil wealth. We saw these nations become the new cartel. And we saw these nations become the battle grounds for countries with huge oil consumption and declining crude production, as when the United States' gained a foothold in the Middle East. In fact, since the early twentieth century, oil demand in these countries has been tied to national security.

Consider the establishment of the Federal Oil Conservation Board in 1924. President Calvin Coolidge said, "It is even probable that the supremacy of nations may be determined by the possession of available petroleum and its products."[1] No wonder, then that under-developed nations thought their oil resources were threatened by the world's super-powers—they were! But what are the stories of the individual oil nations? What are the brains behind OPEC, the muscle to bring Arab countries together, and the Russian bear on the outside, calculating and cold?

Beyond Saudi Arabia's relationship with the United States, there are no more compelling stories, and influential histories in the crude world, than those of these countries: Venezuela, Iran, and Russia. In each of these three countries, the United States, and international oil companies, have sought a foothold in order to claim oil reserves for themselves. This external pressure has had varying degrees of success, and each has a story of oil barbarism that has shaped the country's role in today's war for oil resources. They are unique, politically, geographically, and ethnically.

Venezuela: The Brains behind OPEC

Juan Pablo Perez Alfonzo was the Minister of Mines in Venezuela when the Seven Sisters slashed oil prices in August 1960 after Libyan oil hit the market.[2] Remember the production quotas? The coordinated cuts or increases from OPEC? They were his idea. But let's go back 40 years before Alfonzo's big idea that would unite the oil produc-ing nations of the world, and create one of the most ruthless cartels in crude history.

It's 1920, and the West is talking about oil shortages. Global oil companies installed geologists and other experts in every market in search for more oil, and one of the more promising places was Venezuela. The situation in Venezuela in the early twentieth century was the opposite of what we've seen during Chávez's reign. General Juan Vicente Gómez took control of the Venezuelan government in a coup in 1908.[3] The country was used to generals stealing power over each other, but not much changed for the regular people. They remained poor and scattered, scratching out a living through agriculture. Gómez began the long process of centralizing the government, but he knew Venezuela needed money, and that any money would have to come from foreign investment.

But he wasn't looking for cash to better his country. He was looking for money to line his own pockets.

> Woodrow Wilson called him a "scoundrel," a mild epithet for a man who kept his tight grip on the country through terror and brutality. The British minister to Caracas was more blunt; he described Gómez as "an 'Absolute Monarch' in the most medieval sense of the word." Whatever the state of his literacy, Gómez knew what he wanted, which, in addition to absolute political power, was vast wealth.[4]

And oil was his ticket to riches.

Royal Dutch/Shell was already in the country, drilling its first well in 1912. It didn't take long to realize the potential of Venezuela's oil industry. Standard Oil was next in line, and by 1929, Venezuela was the world's second largest oil producer, and largest exporter.[5] The rush for Venezuelan oil between 1920 and 1935 put oil as the top export by a long mile. In fact, oil exports accounted for only 1.9 percent of Venezuela's GNP in 1920. Want to guess the percentage of exports oil accounted for in 1935? Try 91.2 percent.[6]

These petrodollars did wonders for the economy. Starting in 1936 and continuing for more than 20 years, the country's GNP grew at an annual rate of 7 percent.[7] One of the reasons why Venezuela's GNP grew so quickly—aside from the massive oil production—was because the Hydrocarbons Act was signed into law in 1943. This law stated that foreign companies, like Shell and Standard Oil, could not make greater profits than they paid to Venezuela.[8] This made Venezuelan oil more expensive than new oil from the Middle East.

It is also one of the reasons why Juan Pablo Perez Alfonzo, the Minister of Mines in Venezuela from 1959 through early 1963, wanted to join up with the Middle East. He wanted these new oil countries that were still under the thumb of the Seven Sisters to force oil companies to pay more taxes, thereby increasing the price of oil from the Middle East and making Venezuelan oil more competitive.[9]

Further, each year of the first decade since OPEC was formed (1960–1970), Venezuela's share of oil profits with international oil companies has climbed. In the beginning of the decade Venezuela's share of petro-profits was 56 percent. Companies took 44 percent. By 1970, Venezuela's take was 72 percent versus the companies' 28 percent![10] Sounds like the beginning of nationalization to me.

The Oil Embargo during the October War in 1973 sent oil revenues even higher. According to Gregory Wilpert, author of "The Economics, Culture, and Politics of Oil in Venezuela," "With the Middle East oil embargo of 1973, world oil prices and, along with it, Venezuelan government revenues, quadrupled from 1972 to 1974."[11] Just two years from the massive price shift, Venezuela would first nationalize its oil industry. In 1976, the country paid off the international companies working there and created a national corporation, Petroleos de Venezuela (PdVSA).[12] It's the third largest oil company in the world behind Saudi Arabia's Aramco and ExxonMobil.[13] That's how important Venezuela is, and it is probably part of Hugo Chávez's beef with the United States.

The United States was behind the creation of Aramco: Ar-Am-Co, or Arabian American Oil Company. Before Saudi Arabia nationalized its oil industry, Aramco was run by the United States—or, more correctly—it was run by ExxonMobil's predecessor Standard Oil, and Texas Oil Company, which has since become Chevron.

While nationalization had taken place in 1976, the international companies' assets were just absorbed into the Venezuelan economy. For example, Shell's division became Maraven, Shell's president of the Venezuelan division became the president of the newly nationalized assets, and the company was renamed Maraven.[14] What, then, had really changed in the Venezuelan oil industry?

Miguel Tinker-Salas wrote the following in his *Harvard International Review* article, "Fueling Concern: The Role of Oil in Venezuelz":

> Before his death, Arturo Uslar Pietri Arturo, one of Venezuela's most revered pundits, wrote an article entitled "El parasitismo petrolero," (Petroleum Parasitism) in which he remarked that

the country, between 1976 and 1995, had generated and largely squandered US$270 billion dollars from oil sales.[15]

With international companies still in charge of Venezuelan oil assets, Chávez felt he had no control over the Petroleos de Venezuela (PdVSA). He set about changing that, and went on to renationalize the oil industry and close the newly opened investment pipeline which, in the 1990s, allowed foreign companies to manage oil fields.[16] He put OPEC at the forefront of his push to revitalize the oil industry, which is just a nice way to refer to pumping up craving for more petrodollars.

PdVSA had been producing far above its OPEC quota, and oil prices were becoming depressed. Like his countryman, Juan Pablo Perez Alfonzo, Chávez believed that production quotas could be effectively used to boost prices, and he was right. In early 2000, for the first time since 1985, oil prices topped $27 a barrel.[17] The conflict between the president and PdVSA resulted in a failed attempt to force Chavez out of government. Thousands of PdVSA employees were shut out of oil facilities, when oil production was shut down . . .[18] This resulted in an estimated $3 billion loss in exports.[19]

But Chávez survived—for how long remains to be seen. After the attempted coup in 2002, Chávez ordered that at least 10 percent of PdVSA's investment budget go to fund social programs.[20] But that amount could be falling. According to the Council on Foreign Relations, in 2008, Venezuela was producing only about 2.4 million barrels of oil a day while its "official" record showed a production figure of about 3.3 million barrels a day.[21] A boost in production would need an investment of $3 billion.[22]

Indeed, Chávez's days could be numbered if slacking oil revenues can't contribute enough petrodollars to the president's social programs. And we know what revolutions can do to an oil industry.

Enter Iran . . .

Iran: The Middle East Muscle

Iran's petroleum industry got its start at the turn of the twentieth century, with a 60-year concession for most of the country's territory held by Irishman William Knox D'Arcy. The deal was worth 40,000 pounds, a

16 percent cut of the profits, and a royalty in gold—four gold shillings for every metric ton of oil sold.[23] It was the first deal of its kind in the Middle East, and it was a sought-after prize.

Leonardo Maugeri wrote the following in his book, *The Age of Oil: What They Don't Want You to Know about the World's Most Controversial Resource*:

> Indeed, control of the whole of Central Asia had been the prize behind the almost century-long confrontation between Great Britain and Russia, both countries considering the region key to their security and power. . . . That struggle was still under way when D'Arcy's undertaking took shape, making the Russians the more dangerous candidates to replace the British grip on Persian oil.[24]

It took eight years to hit paydirt, and the British-backed D'Arcy was in near financial ruin. He'd spent hundreds of thousands of pounds on this venture, when suddenly, just days before the whole project was going to be scuttled, at four o'clock in the morning, D'Arcy and his men found a gusher. "A gusher of petroleum," wrote Daniel Yergin in *The Prize: The Epic Quest for Oil, Money & Power*, "rising perhaps fifty feet above the top of the drilling rig, was smothering the drillers."[25]

Nearly a year later, on April 19, 1909, the Anglo-Persian Oil Company went public; and none too soon, either. Great Britain needed secure supplies. As you read in Chapter 7, Winston Churchill, then First Lord of the Admiralty, successfully lobbied for the British Navy to change over from coal-fueled ships to oil-fueled ships. The advent of the internal combustion engine made Iran's oil reserves crucial to Great Britain.[26] And reserves were massive. D'Arcy's gusher turned out to be an oil field bigger than the city of Sacramento, California—more than 10 miles squared.[27]

Admiral Edmond Slade was the former Director of Naval Intelligence and head of a government commission charged with reviewing the Persian concession to see if it was viable enough for the British Navy to rely on. He said in his report after visiting the Abadan refinery—one of the largest in the world at the time—that it would be "a national disaster if the concession were allowed to pass into foreign hands."[28] And that certainly was a danger.

Russia held sway over the northern provinces, and Britain the southern. D'Arcy's oil-producing concessions were right in the middle. And Anglo-Persian was having money troubles. They sought out none other than the British government as a partner, making oil in Iran a national security issue, and making Britain a global player in the oil industry.

But where was Iran on this issue? Iran did not yet exist. In fact, Iran was not even called Iran until 1935. It was known as Persia, thus the name Anglo-Persian Oil Company. The Persians were a collection of tribes that were fractious at best, and threatened on all sides—by the Turks and the Russians at their borders, and from internal struggles from other Persian tribes. Persian leaders from the Qajar tribe were often bought off by foreign powers in order to gain influence in the area, and that's how the British got a foothold in the land.

Iran was using the British as a shield against the Russians, which is why its land was essentially divided between the two superpowers—Russia to the north, Britain to the south. Iran needed money. The continuously weakening Iranian leadership was in constant need of cash. And the only way it could get money was through concessions. Iran became a staging ground for British, German, French, and Russian imperialists trying to gain strategic supremacy in the Persian Gulf. The Iranian government had little to no control over its land, and constantly had to call on one of these superpowers to prevent being completely overwhelmed by outside forces.

World War I saw Iran lose all power and become, essentially, a British state for a few brief years. An Anglo-Persian treaty, which would have made Iran a British protectorate was never signed, and between 1919 and 1921, British and Russian troops were rooted out of Iran.[29] Between 1923 and 1936, Reza Khan, who had assumed control first as Prime Minister, then as Shah, removed the last vestiges of tribal dynasty and attempted to wash Iran clean of foreign influence. He did so with a strong hand (bringing the outlying tribal regions to heel) and a forceful government that implemented revolutionary economic and industrial reforms. Iran was fast becoming a regional power.[30]

But that didn't mean that Iran was cut off from the world's superpowers. On the contrary, Shah Reza offered oil concessions to Britain and the United States, though the Soviet Union called foul, as a 1921 friendship treaty prohibited former Soviet concessions from being granted to other foreign countries.[31] Here's where things get interesting.

In 1932, Shah Reza nullified the Anglo-Iranian Oil Company's (renamed from the Anglo-Persian Oil Company) concession because it wanted a bigger cut of the company's profits. Remember, D'Arcy's deal with Iran said the country would get a 16 percent cut of net profits. This was, in essence, a steal for the British, and now, Shah Reza wanted a better deal.

Great Britain sent warships in order to convince the Shah to reinstate the concession, which it did in 1933.[32] Great Britain conceded a greater share of the oil profits, but this move did nothing to bolster friendship between the two countries, and as Germany was beginning to rise to power, Shah Reza openly courted Adolf Hitler as a balance to British and Russian influence in Iran.[33] With this move, Reza essentially signed his "resignation." In 1941, the British forced Shah Reza out of power and installed his son, Mohammed Reza, as what Leonardo Maugeri puts it, "nothing more than a puppet in the hands of the British government."[34]

That stirred up nationalistic fervor in the Iranians, with the oil industry at the forefront. Horrible working conditions in the industry along with blatantly fraudulent accounting[35] in Anglo-Iranian's (renamed British Petroleum after Shah Reza cancelled its concession) oil books that snookered Iran out of millions in profits thrust calls for nationalizing the whole industry into the political mainstream.

In the spring of 1951, the Iranian parliament put forth a law nationalizing BP's assets.[36] Unfortunately for Iran, the international oil companies were too powerful. These were the Seven Sisters, who controlled all oil movement and nearly all production in the world. Edward Jay Epstein, writing in *New York Magazine*, in June, 1975, put it this way:

> The oil cartel had taken full advantage of wartime allocations administration in both Washington and London to consolidate its control over the world's markets, and by 1951, it had grown so powerful that not even the sovereign governments that supplied it with most of its crude could successfully defy it.

Thus in the spring of 1951, when Prime Minister Mossadegh of Iran unilaterally nationalized the concessions and facilities of the Anglo-Iranian Oil Company, the British company withdrew its technicians . . . from the Iranian wells and refineries, and other cartel members refused to supply Iranians with either tankers or markets for their crude oil.[37]

Indeed, the Seven Sisters effectively kneecapped the Iranian economy to the point that Iran had no choice but to accept a "compromise" in which a consortium of companies would develop Iran's oil reserves. That consortium was, of course, made up of the Seven Sisters, including BP.[38]

During the attempt at nationalization, Iran lost hundreds of millions of dollars in oil revenue. Production dropped from 650,000 barrels a day in 1950 to a paltry 20,000 barrel a day in 1953. Export revenue plummeted from $400 million to $2 million in the same timeframe.[39] It was under this pressure that Iran—just seven years after being near bankruptcy—would join with other oil producers to form OPEC.

Under the thumb of the Seven Sisters, Iran recouped its revenue losses but, in 1959, when the Seven Sisters manipulated oil production, stymieing the flow of cash particularly in the Middle East, Iran sought to join the fledgling cooperation between Arab oil producers and Venezuela: the brains behind OPEC.[40] Though in the beginning international oil companies had more negotiating power, Iran's cooperation with OPEC won countries increased shares of oil revenues (Iran's annual oil revenue topped $500 million by the mid 1960s[41]), and pushed nationalism to a whole new level.

When OAPEC nations instituted the oil embargo against the West for helping Israel in the October War in 1973, Iran did not participate.[42] But that didn't stop the country from making a killing from rising prices.

Ian Skeet, author of *OPEC: Twenty-Five Years of Prices and Politics*, wrote, "In mid-December Iran held an auction for 475,000 b/d and obtained a price of $17.04/bbl."[43] Oil just two months earlier was selling for $5.12 a barrel.[44] Iran's oil export revenue jumped from $1 billion in 1970 to $4 billion in 1974, an annual gain of 75 percent![45] But by 1975, revenues went ballistic, and Iran's oil revenues leaped to

$20 billion![46] Iran was staggering under the weight of all these pet-rodollars. And it used this cash to buoy its economy and infrastructure. It entered into multi-billion dollar deals with the United States, France, and Germany for nuclear reactors. Yes, you read that correctly. Iran, for its abstention from the oil embargo in late 1973 and early 1974, was able to enter into a $15 billion trade agreement with the United States that included building eight nuclear reactors. Its deal with France was for five reactors, and with Germany for one reactor.[47] Such willingness and cooperation with Iran to help build nuclear reactors seems foreign to the West in today's political landscape. In fact, it seems nearly treasonous.

So what changed? On January 16, 1979, Shah Mohammed Reza Pahlavi fled the country amidst civil unrest.[48] This unrest was sparked by the Shah's heavy-handedness to "keep order" and his exile of Ayatollah Khomeini, a popular Shi'a Muslim and activist for true Iranian nationalism.

The Shah was a Western puppet, remember, and the revolutionaries detested the secular government that was focused on capitalism and military might.[49] Iran was torn between oil money and poverty. Maugeri wrote, "Thus, while the oil wealth flowed to a few fortunate enclaves within Iranian society, the majority saw its relative position decline, as the terrible secret police of the shah—the Savak—held in check dissidents and banned any form of protest, usually resorting to torture and killing."[50] There were riots and killings in the streets of Tehran between the haves and the have-nots. After the Shah fled, Khomeini returned like a superstar and ascended to Supreme Leader. He abhorred "Westernism," which meant essentially that democracy and capitalism was out of the picture when he took power.[51] He even said, "Economics is for fools."[52]

His anti-Western stance stymied the relationship with the United States. But it wasn't the only issue. In less than a year came the Iran hostage crisis, when 52 U.S. citizens were held for 444 days at the U.S. embassy in Tehran.[53] *Time* magazine, in an interview with one of the hostage-takers, reported, "The students' aim was to force the U.S. government to extradite the deposed Shah. They genuinely feared . . . that the Shah's arrival in New York City in 1979 for medical treatment was part of a U.S. plot to restore him to power, as was done by a CIA-engineered coup d'état in 1953."[54]

This was the first time that the United States imposed sanctions on Iran,[55] that have since come and gone as relations continued to sour. It was also the first time the United States banned Iranian oil, though most of the sanctions were lifted after the hostage crisis was resolved. In the Iran-Iraq War, the U.S. supported Iraq—sort of.

Geoffrey Kemp, head of the National Security Council's Middle East section during the Reagan administration said, "It wasn't that we wanted Iraq to win the war; we didn't want Iraq to lose. We really weren't that naïve. We knew he (Saddam Hussein) was an SOB, but he was our SOB."[56]

President Reagan signed an executive order banning oil imports from Iran in October 1987, near the end of the Iran-Iraq War. And on March 15, 1995, President Bill Clinton signed executive order #12957 banning U.S. involvement in the development of Iran's petroleum resources.[57] This came only 10 days after a $1 billion deal was inked between ConocoPhillips and Iran to develop the Sirri A and E oil field.[58] We know, of course, that this didn't stop Dick Cheney's Halliburton from continuing to do business with this "blacklisted" country. Iran's oil industry still pulls in tens of billions of dollars every year. Oil production was 4.172 million barrels a day in 2009, and Iran exported more than half of that amount. Oil exports account for 80 percent of the country's total exports, which puts the figure at well over $56 billion.[59]

Over the years, these petrodollars have allowed the country to create the Oil Stabilization Fund, established in 1999, that has a $23 billion piggy bank. Iran uses this cash to make overseas investments in countries like Germany, Brazil, Egypt, but not the United States, obviously.[60]

Russia: Calculating Oil Bear

While Iran's relationship with oil and the United States is emotionally driven and based on mutual distrust, the former Soviet Union has been coldly calculating with its crude. It's all about money and power.

Russia's oil history is a long one, starting back in the second half of the 1800s. Its massive reserves quickly put the country at the forefront of the world's oil production. In fact, it's one of only eight countries outside of the OPEC cartel that has significant oil production.[61] But

Russia and OPEC are on opposite sides of the spectrum. Russia didn't have the International Petroleum Cartel carving up its oil wealth. In the Russian oil industry's heyday, from inception through World War I and up until the country's civil war, Russia supplied half the world's oil.[62]

During World War I, worldwide oil consumption climbed 50 percent, while damages from the war, coupled with the Bolshevik Revolution in Russia, pinched supply.[63] But the oil producers were also sloppy. Whether through inexperience or ineptitude, Russian oil companies were slashing the lifespan of their oil fields. "All this pushed operating costs up sharply," wrote Yergin. "Political instability discouraged the large new investment that was required. . . . Increasingly, Russian oil was a residual, to be bought when other petroleum was not available."[64]

This situation wasn't the straw the broke the camel's back, and sparked the revolution, but it certainly provided ample opportunity for the revolutionaries to nationalize the oil industry in 1919.[65] The state controlled everything, and the oil industry was compartmentalized, regulated, and tied to specific ministries which handled everything. Little control was given to the regions where oil was being pumped, and even less was given back to the people living in that region. In addition, little control went to the companies who previously held interest in the Russian oil industry. In the *New York Times*, Simon Bromley wrote:

> Notwithstanding the British attempt to establish an independent state of Azerbaijan and Standard [Oil]'s contract with its government in 1919, Allied intervention during the Civil War failed either to overthrow the Bolshevik state or to reinstate Western (capitalist) property rights.[66]

This created a turbulent time for the Russian Oil Bear. Boycotts and other hostilities between international oil companies were to become commonplace. Internally, Russia was finding and producing more oil, but its insulation from oil majors made its technology second-rate.[67] In other words, Russia's plentiful supply of new oil that was easy to extract offset the decline of its poorly managed fields. The government did not invest in the industry as smartly as it should have. By the time the Oil Embargo and the OPEC oil price wars hit the West, Russia had become a net exporter. Higher prices, and lack of supply, made the oil industry pay off handsomely. Russia increased production significantly, particularly in Siberia, and it was this new oil production that in 1974 made Russia the world's largest oil producer.[68]

Oil was money, and money was power, because it could buy arms. This was never more apparent than in the nuclear arms race, but Russian military might also played a big role in the Middle East conflict. Remember, it was the Russians who propagated the rumor that Israel had amassed 11 brigades on its northern border with Syria. That rumor resulted in the Six-Day War.

But perhaps the most disturbing acts of oil nationalism come from the Putin Era. Vladimir Putin was a ruthless autocrat, no matter how he protested that title. Though he did not nationalize Russia's oil industry outright, he did control who had access to it.

The West always had concerns about Putin. The *New York Times* reported in 2002 that U.S. officials "have growing doubts about the nature of [Putin's] leadership."[69] But inside Russia, the fear was palpable. In 2003, the *Moscow Times* reported, "Russia is full of fear. Businessmen and politicians are afraid of Vladimir Putin. [Putin] relishes the fear. The greater the fear, the stronger his power."[70] Most particularly telling is the U.K.'s report from its oldest and most respected newspaper, *The Daily Mail*, calling Putin a "brutal despot who is dragging the West into a new Cold War."[71] And one of its deadliest weapons—just as with OPEC—is its oil and gas resources.

Russia sits on over 20 percent of the world's oil and natural gas reserves. That makes it virtually energy independent from the rest of the world, and that's one of the reasons why Russia didn't need to join OPEC. With these reserves, Russia, the lone bear, could go it alone. They're a rogue nation, the largest in the world in fact, that owes allegiance to no one but itself.

"Some believe that we are too lucky to possess so much natural wealth, which they say must be divided. These people have lost their mind," Putin said.[72] And we saw the same thing with Nigeria. Top officials reaped the riches of the lucrative oil industry while the masses lived on just a few dollars a day. But Putin didn't just mean keeping oil profits for himself and his cronies. He meant to keep oil itself, and access to it, out of the West's hands.

Indeed, this kind of rhetoric is par for the course when it comes to Putin. His nationalistic ideology ranged from killing off anti-state journalists to hoarding billions of barrels of oil and gas, ready to cut off supplies at the drop of a hat. The Russian Bear did not make many friends. It's become nearly a tradition. The Petroleum Press Service in 1961 wrote:

> Apart from the obvious risk of security of supply owing to the unpredictable political relationships between East and West, large imports of low-priced Russian oil into Western Europe are apt to upset the international oil market, and so ultimately impede investment and the needed diversification of sources of supply.[73]

In other words, Western Europe would become over-reliant on Russian oil supplies. Indeed, Russia would use its petroleum industry as a gun to the head whenever it felt like it was being underpaid—a shakedown, plain and simple.

In *A History of Modern Russia: From Tsarism to the Twenty-First Century*, Robert Service wrote: "Russia caused fear without gaining friends or admirers. It also worried potential investors. Despite its petro-chemical riches, it needed help in modernizing its drilling and refining facilities—and the Russian government's bullying of foreign companies was scarcely going to hasten this process."[74] That means that the oil and gas industry and the government were in bed together. "Occasional information trickled out about the wealth of ministers. Public office became a ticket to vast wealth," wrote Service.[75] That's no surprise, but with Putin, the knife cut both ways. From Steve LeVine, author of *Putin's Labyrinth: Spies, Murder, and the Dark Heart of the New Russia*:

> Without question, he is willing and able to crush those who offend him. Consider this hallmark of the Putin era: his unyielding pursuit and prosecution of a select group of Russian oligarchs. The most notable target was oil kingpin Mikhail Khodorkovsky, Russia's richest man, who was arrested in 2003 by masked federal agents aboard his private plane on the tarmac of Siberia's Novosibirsk Airport. He was sentenced to eight years in prison, and his oil company, Yukos, was systematically dismantled and taken over by two state-controlled companies, Gazprom and Rosneft.[76]

Gazprom, Russia's behemoth state-owned gas firm, was chaired by First Deputy Prime Minister Dmitry Medvedev, who became Putin's presidential successor. Rosneft, another state-owned oil firm, was chaired by Igor Sechin, the Kremlin deputy chief of staff. Rosneft forced a sale of Yugasnkneftegaz, the production arm of rival YUKOS, below market price. Russian state diamond monopoly, Alrosa, was headed by Alexei Kudrin, former Minister of Finance, who hypocritically called for less government control over the economy.[77] Former German chancellor Gerhard Schröder was rewarded for his support with a directorship of Gazprom. Coincidentally, Gazprom was the company building a pipeline to transport gas directly from Russia to Germany.[78] Other government officials were controlling the oil and gas sector too, in Putin's time.

Sound familiar? Anything like Dick Cheney and Halliburton? Most certainly.

Chapter 15

Drill, Baby, Drill

The Alaska Equation

On Wednesday, September 3, 2008, Michael Steele took the podium at the Republican National Convention in St. Paul, Minnesota. "So, do you want to put your country first?" he asked. "Then let's reduce our dependency on foreign sources of oil and promote oil and gas production at home. In other words: Drill, baby, drill! And drill now!"[1] This became the slogan of the Republican Party—a fitting phrase, as the presumptive candidate for vice president was the governor of Alaska, Sarah Palin.

Alaska has been called the Saudi Arabia of America.[2] Its rich crude resources are so plentiful that Alaskan residents don't pay state income taxes. Instead they get paid by the government just for living there. Guess it's kind of like getting paid off by the oil companies.

It's called the Permanent Fund Dividend, and in 2010, this dividend amounted to $1,281 per adult resident.[3] But as we'll see, this figure could be dropping soon, and Alaskans might not have much to show for their oil industry but a greasy slick on the North Slope, and haunting images of oil-coated baby seals.

The state of Alaska collects oil revenues from companies operating there, and distributes a portion of those revenues to its residents. But it took a while for Alaska to get so much oil wealth.

The oil industry started in the mid-1800s, when Russia still owned Alaska, but they never developed Alaska's vast amounts of oil. There were oil seepages in Iniskin Bay and Cold Bay, but Russia did nothing about them. Indeed, had they tried to develop these sites, they probably wouldn't have ever sold the land so cheaply.

In 1867, Russia sold Alaska to the United States of America, and it wasn't an easy sell . . . Secretary of State William Seward was in charge of getting Congress to approve the annexation at a cost of $7.2 million, and protestors in Congress thought it was far too much. Indeed, they called the deal "Seward's Folly."[4] Even the public didn't understand Alaska's worth:

A few newspapers were most vehement in their denunciation of what they called "Seward's Folly" and "Seward's Ice Box" and referred to Alaska as "Walrussia." Horace Greely, the acerbic editor of the New York Herald, sneeringly advised European potentates with worthless territories to discard that they would find a ready buyer in the secretary.[5]

In reality, it was more of a sweetheart deal than anyone could have ever imagined at two cents an acre.[6]

At first glance, Alaska, though possibly rich in natural resources, was so wild and remote that the government didn't recognize its worth. Consequently, after Alaska came under U.S. control, there was no official government set up, and the territory was controlled by the U.S. military—and not very well, either.[7]

Settlers came and went. Without a centralized local government, there was little to no infrastructure, and settlements dried up as conflicts with indigenous tribes and rowdy military troops made the territory inhospitable.

But things started to change in the late 1800s. It wasn't long before gold was discovered, and this caused a massive rush of people toward

Alaskan territory. They came by the hundreds. By 1881, a monthly boat trip made it easy for prospectors to travel from Portland or Victoria to what's now known as Juneau, Alaska's capital.[8]

A few short years later, though, the first oil claims were filed for territory on the Iniskin Peninsula and Cook Inlet. The first wells were drilled in 1898,[9] but they weren't productive, and oil prospecting was slow to catch on. Even the first producing wells in the early twentieth century at Katalla on the Gulf of Alaska didn't have much of a future, and they were abandoned in 1933 after a refinery fire.[10]

All through the early 1900s, oil companies were moving into Alaska and carving up the land either with mining claims or drillings. The process was similar to the way the Seven Sisters carved up the Middle East.

In 1952, a geological survey was conducted by the U.S. Navy, and the potential for oil on the North Slope was found to be enormous. British Petroleum geologists swept in to take a look for themselves. Bryan Cooper noted in his *Alaska—The Last Frontier,* "BP's geologists noted that on Alaska's North Slope there were geologic structures of Middle East size, measuring 72,000 square miles, larger than BP's entire Iranian concession."[11]

Just the year before, the Iranian Prime Minister Ali Razmara had been assassinated, and the oil industry was being nationalized. Production was slipping dangerously, and international oil companies were looking for other sources.[12] The remote areas of the North Slope weren't looking so daunting anymore.

Oil Companies Swarm the North Slope

By 1957, after the discovery of the Swanson River oil field—the largest of the time—Phillips, Marathon, Unocal, Shell, Mobil, Chevron, Texaco, and Atlantic Richfield Oil Company (ARCO) all started drilling.[13] Two years later, Alaska became a state, and natural resource exploration leases started selling like hotcakes.

The state was allowed to choose for drilling 104 million acres of previously federal land, and the promise of oil was what drove Alaska's choice. It chose a 200km stretch of coastline between the National Petroleum Reserve-Alaska (NPRA) and what's now known as ANWR, the Arctic National Wildlife Refuge.[14] We'll get back to ANWR in a bit.

In 1958, just as Alaska was entering statehood, the Department of the Interior planned to lease 4 million acres on the North Slope in 1,300 tracts.[15] Jack Roderick, author of *Crude Dreams: A Personal History of Oil & Politics in Alaska*, wrote, "Major oil companies, independents, and individuals filed more than 7,000 applications in the 4-million-acre drawing."[16] This was the Black Gold Rush.

But the oil event that changed the face of Alaska came in 1968 with the discovery of oil at Prudhoe Bay. On March 13, 1968, oil was struck. Joe Clyde Truett and Stephen R. Johnson, authors of *The Natural History of an Arctic Oil Field: Development and the Biota*, wrote:

> The location of the strike was the Prudhoe Bay State No. 1 well, just 5 km from the edge of the Beaufort Sea. The flow rate was 2415 barrels of oil and 40 million cubic feet of natural gas per day, providing an initial estimated field size of 5 to 10 billion barrels of oil. Estimates of total reserves were later increased to 23 billion barrels of oil and 26 trillion cubic feet of natural gas.[17]

The initial assessment pegged Prudhoe Bay's reserves at 9.6 billion barrels—more than double the size of the previous largest field ever found on the continent.[18] The amount of oil being produced in Prudhoe Bay made the need for a massive pipeline clear.

Between 1974 and 1977, the Trans-Alaska Pipeline System (TAPS) was built that spanned Alaska from the North Slope to the Port of Valdez.[19] From there, oil could be loaded on tankers and shipped down to the lower 48 states. The companies involved were ARCO, the first to hit the huge reserves in Prudhoe Bay, BP Oil, and Humble Oil, which would later become part of ExxonMobil.[20]

At a cost of $8 billion,[21] it wasn't cheap. (Notice that the price tag for this pipeline is more than the government actually paid for the whole state of Alaska when it bought it from the Russians.) But it was absolutely necessary.

The Prudhoe Bay oil field still supplies between 20 percent and 25 percent of the entire U.S. oil production, and Alaska generates 85 percent of its revenue from the field.[22] That said, the North Slope oil fields have been in decline. According to the American Petroleum Institute,

North Slope oil production peaked in 1988, and in just ten years, dropped by 40 percent.[23] Now oil companies are looking increasingly at another swath of land that has not been explored: ANWR.

Arctic National Wildlife Refuge at Risk

The Arctic National Wildlife Refuge, at 29,730 square miles, is the largest national wildlife refuge in the United States, and was first set aside in 1960.[24] The area is just east of all the North Slope oil, so there has been a huge controversy over the area, particularly as the United States becomes more and more dependent on foreign oil.

The "Drill, Baby, Drill" crowd and oil companies want to open up ANWR to oil exploration. In 1987, the Interior Department said that the coastal plain of ANWR should be opened up for drilling. Even the potential environmental threat to the massive caribou herds and other coastal wildlife couldn't trump the need for secure domestic oil supplies. In March 1989, a U.S. Senate committee approved oil leasing in the coastal plain.[25]

A young environmentalist from Fairbanks, Stan Senner told NPR, "And less than 10 days later, the *Exxon Valdez* oil spill happened, and whatever momentum there was behind that Arctic drilling provision in the Senate, the air simply got let out of the balloon immediately after the *Exxon Valdez* hit the rocks."[26]

In Chapter 17 we discuss this major oil spill, which reigned as the country's largest environmental disaster in its history until the BP oil spill in the Gulf of Mexico in April 2010. But now let's discuss why producers are so keen on opening up ANWR.

In the *Valdez* debacle ExxonMobil fought through the court system to avoid any blame, saying the whole thing was just an accident. After that the public didn't have much appetite for opening up ANWR to drilling. But then came the first Persian Gulf War, and Iraq set the Kuwaiti oil fields on fire.[27] Not only was oil supply back in jeopardy, but the Senate was more concerned about getting U.S. forces what they needed to fight the war. And then, Alaskan Senator Frank Murkowski—father of the present Senator Murkowski who won a write-in campaign against Tea Party candidate Joe Miller in the 2010 midterm elections—pulled an underhanded move. From NPR:

Senner recalled how the junior senator from Alaska seized the moment.

"Then-Sen. Frank Murkowski offered an amendment at midnight to the defense appropriations bill that would have allowed the opening of the Arctic refuge, and the Senate approved that amendment on a voice vote," Senner said.[28]

The measure didn't pass, but Murkowski and his oil-backers didn't stop trying.

In a 1995 budget package, a then-Republican-controlled Congress slipped in the measure to open ANWR to drilling. The budget passed both the House and the Senate, only to be vetoed by President Clinton.[29] So let's take a step back for a second. We've got oil proponents saying we need to open up a wildlife refuge because we're too dependent on foreign oil, particularly from hostile countries. And yet, we've seen government officials doing the hokey pokey between Congress, corrupt oil companies, and the vice presidency, arguing for wars over that foreign oil supply.

Nobody has the best interest of the United States, or you the consumer, in mind. Oil companies have always been and will always be in search of profits—even if they have to get them illegally from no-bid contracts or terrorist nations. And ANWR? This area is no different.

Is It Worth It?

On the eve of George W. Bush's presidency, British Petroleum's CEO John Browne (now famous for his company's oil spill in the Gulf of Mexico), said, "BP is interested in exploring Alaska's [Arctic National Wildlife Refuge] if Bush wins the White House."[30] He said this even though BP has spent millions in settlements in illegal dumping of hazardous waste at Prudhoe Bay.[31]

It's true: Alaska's oil fields in production are being depleted. TAPS, which can support a throughput of 2.1 million barrels of oil a day, is operating at less than 30 percent capacity. And if oil throughput drops to 300,000 barrels a day, the pumps will no longer work and the whole system would have to be shut down.[32] According to the lease laws, once operations cease, the land must be restored, and all traces of oil exploration must be removed.

But here's the thing—geologists can't really agree on the worth of oil in ANWR. Reserve estimates are 10.4 billion barrels,[33] or enough oil to fill TAPS at 100 percent capacity for 13.5 years. In 2009, the United States consumed about 18.77 million barrels of oil a day.[34] At that rate the oil in ANWR would last a year and a half.

The *Exxon Valdez* oil spill, where 10 million gallons of crude oil[35]— or just 1.3 percent of America's daily oil consumption—spilled into the ocean, covered 11,000 square miles, and will take more than a century to clean up.[36] This cost ExxonMobil $507 million in settlement costs,[37] not to mention the $2 billion in clean-up.[38] That's less than $10 a barrel.

Brandon Keim for *Wired Science* wrote on the 10-year anniversary of the spill, "As the *Exxon Valdez* Oil Spill Trustee Council recently reported, oil in many areas 'is nearly as toxic as it was the first few weeks after the spill.'"[39] And this disaster is only the biggest in *Alaska's* history. Oil spills happen more often than you think.

In the late 1990s, BP was responsible for 104 oil spills in the United States' Arctic. These spills totaled 20,000 gallons of oil.[40] On February 20, 2001, BP spilled 9,700 gallons of oil in Prudhoe Bay.[41] Just three weeks later, the company spilled as much as 5,800 gallons of a lubricant mixture[42] used in oil exploration from a pipeline in Prudhoe Bay. But let's not focus just on BP. It's not the only dirty oil company in Alaska.

In 1991, the EPA filed complaints against BP and Exxon for dumping waste at the Valdez Alaska Tanker Terminal.[43] Chevron had an oil pipe crack in 1992 at the Kenai terminal that spilled 47,000 gallons of oil into Cook Inlet.[44] These companies have had to pay hundreds of millions in fines for their oil spills, and Alaska is only one area where negligence and outright illegal dumping activity have gotten Big Oil big fines. But they keep paying, keep pumping, and keep spilling.

Now, as former vice-presidential candidate Sarah Palin is stealing the spotlight with her realty show based in Alaska, and her face backing the up-and-coming Tea Party, Alaska is back "en vogue." Drilling, on the other hand, may not be. Back in 2008 during the presidential election, both Barak Obama and John McCain opposed drilling in ANWR.[45] And in April 2010, British Petroleum unleashed the biggest oil spill in modern history—right in our own back yard: the Gulf of Mexico.

Indeed, "Drill, Baby, Drill!" has become "Spill, Baby, Spill!"

Chapter 16

Black Gold Guardians

Global warming, greenhouse gases. These are phrases the
barbarians of black gold absolutely hate. And they certainly
don't want our government enacting legislation that would
force them to stop polluting our environment. In fact a letter dated
September 14, 2010, signed by 24 lobbying associations, asks members
of the Senate Appropriations Committee to *restrict* the Environmental
Protection Agency's authority to implement the newly established
greenhouse gas emissions rules and restrictions.[1]

Among the signers of the letter are:

- American Petroleum Institute
- National Petrochemical & Refiners Association

But it's not just letters they are sending to Congress to avoid EPA
restrictions. They are spending millions of dollars lobbying against
such actions. Oil and gas special interests groups alone have spent $75
million in 2010 in lobbying activities. Last year, the group spent a
record $175 million, a 30 percent increase from 2008.[2]

Over the past 11 years, those groups have spent a whopping $2 billion on Congressional lobbying efforts. That's about $181 million a year to stop Congress from enacting regulations that would curtail their activities. And the truth is the numbers could be higher. That's because companies spend millions on political advertising campaigns but these types of expenses aren't always allocated directly to lobbying efforts. On top of this, companies that donate money to trade associations are allowed to keep that information secret. So we can't say for sure how much money oil companies actually spend to influence our government. But, as you can imagine, it's a lot of money.

The oil industry's main lobbying agency is the American Petroleum Institute (API). The API represents nearly 400 members involved in all aspects of petroleum.[3] The API describes itself as providing a "unified voice" for the industry and is active in key policy-making forums. Their voice, however unified, is backed by lots of money. The Climate Progress Organization says the API spent $11 million to lobby Congress to defeat pollution reductions and maintain industry tax loopholes.[4] Did their efforts pay off? To date, no legislation has passed, and industry tax loopholes are still in place.

For the oil industry, it seems as if money is no object when it comes to getting their way with Congress. In a *New York Times* article, Anne Mulkern quotes Sam Thernstrom, fellow at the American Enterprise Institute as saying, "When a business's livelihood is at stake, they'll put a lot of money down on the table to influence the policies that will affect it."[5]

Outspoken head of Public Citizen's Energy (PCE), Tyson Slocum says, "Politicians routinely deliver on campaign contributions that are provided to them, by giving goodies to the industry."[6] And that's exactly what the industry is doing: using money to influence policy decisions. But that's the way Congress works. Whoever has the most money generally gets what they want.

In her article, Anne Mulkern says that the government watchdog group PCE says that the millions the industry spends on lobbying *does indeed* bring about concessions. As for regulations related to greenhouse gas emissions, PCE's program director, Tyson Slocum says, "They have the ability to move the issue better than they did a year go."[7]

The API's activities are wide reaching and very effective. Sometimes API instigates rallies in cities across the United States to show Washington that the public sympathizes with the oil industry's issues. The website Polluter Watch showed just how the API uses these tactics to block legislation. Here's a recent blog posting on the site about Jack Gerard of the American Petroleum Institute:

> According to an internal memo leaked in August, Gerard directed API's nearly 400 member companies to mobilize their employees to attend "Energy Citizen" rallies in 20 states to protest a cap on carbon pollution.
>
> To ensure the success of the fake grass-roots protests, Gerard bragged that he had also enlisted a bevy of polluting allies— including the U.S. Chamber of Commerce and the National Association of Manufacturers.[8]

Polluter Watch says that in the memo, Gerard urged members to treat the information as sensitive so that critics wouldn't know the game plan. One of these "energy citizen" rallies was aimed at the Waxman-Markey Climate bill also known as the American Clean Energy and Security Act of 2009. The American Petroleum Institute opposes the bill.

The act, sponsored by Henry Waxman of California and Ed Markey of Massachusetts, aims to create clean energy jobs, reduce consumer's energy costs, cut global warming pollution, and increase America's energy independence. Major elements of the bill include a requirement that 20 percent of electricity come from renewable fuels by 2025; smart grid and electrical car provisions; and higher energy efficiency standards for buildings, lighting, and appliances. However, the most significant element in the bill is a proposal to put an absolute limit on global warming pollution and start ratcheting that pollution down. It aims to reduce pollution by 20 percent by 2020, 40 percent by 2030, and 80 percent by 2050.

The oil industry, backed by the API, says any type of cap-and-trade regulation would cause companies to incur higher costs. API claims those costs will lead to increased gas prices which in turn would harm the economy as well as hurt the jobs market. The industry seems to be getting its way. According to MapLight, a non-profit organization that tracks donations given to elected officials, members of the house who voted against this bill received 5.7 times as much in donations as those who voted for it.[9] The bill has not yet made it to the Senate.

Binding Ties

The old saying "It pays to have friends in high places" couldn't be truer for the oil industry, especially when George W. Bush was President. In 2005, Bush signed an energy bill that gave $14.5 billion in tax breaks for the industry. Interestingly enough, at the time, Bush received more money from the oil and gas industry than other politician.

But here's what truly demonstrates the political connection to the oil industry. During his presidency Bush asked Vice President Cheney to head up a special task force to help develop the country's energy policies. Many of the components in the energy bill Bush signed were recommendations made by the task force. In addition to tax breaks for the industry, the task force did away with exemptions that the industry didn't consider beneficial. In similar style, Cheney recruited executives from ExxonMobil, ConocoPhillips, Shell, BP, and Chevron to sit in on his special task force. In reality, the task force was a meeting of the big oil companies to enact regulations that favored their industry.

When information about the task force became public, many of the company officials denied they had attended any meetings. In hearings held in 2005 before both the Senate Energy and Commerce committees, executives said they had not participated in meetings with Cheney or were not involved in the task force. However, the *Washington Post* had obtained documents that showed otherwise:

- On April 17, the task force met with Royal Dutch/Shell's chairman, Sir Mark Moody-Stuart, and two other oil company executives.
- The group met again on March 22, this time with BP regional president Bob Malone, chief economist Peter Davies, and company employees Graham Barr and Deb Beaubien.

Questions arose about the task force when environmentalists complained they were not allowed to participate. Actually, the task force meetings were held in secrecy. Of the matter, Senator Frank

Lautenberg, Democrat from New Jersey, said, "The White House went to great lengths to keep these meetings secret, and now oil executives may be lying to Congress about their role in the Cheney task force."[10]

The binding ties of the oil industry to Congress run deep and are particularly tied to the Gulf States. For example, the oil industry has been "heavily invested" in the state of Louisiana. Louisiana Senator Mary Landrieu has received $758,000 from the industry.[11] There seems to be a long list of BP officials who have donated generously to Landrieu. The current president of BP America, Lamar McKay, gave $1,000 to Landrieu's 2008 reelection campaign. Robert A. Malone, previous president of BP America, gave $2,300 to Landrieu's campaign.[12]

That's not all. Margaret Hudson, BP America's vice president gave $1,100. Benjamin Cannon, BP America's federal affairs director, gave $2,300. The truth is, Landrieu topped the list of members of Congress who received money from BP. In return, she's become one of their biggest allies and a champion for offshore drilling.

In the days following the BP *Deepwater Horizon* oil spill, Landrieu is reported to have minimized the spill. In describing the slick, Landrieu told fellow senators, "The slick contains only 3 percent thick emulsified crude that exists as a very thin layer, only as thick as a couple of strands of hair."[13] Chris Bowers of Open Left says, "If people like Mary Landrieu were Senators from Chernobyl, back in 1986, in the days immediately after the disaster, they would probably have been arguing that the meltdown shows the need for lower regulations on nuclear power plants."[14]

Jim Hightower, writing for the Common Dreams organization, describes the relationship between big oil and congress, specifically Republicans, as a "perfect genetic link."[15] In his article, Hightower lists several incidents of big oil's connection to Republicans. For example, he says that only hours after winning a seat in the Kentucky state election, Rand Paul was calling President Obama un-American for demanding that BP be held accountable for its destruction in the Gulf of Mexico. In another incident, Hightower says that Michelle Bachmann of Minnesota said that "BP shouldn't have to be fleeced and made chumps to have to pay for the perpetual unemployment and all the rest."[16] Hightower also talks about Texas Republican, Joe Barton, who said he was ashamed to live in America, after Obama got BP to agree to set aside $20 billion for damages. Barton called it a "shakedown."[17]

The Center for American Progress wanted to know if there was indeed a link between donations from oil companies and how elected officials vote on bills. Their findings came as no shock. The Center looked specifically at the Renewable Energy and Energy Conservation Tax Act of 2007 (the bill that would remove about $16 million worth of tax breaks to the industry) and found that members of Congress who voted against the bill received on average four times more money in campaign contributions from the industry than those who voted for the bill.

Money talks. The bill died.

Sometimes the connections are more than just monetary. This is particularly true in the case of a particular agency tasked with overseeing certain aspects of the oil industry—the Minerals Management Services—which has long been criticized for its lack of oversight and not-always-appropriate behavior.

Even President Obama acknowledged the relationship wasn't up to par. In responding to the *Deepwater Horizon* disaster, Obama said, "For too long, for a decade or more, there has been a cozy relationship between the oil companies and the federal agency that permits them to drill."[18] For example, *U.S. News* says that a 2008 inspector general's report found that MMS workers were holding sex and drug parties with oil industry representatives.[19] Talk about barbaric!

Other questionable behavior includes MMS inspectors tracing over penciled-in inspection forms filled out by oil industry workers. It was also discovered that MMS workers were accepting meals and hunting trips, and sometimes, all expenses-paid trips to the Peach Bowl.[20]

These deep bonds are hard to break. But what's sad about the connection of elected officials to big oil is that it will cripple our chances of becoming less dependent on oil.

The alternative energy industry doesn't quite have the voice or the money to lobby elected officials. The Clean Economy Network, which calls itself the country's largest "clean tech" organization, spent a paltry $1.3 million on lobbying. Compare that to big oil, which since 1998 has *never* spent less than $50 million on lobbying in any given year.[21] How can the United States move forward and develop better alternative energy sources and become a "greener" country when big oil's pockets run so deep?

Big Budgets

A 2010 ruling by the Supreme Court made it impossible for the U.S. government to ban political spending by corporations in elections. The ruling overturned a 2002 law that banned the broadcast, cable, or satellite transmission of electioneering communications paid for by corporations or labor unions from their general funds. President Obama said the ruling was a major victory for big oil, Wall Street banks, health insurance companies and the other powerful interests that marshal their power every day in Washington to drown out the voices of everyday Americans.[22] Their voices are loud, because their pockets are deep. Oil companies with the largest lobbying expenditures are ExxonMobil, ConocoPhillips, Chevron, BP, and Shell.

Even in the wake of BP's *Deepwater Horizon* oil catastrophe, the company still spends money on lobbying. From January through September of 2010, the company has spent a total of $5.18 million on lobbying.[23] In 2009, BP ranked 20th among highest spenders. BP has become one of the oil industry's 10 largest political spenders. Elected officials who receive money from BP include Republican Don Young of Alaska, who received $73,300 during his tenure; Republican Senator George Voinovich of Ohio, who received $41,400; and former presidential candidate Senator John McCain, who received $44,899.[24] Most notable of all is President Obama, who received $77,051 during his time as a Senator and while running for president.

A good portion of BP's lobbying money went to lobbying efforts to open U.S. waters for offshore drilling. ConocoPhillips has a big budget for lobbying as well. In the second quarter of 2010, the company spent $5.5 million in lobbying efforts. The money went to convince Congress to lift moratoriums on offshore drilling. But it also went to oil sands projects.[25] ConocoPhillips has ownership of several oil sands ventures in Canada. Interestingly enough, oil sands projects generally release more greenhouse gas emissions than other traditional forms of drilling. It wouldn't take much guessing to figure out why ConocoPhillips is lobbying Congress about oil sands projects.

Chevron spends money on lobbying as well. The Center for American Progress puts Chevron third on the list of largest lobbying spending. From January 2009 through June 2010, the company spent $27.8 million.[26] In California, Chevron lobbied hard against legislative proposition 87, a measure that would have taxed the petroleum industry and used the money in a variety of alternative energy measures. The industry banned together and in total spent $94 million to make sure the proposition never made it onto ballots.[27]

Shell does its fair share of lobbying too. In the second quarter of 2010, the company spent $4 million lobbying the government on off-shore drilling. From April to June, Shell lobbied members of Congress, the Environmental Protection Agency, the Interior Department, and the National Oceanic and Atmospheric Administration.[28]

There's no denying that big oil and our elected officials work together on issues that benefit the industry from tax breaks to the environment. Ralph Nader describes the tie-in best. Of the money big oil companies spend lobbying, Nader says, "The corporate lobby in Washington is basically designed to stifle all legislative activity on behalf of consumers."[29]

Part Five

DANGEROUS ADDICTION

Chapter 17

Dirty Business

"I'm scared," she said.

"I'm scared too," he replied.

"What are we going to do?" she asked. "We're gonna burn. Or we're gonna jump."[1]

That was the last conversation Mike Williams, a crewman on BP's *Deepwater Horizon*, had with female crewmate Andrea Fleytas before the two jumped 100 feet into the oil-infested waters of the Gulf of Mexico. The explosion and horrific oil spill that followed would make headlines around the world.

Researchers estimate 4.4 million barrels of oil spilled into the Gulf of Mexico after the deep water well ruptured in April 2010.[2] It is considered the worst marine oil spill in history. But this isn't the only problem BP has had with the platform. In June 2005, human error was blamed for the 15 gallons of diesel fuel that overflowed on the platform and sparked a fire. Somehow the crane operator forgot that he was in the middle of a refueling operation.

In November 2005, about 212 barrels of an oil-based lubricant leaked into the ocean. Uncertain whether it was human error or equipment failure, experts from the Minerals Management Service (MMS) say the spill was probably caused by pipes not tightly screwed together and or improper alignment of the rig.

Then there's the 267 barrels of oil that spilled into the Gulf waters in February 2002, from a hose failure.

In June 2003, 944 barrels of oil spilled out when the rig floated off course. Minerals Management Services said the incident happened because of bad weather, but also because of poor judgment from the rig's captain.[3]

Experts also say that it is not unusual for rigs to have problems, especially considering they operate 24 hours a day in rough water conditions. But they also say if problems go unfixed, these types of incidents could mushroom into much bigger concerns. Obviously the explosion and massive oil leak in April qualify as "bigger concerns." It seems the rig was destined for failure.

From 2000 to 2010, the Coast Guard issued six enforcement warnings, a notice of violation, and a civil penalty to the *Deepwater Horizon*, which is owned by Transocean Ltd. BP contracted Transocean, the largest offshore drilling company to operate the rig in the Gulf area. The vessel had been cited on at least 18 different occasions for "acknowledged pollution source." Guy Cantwell, a spokesperson for Transocean Ltd., says, "Any prior incidents were investigated. Any speculation that they are related to the *Deepwater Horizon* incident is speculation."[4]

It's hard to think these previous incidents aren't related. Mike Williams, chief electronics technician and survivor of the blowout, says the destruction of the *Deepwater Horizon* had been building for weeks in a series of mishaps. Williams also claims that four weeks before the explosion, there was an incident on the rig that damaged one of its vital pieces of safety equipment. The incident was not reported. According to Williams, a blowout preventer, which is used to seal wells shut in order to test their pressure and determine if gas is seeping, was accidentally bumped by a 15-foot-long piece of drilling pipe.

A blowout preventer is an important component. As its name implies, it helps prevent horrific blowouts. When the preventer, which has a rubber gasket, was bumped, it was broken. A broken blowout preventer meant the well wasn't sealed shut. It could also mean that dangerous gas was leaking out from the well. Unfortunately the supervisors on the rig didn't see it as a problem, and all operations resumed.

Researcher and veteran engineer Dr. Robert Bea, who has been investigating disasters, says the accident was the result of a series of mistakes and flawed decisions, which compromised safety. Bea writes, "This disaster was preventable, had existing progressive guidelines and practice been followed."[5]

In September 2010, BP released an internal report blaming itself for the disaster but also its partners, specifically, Transocean Ltd. But Transocean couldn't stand being named as key partner in blame and they fired back, "This is a self-serving report that attempts to conceal the critical factor that set the stage for the Macondo incident: BP's fatally flawed well design."[6]

The two companies will probably continue to battle it out. But one thing's for certain: The oil industry has a history of creating some of the worst disasters on record.

100 Million Gallons of Oil

Before the Gulf of Mexico spill, most people assumed that the *Exxon Valdez* spill in Alaska was the worst spill on record, with 10 million gallons. Yet it ranks as the 34th worst spill worldwide. In fact according to Ocean World, oil spills from oil tankers account for only 7.7 percent of oil in the ocean. The worst spill from an oil tanker is from the *Atlantic Empress*, operating off the coast of Tobago, which spilled 287,000 tons of oil.[7]

Much larger spills with far larger amounts of oil have received less attention from the press, but their effects have been just as damaging. One of those spills happened in 1979. At the time the Ixtoc 1 oil spill was considered the largest in history. When Wes Tunnel, a marine biologist, surveyed the spill he thought to himself, "This is horrible. It's all going to die."[8]

The oil came from an offshore well located in the Gulf of Campeche, known as Ixtoc 1. Mexico's Pemex Oil Company owned the well. Pemex is Mexico's largest oil producer and they are in a desperate situation. One of their oldest and largest oil fields, Cantarell, is declining in capacity. A recent report showed that the field reached its peak in 2004.[9] This puts pressure on the global oil supply. Reduced capacity is one reason the company began exploring for oil in other areas, including the Gulf of Campeche.

The similarities of the *Deepwater Horizon* disaster and the Ixtoc oil spill are eerie. First, the Gulf of Campeche (also referred to as Bay of Campeche) sits directly below the Gulf of Mexico. The Ixtoc spill began with a burst of gas, followed by an explosion that caused a massive amount of oil to leak into the Gulf waters. Experts estimate that as much as 100 million barrels leaked.

Just as with the *Deepwater Horizon* well, several attempts were made to plug the well to prevent more oil from spilling into the ocean waters. Plugs of mud, debris, and chemical dispersants were used to no avail. It took 10 months to finally cap the well. During that time, the oil floated to the shores of southeast Mexico and Malaquite Beach, Texas. It destroyed a great deal of marine life. In some areas as much as 50 percent of marine life was destroyed; in others it was as much as 80 percent.[10] The fishing industry in the area was shut down entirely. Even fishing ports 60 miles away from the well were affected. To this day, local fisherman in the area say the fish never really came back.

Meanwhile tourism in Texas' Corpus Christi area declined. The oil hit 150 miles of beach. On some beaches, the oil was 12 to 15 inches thick. Thirty years after the spill, marine biologists and scientists say that in the short term, things look okay for the area. But Jeffrey Wozniak, a researcher at the Texas Research Institute for Environmental Studies, says the concern is long term. Wozniak says once the oil was gone, most scientists left the area and their research was discontinued:

> These ecosystems can take some big hits. They can take pressures that humans put on them, but if we push too hard they are going to break. Is it going to take a breaking point for us to open our eyes? We keep seeing big storms and spills like this but it is not quite enough to make us realize that we are nearing what could be a major ecological tipping point.[11]

The Norway Incident

Oil spills don't occur just near the Gulf of Mexico. They occur all over the world. The Norwegian Continental Shelf was the scene of an oil spill that leaked roughly 202,380 barrels.[12]

The field was known as the Ekofisk and was discovered in 1969. The field is located in the Norwegian sector of the North Sea. One year after the oil was discovered, production began, and a pproximately 29 platforms operated in the area.

On April 22, 1977, well B-14 blew out. Oil and mud gushed 180 feet into the air. The oil leaked into the ocean waters at an esti-mated rate of 1,170 barrels per hour.[13] This was the area's first major blowout.

Just before the blowout happened, production tubing was being pulled from the B-14 well. But the "blowout preventer" had not yet been installed. Suddenly the well kicked, and the safety valve was turned on but, unfortunately, it was turned on the wrong way. Official investigations into the incident showed that human error had caused the blowout when the safety valve had been incorrectly installed. The investigations also showed that improper planning and improper well control were a major contributing factor to the blowout.

When he arrived on the platform the next day, Richard Hatteburg, a well control specialist, said, "Oil was spewing all over the place."[14] Hattburg was sent to the platform with other well specialists to help resolve the situation, but there was little Hatteburg could do.

Hatteburg says, "They had put the blowout preventer upside down and tightened it up with a couple of bolts. It was studded, so we couldn't pick it up. We couldn't pump into it. We couldn't do anything with it at all."[15] It took Hatteburg and his workers seven days to cap the well. They stopped the leak by reworking the blowout preventer just enough to enable kill-weight fluid to contain the flow.

The Norwegian Office of Response and Restoration says that as much as 79 percent of the spilled crude oil either evaporated or was skimmed or burned off, minimizing the total spill amount. But not everyone agrees. The Woods Hole Oceanographic Institute of Massachusetts released a study suggesting that a considerable "plume" of oil is still circulating in the water, far below the surface.

This means scientists can't be sure of the long-term impact of the oil. Yet it's highly unlikely much will be done to figure this out. Drilling continues in the North Sea. Many of the wells are owned by ConocoPhillips. In fact, the Ekofisk Bravo Platform, where the spill occurred, is operated by ConocoPhillips. The company got approval for development of the Ekofisk field in March 1972. But it had been exploring for oil in the area for at least two years. During that time, it drilled 11 dry holes before it found oil.[16]

The Ekofisk field was the biggest find in the area, so big that in 2009, the field is estimated to have produced 66.2 million barrels of oil. Peak production occurred in 2002, with 127.2 million barrels produced.[17]

All of Norway's oil reserves are located offshore: the North Sea, the Norwegian Sea, and the Barents Sea. The bulk of the country's offshore oil production occurs in the North Sea. Crude oil and natural gas account for almost 50 percent of the value of Norway's exports. According to the *Oil and Gas Journal*, Norway had 6.8 billion barrels of proven oil reserves as of January 2, 2010.[18]

The Santa Barbara Blowout

Santa Barbara, sometimes called the American Riviera because of its beautiful beaches and luscious mountain views, was the gold rush capital of the United States. But when oil was discovered in California in the 1800s, it became part of the oil boom. In fact the Santa Barbara channel is rich in petroleum.

The first offshore field was discovered in 1896 off a pier. The first offshore oil platform, Hazel, was erected in 1958. Then, in the early and mid 1960s, four significant offshore fields were discovered: Conception field, Summerland field, Carpinteria field, and South Elwood field. Production of the fields peaked in 1964 at 8.9 million barrels.[19]

Today there are 20 platforms in the Santa Barbara channel. The oil-rich area is called the Venture Avenue Anticline. The MMS estimates the risk of a major oil spill of 1,000 barrels is 41.2 percent over the next 28 years.[20] In 1969, little did the MMS know that the offshore oilfield would indeed experience a massive oil spill.

It was the afternoon of January 29, 1969 that Union Oil Company's platform A, stationed six miles off the coast, experienced a significant blowout. Earlier in the day, workers had drilled a well down to about 3,500 feet; then the riggers took over. They were retrieving the pipe in order to replace it with a drill bit. But what they didn't realize is that the mud used to maintain pressure at the well was dangerously low.

The pressure difference in extracting the pipe and pumping the mud was not properly calculated. When the pressure mud was pumped back down, it caused a dramatic increase in pressure. The increased pressure caused a massive blowout, spilling 200,000 gallons of oil that formed an 800-square-mile slick.[21] Tides brought the thick oil to the shoreline. The oil touched almost 35 miles of coastline. It took workers eleven and a half days to stop the leak. Chemical mud was pumped down the shaft at a rate of 1,500 barrels an hour. Finally, a cement plug was used to cap the well.

Investigations showed that using inadequate equipment caused the blowout on platform A. Union Oil would even agree. As it turns out the Union Oil Company had been given permission by the U.S. Geological Survey to use protective casings that were deemed below federal standards.

What's going on here? Because the rig was located outside the California three-mile coastal zone, federal standards didn't apply. So Union Oil could use substandard casings. Just as blowout preventers are important components in the rigs machinery, so too are casings. Casings are reinforcing elements that help prevent blowouts. In this incident, when the pressure increased from the mud being pumped down the pipe, the casings at the top of the well started to strain. The pressure caused a natural gas blowout, which ruptured the substandard casings.

According to a report released by the University of California, 3,686 birds were killed as a result of the spill. Dolphins, fish, seal and most other marine life were also killed.[22] The spill prompted environmental legislation, which led to the creation of the Environmental Protection Agency.

Worst Oil Spills

While the spills in the Gulf of Mexico, the Bay of Campeche, and Santa Barbara are certainly huge they are not the only spills in the world. Our hunger for oil means we have no choice but to deal with dangerous oil spills.

What's worse is that not all spills are caused by human error. Some are deliberate, which is the case with the Arabian Gulf/

Kuwait oil spill. During the Gulf War, Iraqi forces opened up values at an offshore oil terminal, dumping oil from tankers. They were dumping the oil to prevent U.S. soldiers from landing. The spill created a 4-inch thick slick that spread across 4,000 miles in the Persian Gulf.

George Draffan, founding member of Conservation Northwest, as well as co-author of several books including *The Elite Consensus: When Corporations Wield the Constitution; Welcome to the Machine: Science, Surveillance, and the Culture of Control;* and *Railroads and Clearcuts: Legacy of Congress's 1864 Northern Pacific Railroad Land Grant,* has compiled a list of the worst oil disasters dating back to 1967. (You can get a complete list of oil spills at endgame.org.)

The spills that top his list include:

- The Gulf of Mexico spill.
- The oil tanker, *Prestige,* carrying 20 million gallons of fuel oil, broke up off the Spanish coastline in 2002.
- The Ecuadorean ship *Jessica* spilled 175,000 gallons of diesel oil into the sea off the Galapagos Islands in 2001.
- The carrier, *Treasure,* leaked 1,400 tons of heavy fuel oil off Cape Town in 2000.
- A ruptured pipeline spewed 340,000 gallons of oil into Guanabara Bay in 2000.
- The tanker *Erika* sank off the coast of France carrying 25,000 tons of fuel oil in 1999.
- The Russian tanker *Nakhodka* spilled 19,000 tons of oil in the Sea of Japan in 1997.
- The tanker *Sea Empress* hit rock near Wales and spilled 72,000 tons of oil in 1996.
- The Seki tanker collided with a UAE tanker and spilled 15,000 tons of crude oil into the Arabian Sea.[23]

The oil business is a "dirty business." Its history is littered with spills that have caused great environmental damage. Until we break from the oil addiction imposed upon us by modern-day oil barbarians, oil spills will always be with us. And it may take years to know their effects on the environment, not mention costs.

In fact, according to an MMS 2007 report, blowouts were common in offshore drilling. In their report, the MMS said that from 1992 to 2006, there were 5,671 wells drilled in the Outer Continental Shelf. During that time, 39 blowouts occurred (that's one blowout for every 387 wells).[24]

Cleaning Up the Mess

Clean-up costs vary with the amount of oil spilt as well as location. The OSIR International Oil Spill Database estimates that on average, it costs about $3,637 per ton of oil spilled to clean up what is considered minimal spillage.

Moderate spillage costs $4,513 per ton. Heavy spillage costs $25,111 per ton.[25] The *Exxon Valdez* oil spill cost roughly $2.5 billion (including fines, penalties, and settlement claims). However, some estimates put the total amount at $7 billion.[26]

Another costly clean-up came from the Amoco *Cadiz* spill in 1978. The *Cadiz* was a tanker that ran aground off the coast of Brittany France. Reports suggest the spill cost the United States $282 million, of which half was for legal fees and accrued interest.

A spill from the *Braer*, an oil tanker which ran aground off the Scotland in 1993, cost roughly $83 million.

The cost of cleaning up after the *Sea Empress* in 1996 was $37 million. The spill occurred near Wales, when the tanker was heading to the Texaco oil refinery near Pembroke. However, once all damages were settled, total costs ran more than $60 million.

Another expensive clean-up was for the *Nakhodka* oil tanker spill near Japan in 1997. Compensation claims were settled at approximately $219 million.

And claims are still being processed for the spill that happened when the oil tanker *Erika* broke in two 40 miles off the coast of France in 1999. Experts suggest the cost could exceed $180 million.

BP says so far it has spent $11.2 billion cleaning up the spill from the *Deepwater Horizon* blowout. The company says it has paid out $399 million in claims related to the incident.[27] But although we may know the costs to clean up for these oil spills, we may not fully know the impact they'll have on our environment. The problem scientists face is that they can only draw conclusions from past spills, which haven't always been identical in nature and makeup.

Myron Fischer, director of Louisiana's marine biology lab says, "Leading scientists can build a model for what they think is going to happen, but we may wake up the next morning and not know exactly what to expect."[28]

For example, in Ecuador many of the thousand indigenous tribes living in the area have been reduced to a few hundred. This is a direct result of the pollution caused by oil exploration. Water contamination has led to increased risks of cancer, dermatitis, fungal infection, headaches, and nausea.

Thousands of acres of rainforest have been chopped down, destroying natural habitats and fouling rivers. Some estimates say that at least 2.5 million acres of rainforest have been wiped out.

In Nigeria, the 12 million barrels of oil the country exports has come from 12 percent of the country's land.[29] Oil exploration has led to the destruction of wildlife, loss of fertile soil, air and water pollution, and damage to aquatic ecosystems.

An independent investigation found that Shell, the largest oil company in the area, has spilled 1,626,000 gallons of oil in the area.[30]

There's no doubt that our desire to find more sources of oil is threatening our environment. Even if governments impose stricter regulations on oil companies, we'll always be at risk for oil spills and disasters. But one way to reduce this risk is to push for alternative energy sources to reduce our addiction to oil.

In later chapters, you'll learn how it's possible to be less reliant on oil. A tiny island off the coast of Denmark has paved the way.

Chapter 18

Big Oil's Sidekick

I t's fast and has the best engine possible. It even has all the latest gadgets including electronic windows, power steering, sunroof, and heated seats. It will even park itself. Best of all, it's got the one thing Big Oil likes most: low fuel efficiency.

For years, the auto industry has dragged its feet on producing cars with higher fuel efficiency. The industry says it sells the kind of car the public wants and so far, fuel efficiency just isn't in demand. But the Consumer Federation of America says a national survey shows that most consumers support 60 mile-per-gallon (mpg) fuel economy standards.[1] Where are these cars?

The Department of Transportation (DOT) and the Environmental Protection Agency (EPA) say we might get those cars in 2025. That's the target date they've set for the auto industry to produce cars that can meet the 60 MPG target. The current target is 35.7 MPG by 2016 for cars and 31.8 for trucks.

Is it possible to make cars that achieve these kinds of fuel efficiency standards? Does the technology already exist to produce more fuel-efficient automobiles? A spokesperson for the Alliance of Automobile Manufacturers recently told trade publisher Platts, "There's no question that the technology exists or that the technology will exist to achieve these goals."[2]

In fact the industry has already shown it can improve fuel efficiency. The first standards went into place in 1978. The goal was to double the 1974 passenger car fuel economy average to 27.5 mpg by 1985. Operating under the Energy Policy Conservation Act, passed in 1975, automakers had to improve the average fuel efficiency of passenger cars. Until passage of the act, Americans drove gas-guzzling cars. But when the Arab oil embargo occurred in 1973–74, efficiency became a government mandate.

Standards known as corporate average fuel economy were set and administered by the National Highway Traffic Safety administration. Failure to meet the new standards meant automakers could be fined $5.50 per tenth of a mile per gallon for each tenth under the target times the total volume of those vehicles manufactured for a given year.

The standards were set for each year:

1978 = 18 mpg
1979 = 19 mpg
1980 = 20 mpg
1981 to 1984 = 22, 24, 26, and 27 mpg
1985 = 27.5 mpg[3]

Although the standards increased to 27.5 mpg, the auto industry isn't jumping for joy. Automakers say that increasing fuel efficiency means costs will rise. When the new standards were adopted in 2010, Ed Tonkin, chairman of the National Automobile Dealers Association said:

Under these new mandates, the price of new cars and light trucks will rise significantly, meaning fewer Americans will be able to buy the new vehicles of their choice.[4]

They also say cars will be less safe. The industry says that in order to build more efficient cars they will have to be made from lighter materials, reducing the weight of the vehicles, which will make them unsafe in an auto accident.

But David Friedman, engineer and director of the Union of Concerned Scientists (UCS), has been studying these types of issues and doesn't agree. The UCS group designed a minivan, using the same current technology available to automakers that achieved higher fuel efficiency and lower greenhouse emissions without altering the weight of the vehicle. To reinforce the point, Freidman says a study done by the National Academy of Sciences in 2002, showed that the auto industry could be making midsize SUVs that achieve 34 mpg, a minivan that gets 37 mpg, a pickup truck that gets 30 mpg, and a family car that gets 40 mpg.[5]

Laura Schewel, an environmental engineer for the Rocky Mountain Institute, agrees that the industry is capable of achieving better fuel efficiency without reducing car weight. Schewel says the driver of a Chevrolet Blazer is 26 times more likely to die in that vehicle than someone in a Toyota 4Runner. Although both are mid-size SUVs, the 4Runner is 200 lbs. lighter.

The EPA and DOT say that the new standards will save 1.8 billion barrels of oil a year.[6]

Looking Over Seas

Although the industry has made strides, it hasn't done enough. In 1908, when Ford introduced the Model T, it averaged about 17 mpg. Seventy-seven years later, 27.5 mpg became the average. This means automakers have managed to increase the average mpg only by as little as *.35 for each year*. However, during that same time span we've seen better aerodynamics, more powerful engines, improved safety, and a host of other technological advances, including built-in GPS systems and Bluetooth capabilities.

Fuel efficiency falls at the bottom of the list. To make matters worse, even the new fuel efficiency standards lag behind most of the developed nations. Take China for example. China requires an average fuel efficiency of 35.8 mpg. Some people argue that U.S. and Chinese standards can't be compared because China's cars are smaller than U.S. cars. Although this is true, China has the same basic problem as the

United States, but seems to be ahead of us in tackling it: a growing desire for oil.

By having higher standards from the get-go, the Chinese government is sending a message to its auto industry that fuel efficiency is of the utmost importance. China is the world's most populous country with 1.3 billion people. The country has been undergoing a major industrialization growth spurt, and has averaged 9 percent growth for the past two decades. It just surpassed Japan as the world's second largest economy.

It is the second largest consumer of oil in the world, second only to the United States. Its need for energy is expected to increase 150 percent by 2020. Its oil consumption grows 7.5 percent per year or seven times faster than the United States.[7]

In 1993, China became a net oil importer, which means it consumes more oil than it produces. The International Energy Agency projects China's net oil imports will jump to 13.1 million barrels per day by 2030.[8] Part of that need for oil comes from an increase in cars. China used to be a "country of bicycles." But as the country makes its way into the twenty-first century, pushed by a growing middle class, cars are now the transportation mode of choice.

Although the United States bought an average of 17 million cars from 1997 to 2007, the Chinese market is just getting started. In 2009, more cars were sold in China than in the United States. Experts predict that auto sales could surpass 17 million in 2010.[9] The number of motor vehicles in China is 199 million, and the number of drivers is expected to increase as well. Right now, 144 million Chinese have a driver's license, but that number is expected to increase by an additional 22 million.[10]

The Chinese government has been much more aggressive in setting fuel efficiency standards than the United States. In anticipation of rising energy needs, China has recently drafted plans to increase fuel efficiency in cars. By 2015, the Chinese government wants efficiency standards raised to 42.2 mpg, a 17.8 percent increase. And their car boom has only just started. They are taking a much tougher stance on fuel efficiency than the United States.

How do increasing standards sit with automakers? Michael Dunne, managing director for China at J.D. Power & Associates, says, "Global automakers care so deeply about this market, that they'll do whatever it takes and adjust."[11]

What's interesting is that some of the most popular cars in China are U.S. models. For example, in China, the Chevrolet Cruz is a popular compact sedan. In September 2010, 17,300 units of the Cruz were sold. Because it's selling so well, the Cruz is getting an upgraded engine. Chevrolet is taking the 170 bhp 1.6T engine from the Buick Excelle, another popular model in China, and installing it in the Cruz.[12]

Last year, GM China sold more cars than GM USA. The Chinese-GM joint venture company sold 181,148 vehicles in China. At the same time, 156,674 cars were sold in the United States.[13] In total GM sold 1.8 million vehicles in China. GM China president Kevin Wale said, "Despite the sales records in 2009, it looks as if 2010 will be even stronger."[14]

Even though the United States has upgraded its fuel efficiency standards, it still lags Europe, which has a standard of 43.3 mpg. Japan is already talking about raising its standards closer to 50 mpg. If U.S. fuel efficiency standards had been raised after 1985, it's possible we could have saved 3.3 million barrels of oil a day.[15]

Government-Backed Addiction

Our addiction to gasoline isn't 100 percent self-induced. As you might suspect, the oil industry gets a little help from the government. What most people don't realize is that the government subsidizes the U.S. oil industry, and these hidden subsidies are roadblocks to better fuel efficiency in automobiles, along with alternative fuel methods.

This is how these subsidies work. There are environmental costs associated with motor vehicles known as externalities. An externality is an economic term that describes an effect of one individual's actions (or group) on the well-being of another individual (or group), whether for better or worse. For example, if your neighbor renovates his house and is able to sell it a higher price, in essence, he has raised the market value of all the homes in your neighborhood. This is a positive externality.

Sometimes the effects of another person's actions can be negative, and those negative effects often must be paid for. An example of a negative externality is when a factory emits soot that dirties surrounding buildings. The buildings have to be cleaned, but the building owner can't necessarily charge the factory directly for the additional cleaning expense, because the soot is considered pollution.

The oil industry doesn't have to pay for pollution. You do. Since pollution impacts everyone, these types of negative externality costs are passed on to society as a whole in the form of taxes, fees, or sometimes as higher insurance costs. These costs are enormous. These hidden external costs amount to about $558.7 billion to $1.69 trillion per year.[16]

How does the oil industry benefit from government intervention? One way is through tax breaks and incentives it receives from the government. These include the Percentage Depletion Allowance, the Nonconventional Fuel Protection Credit, the Enhanced Oil Recovery Credit, Foreign Tax Credits, Foreign Income Deferrals, Accelerated Depreciation Allowances, and the immediate expensing of exploration and development costs. These alone add up to about $10.4 billion a year. Greenpeace suggests that the U.S. subsidies amount to between $15 and $35 billion a year, compared to the European market, which averages about $10 billion.[17]

But most experts say the number is hard to quantify precisely because the number of programs and benefits the industry receives can easily be categorized as a subsidy or incentive. Cleantech says some of those incentives include:

- Construction bonds with low interest rates (or tax free)
- Research-and-development programs at low or no cost
- Below-cost loans with lenient repayment conditions
- Income tax breaks, especially featuring obscure provisions in tax laws designed to receive little congressional oversight when they expire
- Sales tax breaks—taxes on petroleum products are lower than average sales tax rates for other goods
- Relaxing the amount of royalties to be paid[18]

And it's not just tax breaks and incentives that cost us dearly. Our oil addiction, especially from countries that are unstable or at direct odds with the United States, such as Iran, also has cost implications. According to the U.S. Department of Energy, disruptions in supply and sudden price hikes have costs the U.S. $7 trillion over the last 30 years. The DOT also estimates that each $1 billion of trade deficit costs 27,000 American jobs. Oil imports account for one-third of the total U.S. deficit.[19]

The National Defense Council Foundation (NDCF), a Virginia-based research and education institution, also studies the impact of the oil industry on the U.S. economy. In recent testimony before the House Committee on Foreign Affairs, NDCF Chairman James Martin noted that the Council had determined that the direct loss of economic activity arising from U.S. oil import dependence amounted to $117.4 billion. He also said that importing oil costs 2.4 million American jobs.

Mr. Martin also noted that the United States was capable of reducing imports by 40 percent, but that number could reach 75 percent in 15 years. He says it will not be easy, but can be done. Martin added, "If we do not, America will see the hemorrhage of cash for oil imports grow and its enemies strengthened."[20]

No Push for Alternative Fuel

Keep in mind that sometimes these subsidies *prevent* the industry from seeking alternative fuel methods. In other words, it would be too costly to give these incentives up in favor of developing different fuels for consumers.

One example is ethanol. Ethanol has many advantages over gasoline in that it is environmentally friendly, mixes well with gasoline, and can be used as an alternative fuel to oil. When George W. Bush was president, he set a target date of 2025 for reducing Middle East oil imports by 75 percent with ethanol. Everyone applauded his aggressive goals. Unfortunately we're not yet at the point where we can rely on ethanol. Yet, other countries have shown it's entirely possible.

Take Brazil for example. The country relies on bio-fuels to met 16 percent of its energy needs. This makes ethanol Brazil's second largest energy source.[21] The Brazilian government encouraged the use of more alternative fuels by launching the National Alcohol Programme in the mid 1970s as a way to curb its growing oil addiction. As the government pushed for ethanol, it took the country about 10 years to get fully immersed in the pro-ethanol program. During that time, ethanol production increased 35 percent.

Sales of vehicles powered by hydrous ethanol made up 90 percent of countrywide auto sales. By 1979, there were 104 distilleries operating.[22] The Brazilian government provided the industry with incentives and subsidies to strengthen the growth in the use of ethanol as an alternative fuel. Now, there are approximately 303 ethanol distilleries, and ethanol has become one of the country's leading exports.

But for the United States, it's a different story. Although Bush set a goal for increased use of ethanol, the U.S. government still favors big oil. In fact an organization known as DTN/The Progressive Farmer, a leading agricultural information services provider, found that the oil industry receives many more subsidies than the ethanol industry. Both receive government subsidies, but the oil industry receives the largest share of taxpayer dollars. DTN says the oil industry receives exclusive incentives that amount to roughly $17.9 billion a year. The ethanol industry receives just $7.1 billion in incentives.[23]

DTN has found that the oil industry also benefits from indirect taxpayer support including U.S. military spending. Most of this comes from military spending in the Persian Gulf. Mark Delucchi, a research scientist at the Institute of Transportation Studies at University of California says that oil's share of that protection benefit ranges between $6.9 and $28.9 billion.[24]

The truth is the United States ranks as the number-one oil-subsidizing nation in the world. If these subsidies were cut out, oil demand would decline by 6.5 million barrels a day. The industry says that cutting back on government-sponsored subsidies would mean the inevitable—higher energy prices.[25]

Even though the oil industry is cash rich and could easily afford to do without the subsidies, the subsidies will remain intact, because Big Oil has Big Clout with Congress.

When Rep. Joe L. Barton of Texas, and long time oil industry friend, introduced a $50 million annual earmark to the 2005 Energy Policy Act in favor of supporting technical research for the industry along with billions of dollars in tax and royalty relief for drilling in the Gulf of Mexico, some members of Congress questioned whether it was necessary.

Representative Edward Markey of Massachusetts was one of those members. He suggested the government didn't need to subsidize the oil industry's work, and amendments should be made to reflect this change. However, he was quickly overruled. The bill was passed in both houses. At the time, then–Senator Barrack Obama voted in favor of the bill.[26]

Former White House counsel to George W. Bush and former ambassador to the European Union, C. Boyden says:

> What's happened historically, for national security reasons, is that the oil companies were made quasi–partners and have become engrained. So the preferences they receive are just part of the fabric of our country.[27]

His statement couldn't ring more true. While the oil industry has made itself a permanent part of our history, it has had a profound impact on our political leaders. In fact the sad truth is the oil industry helps dictate our country's energy policy.

According to Raymond J. Learsy, author of *Over A Barrel: Breaking Oil's Grip on Our Future*, says that the oil industry coughed up $35 million in political donations to George W. Bush and fellow republicans. In fact, from 1998 to 2004, the industry ponied up $440 million in political contributions.[28]

But it gets worse. Learsy says the industry acts under a veil of secrecy, especially multinational companies, when it comes to reporting the money they pay for oil drilling rights in foreign countries. Learsy says that at least 34 companies paid money to the Angolan government to drill for oil in the country. But how much, to whom, and for what are company secrets?

To increase transparency, George Soros, through his Open Society Institute, advocates a "publish what you pay" initiative that would force publicly listed oil companies to publish the details of their payments. Thomas Palley, a member of the Open Society Institute, says, "Sadly, U.S. oil companies have thus far resisted."[29]

It is possible to figure out some of the details of what happens in these transactions. Learsy says following the money flow provides clues. One of those clues takes us to the Riggs National Bank of

Washington, D.C. A small bank by many standards, it specializes in handling the transactions of Washington's foreign embassies and consulates worldwide. One of the bank's larger clients was dictator Brigadier General Teodoro Obiang Nguema Mbasogo, of Equatorial Guinea.

Equatorial Guinea is an oil-rich country, which is ruled by Mbasogo. According to the U.S. State Department, torture and arrests are regular methods used by the dictator to "rule his people." Under his leadership, smashing skulls with iron rods, chopping off ears, and smearing bodies with substances that attract stinging ants are tactics routinely used.

Following the money flow, it was discovered that Marathon Oil and ExxonMobil had paid a few billion dollars to the country. ExxonMobil, probably the largest oil company in the area, supplied cash to Mbasogo as part of a profit-sharing arrangement.[30] Of course, the details of the transaction remain confidential.

The International Monetary Fund says the money collected by Mbasogo is not being used for the good of the people or the country. Conditions are so bad that life expectancy in the country is now set at just 44 years.

This is the barbaric side of the oil business that goes unreported. The barbarians won't clean up their actions until we've stopped our addiction to oil.

Chapter 19

The Red Dragon's Thirst for Oil

C hina's thirst for oil is unprecedented. In 2009, China consumed 8.6 million barrels of oil per day and that number will probably be much higher by the end of 2010. In fact the International Energy Agency (IEA) says that Chinese demand for oil jumped an astonishing 28 percent in January 2010, compared to January 2009.[1]

China ranks second only to the United States in demand for oil. In the United States, Americans consume about 10 times as much oil as their Chinese counterparts. But the Chinese are catching up. Most experts predict that China's oil imports will grow substantially over the next few years, and at some point, could outpace the United States. Some experts suggest that between 2010 and 2020, Chinese oil consumption could increase 150 percent.[2]

Oil Consmption (Million Barrels per Day)

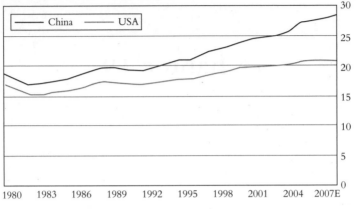

Figure 19.1   Oil Demand, U.S. and China
SOURCE: Energy Information Administration.

The U.S. Department of Energy now predicts that China will overtake the United States as the world's leading oil importer around 2030.[3] Figure 19.1 compares China's need for oil to that of the United States.

There's no doubt China needs oil. And they're doing whatever it takes to make sure those needs are met. For example, just recently China signed a $23 billion dollar oil deal with the government of Nigeria. The deal makes it possible for China to build three oil refineries and a petrochemical plant. The three refineries will be built in Lagos, the commercial capital of the country, and the refineries will have a combined capacity of 900,000 barrels of oil per day.[4]

But there are more deals on the table. In 2009, Yar'Adua, then-president of Nigeria, received a letter from the China National Offshore Oil Corporation (CNOOC) that expressed the company's desire to buy up as much as six billion barrels of Nigerian reserves. The CNOOC is considered one of the world's largest independent oil exploration companies. In addition to expressing an interest in Nigeria's reserves, the company also showed an interest in 23 percent of the country's prime offshore fields. Yar'Adua was forced to reject the offer when the letters were leaked to the press. However, negotiations continued. The price tag on the deal is estimated between $30 and $50 billion.

Initially China opened the door to oil deals in Nigeria when it bought the country's state-owned telecom company. China has used this tactic of first acquiring infrastructure and then oil to set up deals in other oil rich countries including Angola and Sudan.

China also has deals in South America for oil fields in Argentina, Bolivia, and Chile. In early 2010, CNOOC paid $3.1 billion in cash for a stake in one of Argentina's largest oil explorers, Bridas Energy. Bridas has proven reserves of 636 million barrels of oil, and puts out about 92,000 barrels a day.[5]

China is also planning deals with Brazil's leading energy company, Petrobras. Petrobras is the fourth biggest energy company in the world. It produces about 1,978,000 barrels of oil a day with proven reserves of 11.19 billion barrels.[6] Petrobras signed an oil export contract with Unipec Asia Ltd, a subsidiary of CNOOC to export about 100,000 barrels of oil a day. The deal is estimated to be worth $10 billion.[7]

China even has a deal worth $7 billion with Spain's Repsol YPF, the country's largest oil company. It operates five refineries in Spain and one in Peru. Repsol controls Argentina's number-one oil company but also has operations in 30 other countries including in the Middle East and North Africa. China was attracted to Repsol because it has proven oil reserves of 2.2 billion barrels.

China has been consistently buying oil assets for the past 10 years and has landed deals in Africa, Asia and the Middle East.

Strained Relationships

China isn't just making deals for oil in foreign countries either. The CNOOC is investing in U.S. energy reserves stockpiled in Texas. In October 2010, the country's state owned oil-company announced a 33 percent interest in Chesapeake Energy Corporation's oil leasehold acres. The deal is worth $2.16 billion.

Chesapeake Energy Corporation already has 10 rigs operating in the leasehold area and anticipates, with the infusion of capital from CNOOC, increasing that number to 40 rigs by the end of 2012.[8] If the deal is approved it would mark a major milestone for China. For years the country has tried to establish ties with American-based oil and gas companies.

Five years ago, China tried to buy American-owned oil company Unocal. It successfully outbid other companies with $18.5 billion and was in top position. But the deal came under intense pressure and scrutiny from Congress and lobbyists, and CNOOC backed away. The issue was whether a strategic American asset should be sold to a foreign country, especially China, which was rapidly outpacing U.S. oil consumption needs.

The U.S. government has always placed restrictions on the extent of foreign ownership in a variety of industries, including airlines, media, and military contractors. The government approves these types of deals through its Foreign Investment Committee, which determines whether these types of deals pose a national threat to our security. Some previous deals have been approved such as the $1.75 billion sale of IBM's personal computer business to Lenovo, a Chinese company. But the Unocal deal was considered more risky to the United States, considering it is the largest consumer of oil in the world.

China used to be a net exporter of oil, meaning it was able to keep up with internal consumption. But as the nation's economic growth took off, so did its thirst for energy, particularly oil. The Chinese government has taken a proactive role in encouraging its national companies to look for ways to satisfy its oil needs, and it has the cash to make as many deals as possible. It has about $2.2 billion dollars stashed away. Jiang Jemin, chairman of Petrochina, a subsidiary of CNOOC says, "Low share prices of some global resource companies provide us with fresh opportunities."[9]

In fact China is so dedicated to buying foreign oil reserves and companies that it created the China National Energy Administration. The new institution consists of nine departments, with 112 personnel. The China National Energy Administration's main responsibilities include drafting energy development strategies, proposing reform advice, implementing management of energy sectors, and creating policies related to exploring new energy sources. The Administration even established a special fund for China's three state-owned energy companies, including Petrochina, Sinopec, and CNOOC to buy oil and gas firms from around the world. So far, the three companies have put together deals in 30 countries.

That may not be enough. Robin Geffen, chief executive of Neptune Investment Management, which runs a Chinese investment fund, suggests that China would need to buy two companies the size of BP each year for the next 12 years to meet its growing domestic energy demands.[10] Their need for energy could be seen as a direct threat to the U.S. As supplies of cheap oil are being quickly used up or depleted, China is creating competition with the U.S. for oil sources.

Right now 60 percent of China's oil comes from the Middle East. Experts say that is expected to increase to 500 percent by 2030.

Oil for Weapons

One of the main problems with China getting oil from the Middle East is the country's relationship with Iran. Iran has a huge supply of oil. In fact, oil exports provide half of the Iranian government's revenue. The U.S. Energy Information Administration reports that as of January 2010, Iran has proven oil reserves of 137.6 billion a day. That's approximately 10 percent of the world's total reserves. Iran is OPEC's second largest producer, behind Saudi Arabia.[11]

China imports about 430 million barrels of oil a day from Iran and that number is growing. In March 2010, China increased its Iranian oil import by 14.8 percent,[12] and Iran is the third largest supplier of oil to China. Experts say that this dependence on Iranian oil is making the Chinese government reluctant to implement sanctions against Iran.

That doesn't make the United States happy as it pushes the Chinese government to provide sanctions against Iran. Currently the United States, Japan, South Korea, Australia, Canada, and the European Union have passed laws that restrict investing in Iran's energy sector. China is not on that list. Although the country has signed on to United Nations Security Council resolution that punishes Iran for its nuclear weapons program, China isn't using sanctions against the country.

China doesn't believe its current deals violate the resolution and has often voiced opposition against Iranian sanctions. He Junke, Deputy Head of China's Youth Federation, commented, "China is always opposed to sanctions against Iran. The sanctions method does not help settle the problems as China developed its defense industry in time of sanctions."[13] Jiang Jiemin, president of state-owned China National Petroleum says, "We will implement our projects in Iran as usual."[14]

In fact after most U.S. companies withdrew from the area, CNOOC did indeed strengthen its position in Iran. For example, China's state owned Sinopec (also a subsidiary of CNOOC) has a $70 billion deal with Iran. The deal allows Sinpoec to buy 250 million tons of liquefied natural gas for 30 years from Iran along with development rights in Iran's Yadavaran field.

CNOOC is also in various phases of developing three other fields in Iran, including work on one of the world's biggest natural-gas fields, and on enhancing recovery from a small, older oil field. CNOOC expects production from the older field to hit around 20,000 barrels a day later in 2010.

In addition, Iran is committed to providing China with 150,000 barrels of oil a day for the next 25 years. Iran oil Minister Bijan Zanganeh has publicly stated that Iran is China's biggest oil supplier and wants to be its long-term business partner.

The U.S. is also accusing the Chinese of violating sanctions against Iran. According to an article in the Washington Post, the Obama administration has concluded that Chinese companies are helping Iran improve its missile and nuclear weapon technology.[15] In 1997 China expressed its commitment to end involvement in supplying Iran's nuclear program in an official policy declaration. However, the U.S. believes China isn't aggressively following through on their commitment. In 2007, the Defense Intelligence Agency (DIA) director stated that China appears to be adhering to its commitment to limit nuclear-related cooperation, but that, "Chinese entities continue to supply key technologies to countries with WMD and missile programs."[16]

Additionally the U.S. director of central intelligence says that assistance from Chinese entities has in part helped Iran move toward self-sufficiency in the production of ballistic missiles.[17] And we're not alone in this thinking. Israel believes there is a link to China and Iran missile technology. The International Assessment and Strategy Center released a report a few years ago that showed Hezbollah munitions were mainly rockets and missiles that could be traced back to China.[18] Most notable are the C-802/Noor anti-ship missiles which were sold by China to Iran in the mid-1990s.

But the list of Chinese-related weapons runs deep. They now include the Shahab series of medium range ballistic missiles, solid-fueled missiles, long-range land-attack cruise missiles, short-range anti-ship and man-launched anti-aircraft missiles, optically guided missiles, deadly fast-rising naval mines, and very fast missile-armed attack ships.[19]

China's involvement in Iran's nuclear program goes back to the mid-1980's when the two countries cooperated on missile technology. Then later on in the 1990s, China served as a source of raw supplies, providing Iran with nearly two tons of natural uranium.

The United States has tried to put a halt to China's involvement in Iran's nuclear programs. Between 2001 and 2007, the United States imposed sanctions in fifty-two instances against Chinese parties under the Iran Nonproliferation Act (INA) and the Iran and Syria Nonproliferation Act (ISNA).[20]

It's not just China's aid to Iran that worries the United States, it's also the country's ties to Sudan. Sudan supplies China with 7 percent of its oil. Sudan is an oil-rich country with an estimated 5 billion barrel reserve. That's a lot of oil for energy-desperate China, and therefore the Chinese have invested billions of dollars in joint exploration contracts in Sudan, including the building of a 900-mile pipeline.

In return for oil, China sells small arms to Sudan; assault rifles are the most common weapon. In September 2004, the UN Security Council passed resolution 1564, threatening Sudan with oil sanctions unless it curbed its support for militia groups in Darfur.[21] However, to protect its oil interests in Sudan, the Chinese government said it would veto any bid to impose such sanctions.

According to Human Rights First, because of the increase in arms, violence in Darfur has escalated. Khartoum is the capital of Sudan, and the Human Rights First says China has topped the list as biggest supplier of arms to Khartoum, at 90 percent. China denies such charges and says it is one of seven countries supplying weapons to Sudan. Betsy Apple of Human Rights First says,

> So long as it continues to sell massive quantities of small arms to Khartoum, the government of China has created a virtual supply line from the small arms factories in China to the Sudanese government-sponsored militias killing civilians in Darfur.[22]

It's highly unlikely China will stop selling arms to Sudan, not as long as the country has oil. As China's oil consumption grows, China will use every avenue to fulfill that need, regardless of the number of lives lost.

Like Charlemagne, classified as the clandestine barbarian in *Barbarians of Wealth*, so too could China be considered a clandestine barbarian, except its oil-for-infrastructure, oil-for-arms are fairly transparent.

India: Forgotten Stepchild

Although China just replaced Japan as the world's second-largest economy, we can't forget about India. From FY 1980 to FY 1989, the economy grew at an annual rate of 5.5 percent. By the early 1990s, economic changes led to a dramatic growth in the number of Indians with significant economic resources. More recently, India's growth rate hit the 8.8 percent mark. India is now the second-fastest-growing economy in the world.

About 10 million Indians are considered upper class, and roughly 300 million are part of the rapidly increasing middle class. In 1984 and 1985, India's middle class constituted less than 10 percent of the population, and since then, it has more than tripled. Experts predict that half of India will turn middle class between 2020 and 2040. McKinsey Global Institute (MGI) suggests that if India continues its recent growth, average household incomes will triple over the next two decades, and it will become the world's fifth-largest consumer economy by 2025.[23]

India's middle class likes to shop. They buy the same things that we do, including mobile phones, televisions, and cars. In fact the automobile industry in India is the ninth largest in the world.[24] On top of all this unprecedented growth in India's economy and its middle class, is the population itself. India holds 15 percent of the world's population. This means the country's energy needs are massive. India is currently the world's fifth largest energy consumer and is expected to take third place by 2030, behind the United States and China. In 2009, India consumed nearly 3 million barrels per day of oil.

Despite the global economic recession, India's need for oil has continued to rise, but it can't domestically fulfill its energy needs. According to the Energy Information Administration, India has approximately 5.6 billion barrels of proven oil reserves, the second-largest amount in the Asia-Pacific region after China.[25] To keep pace with demand, India will need to import oil from other countries. Now oil accounts for nearly 24 percent of total energy consumption. Nearly 70 percent of India's crude oil imports come from the Middle East, primarily from Saudi Arabia.

India is in the same situation as China and seems to be following the same path of actively pursuing oil deals in other countries. Recently India's Oil and Natural Gas Corporation (ONGC) acquired a 40 percent stake in a $19 billion project to develop crude oil in Venezuela. An official said the group would pay $1.05 billion to Venezuela as the signing amount and then invest another $9 billion in developing the field, which is expected to produce 400,000 barrels of oil per day.[26]

Another India-based oil company, Videocon, has a 10 percent stake in an offshore oil block in Mozambique, and the deal is worth $75 million.

Reliance Petroleum, another India company, is scouting for deals in Latin America and Africa. Indian Oil Corporation (IOC) is in talks to acquire Gulfsand Petroleum, a U.K. company active in Syria. In 2009, the ONGC bought another U.K. company, Imperial Energy, for $2.1 billion so it could gain access to West Siberia oil fields.

India is also considering Central Asia as a source to fulfill its energy needs. The Central Asia region, which consists of the republics of Turkmenistan, Kazakhstan, Uzbekistan, Kyrgyzstan, and Tajikistan, is emerging as a viable energy source. CK Santhanam, President of India-Central Asia Foundation, an organization formed to promote initiatives in Central Asia, says, "Central Asia could be a key region for fulfilling our rapidly expanding energy requirements."[27]

India doesn't have the cash reserves that China has, so its deals are smaller in size and scope. But that doesn't mean the country is following in step with China. In fact, India, like China, also has ties with Iran. The United States says India's two leading energy companies ONGC and Indian Oil Corporation (IOC) along with three others have oil-related ties to Iran. These ties, however, violate the UN agreed-upon sanctions against Iran. Those who violate the sanctions run the risk of sanctions themselves. This means the United States could impose sanctions against India. However, the reality is that since

1998 the United States has not imposed sanctions against any country violating the Iran Sanctions Act.

India doesn't see its ties with Iran as a violation. A senior Indian official says that the oil companies are not in violation, stating, "Whatever we are doing is fully compliant with the Government of India policy. We have not violated any rule by investing in Iran."[28]

As much as the United States would like countries like China and India to stay out of Iran, it's not going to happen. These countries are on a hunt for oil. Just as a junkie needs to supply his or her daily heroin addiction, China and India will get their oil fix anywhere they can, even if that means supplying weapons to Iran.

Chapter 20

Petro Landgrab

The Fight for African Oil

Africa is a continent rich in history. The remains of the first creatures to be classified as part of the human species, dating back two million years ago were found in Africa. In Namibia, you can find paintings on stone slabs that date back nearly 30,000 years.[1] North Africa is home to one of the greatest civilizations of the world: Egypt. Another early first civilization known to man was located in Ethiopia.

Africa is the world's second largest continent, after Asia, and is made up of 53 countries. The continent covers one-fifth of the total land surface of the earth. The Sahara Desert, larger than the United States, divides North Africa and Sub-Saharan Africa. The Nile is the longest river in the world. It runs from Uganda all the way to Egypt, for 4,132 miles.

Africa was known traditionally as the "dark continent." Unfortunately its natural beauty is often overshadowed by its political and economic struggles. In 2001, addressing the British Labour Party, Prime Minister Tony Blair described Africa as a scar on the conscience of the world.

A majority of the world's poorest countries are in Africa. Africa has a population of 888 million people, and most of those people are living in poverty. For example, in Sub-Saharan Africa alone, more than 218 million people live in extreme poverty, and the situation is getting worse. Experts say that the incidence of poverty in Sub-Saharan Africa is increasing faster than the population.[2] In the last half of the century, the country has received over $1 trillion in aid. Yet, over the past 30 years, the number of poor inhabitants has grown, and roughly 300 million Africans live on less than $1 a day.[3]

It's not just poverty that touches most people living in Africa; diseases like AIDS, cholera, and malaria are widespread. Health experts say that malaria is reemerging at an alarming rate. In the 1950s and 1960s, malaria was considered controlled through aggressive eradication programs, but the disease is making a dramatic comeback. An estimated 300 to 500 million cases each year cause 1.5 to 2.7 million deaths.[4] AIDS ravages the lives of people living in Sub-Saharan Africa. An estimated 22.4 million people there are living with HIV, which equates to around two-thirds of the global total.

Not all countries suffer from disease and poverty in Africa. South Africa and Egypt are two of the richest countries in the continent. In 2009, South Africa's GDP was $488.6 billion. Egypt's GDP was similar at $470.4 billion. Because of this, Africa is a paradox, blending rich and poor. Many of its people are poor and live in extreme poverty, yet the continent is rich in natural resources including cobalt, platinum, uranium, and gold, and the continent is the world's largest producer of diamonds. Until recently, no one realized the continent held another resource—one that could ignite a resource war between the world's biggest superpowers: oil.

Africa's Hidden Secret

Located on Africa's west coast, the Niger Delta is 60 million years old and stretches nearly 150 miles. The Niger Delta is one of the largest wetlands in the world. The Niger River snakes through the wetlands forming creeks, rivulets, and tributaries. Annual rainfall ranges from 150 inches to 400 inches, which makes the area easily susceptible to flooding.[5] The intertropical front winds collide with a mix of dry and humid air masses, making the area thick with humidity. The forests in the delta are dense.

Niger is the largest country in West Africa. No one suspected oil would lie beneath the delta's surface, but in 1956 vast quantities of commercial oil were discovered in the small town of Oloibiri, about 60 miles west of Port Harcourt. The search for oil started a few years earlier in 1953. Chief Sunday Inengite remembers the day the oilmen came hunting for oil. Members of his village weren't sure what the men were after, and most thought they were hunting for palm oil. Inengite says, "It wasn't until we saw what they called the oil—the black stuff—that we knew they were after something different."[6]

But this was not the first time the local villagers dealt with oilmen. Oil was being actively sought from 1907 to 1914. In 1907, the German Nigerian Bitumen Corporation, a German-owned company, was granted the rights to explore and drill for oil. This in itself is worth noting, because the grant to drill oil would have been given by the British government, which ruled over the area. At the time, the British were already exploring and finding oil in Persia and Russia, so Nigeria oil exploration seemed irrelevant to the British government, because oil exploration in the area was considered speculative.

But the Germany owned company thought otherwise. They drilled the first oil wells in the vicinity of the tar seep deposits in the northern portion of the delta. But their efforts yielded no oil and the German Nigerian Bitumen Corporation was forced to abandon the project because of the outbreak of the War World I. After the War was over, the company tried to resume operations but Britain no longer wanted companies that were not British-owned in the area. The German Nigerian Bitumen Corporation had shown the British government that Nigeria was indeed an oil-rich country.

The British government then granted licenses to two British-backed companies, the D'Arcy Exploration Company and the Whitehall Petroleum Corporation. However, by 1923, both companies surrendered their licenses because they could not find oil in commercial quantities. All oil searches were abandoned until the late 1930s when the Royal Dutch Shell Company and British Petroleum were granted a license to explore for oil in the Niger territory. In 1951, drilling commenced.[7]

In Nigeria, they first found oil in Akata, but that find was quickly overshadowed by Royal Dutch Shell-BP's discovery of oil in Oloibiri in 1956. By the end of that same year, the company struck oil a second time in the area of Afam. Several more wells were discovered in the Niger Delta including the Bomu oil field. By 1958, Royal Dutch Shell-BP was exporting large quantities of oil from Africa. Estimates put the output at 400,000 barrels a day. By 1959, they had 53 wells operating in the area and had secured a monopoly of oil exploration in Nigeria.

Oil quickly became one of Nigeria's most lucrative exports. By 1960, 847,000 tons of oil was exported. In 2009, total oil production in Nigeria was 2.2 million barrels a day, making it the largest oil producer in all of Africa. Figure 20.1 shows the growth of Nigeria's oil production over the past nine years.

Oil exports are growing. In the first four months of 2010, oil exports from Nigeria averaged 2.10 million barrels per day, up from its average of 1.90 to 1.95 million barrels a day.[8]

But African oil doesn't come just from Nigeria. The most oil rich regions besides Nigeria are Libya, Angola, and Equatorial Guinea.

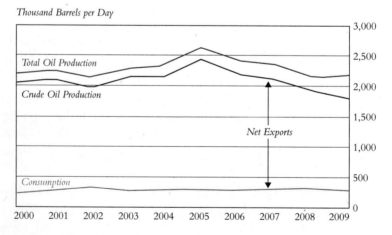

Figure 20.1 Nigeria's Oil Production and Consumption, 2000–2009
SOURCE: Energy Information Administration, International Energy Annual, Short Term Energy Outlook, June 2010.

Then there's the oil in the Gulf of Guinea, which is expected to become the world's leading deep-water offshore production center. Experts say the area could hold as much as 24 billion barrels of oil.[9]

The truth is, Africa is oil rich. According to Energy Information Administration, Africa has proven reserves of 117 billion barrels of oil.[10] Compared to the Middle East, Africa's oil supplies account for 9 percent of the world's total reserves. But most experts say that outside of OPEC, Africa will become the major source of oil. In fact in the last five years alone, Africa's west coast accounted for about one-third of the world's new oil discoveries. For example, a major oil discovery was found at the deepwater Jubilee oil field in the Gulf of Guinea in 2007. The field is expected to produce 550 million barrels of oil a day.

Another discovery was found in the oil rich region of Tweneboa off the shore of Ghana. This area is said to hold 800 million barrels of oil. The area is also rich in natural gas.

In September of 2009 in the Sierra Leone region, another major oil field was found. That discovery sparked intense exploration programs off the coasts of Liberia, the Ivory Coast, and Equatorial Guinea.

Oil was also found in East Africa. Lake Albert, on Uganda's western border, proved a significant find with expectations of producing two billion barrels a day. Oil has even been found in the Sahara desert in the Murzug Basin. The newly discovered oil field already has a preliminary output of 4,650 barrels per day.[11] And it's expected to continue to grow.

Sub-Saharan oil fields already produce as much as Iran, Venezuela, and Mexico combined. The Sudan area produces over 186,000 barrels a day.

Angola has become the second largest producer of oil in Africa. Its output has been steadily climbing since 2001. Angolan oil is anticipated to reach 3.2 million barrels a day by 2020.[12]

Oil Dominance in Africa

The truth is, Africa has long been considered a "shared" continent with Britain, France, Germany, Belgium, Italy, Portugal, and Spain all having claims. Each country scrambled to own a portion of Africa's rich natural resources including copper, tin, coffee, gold, and of course, manpower in the form of forced slavery. With the discovery of significant oil fields, once again, countries are scrambling to get a foothold into Africa. China is one of those countries.

China has maintained economic ties to Africa since the 1950s. Since that time, China has made deals with 53 African countries including interest-free loans and grants. But deals for oil and minerals have been the biggest deals made to date.

China doesn't like to be seen as an oil monger. It would prefer the world to view its relationship with Africa as mutually beneficial. In fact, Chinese Ambassador Gong Jianzhong describes the relationship as one built on equality and trust.[13] Of course, Mr. Jianzhong doesn't mention that the relationship is also built on oil . . . and lots of it.

China is already getting a large portion of oil from Africa. Roughly 30 percent of Africa's oil exports go to China, and most of that comes from deals China made in the past few years. For example, in April 2006, China National Offshore Oil Corporation (CNOOC) bought a stake in a Nigerian offshore field for $2.7 billion.

In July 2005, China had previously signed a deal with the Nigerian government to supply China with 30,000 barrels of oil a day.[14] The country anticipates it will increase that amount by 25 percent over the next 10 years.[15]

But new deals are already being made and wells being dug. For example in September of 2010, the China Development Bank and the China Exim Bank signed a deal with Ghana, loaning it $12.87 billion to fund oil and other infrastructure projects in development.

CNOOC and Sinopec agreed to purchase a stake in an oil block in the Angolan offshore oil field. The deal is said to be worth $1 billion.

These aggressive oil deals worry the U.S. government. A Pentagon analysis of the world's oil supply suggests we'll see dark days ahead with possible armed conflict with China over oil. The Pentagon's concerns were released in a recent Joint Operating Environment (JOE) periodic analysis. The analysis reveals that, "By 2012, surplus oil production capacity could entirely disappear, and as early as 2015, the shortfall in output could reach nearly 10 million barrels per day."[16]

The JOE report also says, "The presence of Chinese 'civilians' in the Sudan to guard oil pipelines underlines China's concern for protecting its oil supplies and could portend a future in which other states intervene in Africa to protect scarce resources. The implications for future conflict are ominous."[17]

It's not just countries in Africa that have the United States concerned. China has been buying oil assets in other oil-producing nations such as Brazil, Venezuela, and Russia. In 2010, China and Russia agreed to the construction of a major oil pipeline. The pipeline would ensure Russian oil supplies to China for 20 years. This would make Russia China's third major oil supplier.[18]

In 2009, the China Development Bank agreed to lend Brazil's largest oil producer, Petrobras, $10 billion in exchange for a long-term commitment to send oil to China. In April, China signed a series of deals with the government of Venezuela. The two countries agreed to an oil exploration and processing joint venture. Venezuela is now China's fifth-largest trading partner.

Oil-needy countries like China aren't shy about the oil prospects in Africa; neither is the United States.

The U.S. Fight for African Oil

In his 2001 National Energy Policy Report, Vice President Dick Cheney highlighted the importance of African oil to the United States. He said, "West Africa is expected to be one of the fastest growing sources of oil and gas for the American market."[19]

Ed Royce, chairman of the U.S. House of Representatives Subcommittee on Africa said, "African oil should be treated as a priority for U.S. national security post 9/11. I think that post 9/11 it's occurred to all of us that our traditional sources of oil are not as secure as we once thought they were."[20]

The Energy Information Administration agrees that Africa will be vital to the growing oil needs of the U.S. In its 2005 International Energy Outlook, it projects that oil imports from Africa will increase to 6.2 million barrels per day in 2025. That represents a 91 percent increase over 20 years.[21]

Already African has shown its importance to the United States in satisfying its oil needs. Nigeria has become the United States' fifth-largest source of oil.

The United States is trying to find a way to lessen its dependence on Middle East oil. Whether it can actually accomplish that is unknown. But the United States knows it needs to protect its oil interests in Africa. In February 2007, President Bush stated the Department of Defense (DoD) established a regional command for Africa, named AFRICOM. In 2008, AFRICOM became operational. Basically, AFRICOM was created so that the oil-related interests in Africa would receive military attention and initiatives.

Prior to AFRICOM, U.S. military involvement in Africa was divided among three groups: U.S. European Command, U.S. Central Command, and U.S. Pacific Command. Under AFRICOM, the efforts are centrally coordinated and controlled. The commander of AFRICOM reports to the U.S. secretary of defense, who reports to the President of the United States. AFRICOM receives significant funding: In 2007, it was slated to receive $50 million; in 2008, that number jumped to $75.5 million; and in 2009, the funding skyrocketed to $310 million.[22]

The United States is turning to continents like Africa to escape the tight oil grip of the Middle East. But depending on African oil isn't problem free. Nigerian militants routinely attack oil facilities, disrupting the flow of oil. Nigeria has had nearly a third of its oil production capacity shut down from attacks, and these attacks happen both on land and at sea. Some reports say that piracy in the Gulf of Guinea is far worse than pirate attacks off the Horn of Africa. Pirates often attack oil tankers and oil platforms. During a September 2010 attack, three employees were kidnapped and held hostage. Most hostages are released without injury after ransom is paid.

Most of the attacks are lead by the rebel group, Movement for the Emancipation of the Niger Delta (MEND). The group says the region doesn't receive any benefits of oil being pumped from their area. Most of the people living in the area live well below poverty levels. These attacks often result in higher prices for oil, for example, in November 2008, when Somali pirates captured an oil tanker, the price of oil rose by $1 a barrel.

Authors Jennifer Giroux and Caroline Hilpert, writing for the *Journal of Energy Security*, say there is a definite relationship between energy infrastructure attacks and crude oil prices. Known as a "risk premium," oil companies raise the price of oil from $4 to $25 a barrel.[23]

In May 2008, *Time* magazine ran an article titled, "The Nigerian Rebel Who 'Taxes' Your Gasoline."[24] The story was about Henry Okah who heads up MEND, was extradited from Angola, and now is in prison for leading the attacks. He has to appear before a Nigerian court, and his lawyer thinks Okah will be convicted and sentenced to death. If that happens, members of MEND have said that his death will be a disaster for the Nigerian oil industry.

India Steps In

While Africa may hold the key to helping to satisfy the United States' and China's desire for oil, India has not only a very large population, but its economy has posted a 7 percent growth rate over the last decade.

As we mentioned in Chapter 19, India's energy needs are immense. It is the fourth-largest consumer of oil in the world and the second-fastest-growing energy market. The need for oil is driven the country's rapidly expanding transportation sector. In 2007 alone, the sector contributed about 5.5 percent to the nation's GDP, with road transportation contributing the lion's share.[25] The budget for the sector for 2009 through 2010 is $1.8 billion. The government plans to continually increase this amount over the next five years.[26]

India can't support its rapid growth in the transportation sector without oil. Now 30 percent of India's energy needs are met with oil. But much of the oil it uses is imported, as much as 70 percent comes from imports. The Energy Information Administration says that India will need to import 90 percent of its oil to meet its growing energy needs.

Like China, India is spending money to line up oil deals in Africa, and like China, India is willing to offer economic and infrastructure aid in exchange for access to oil. Over the last five years, India-Africa trade has grown to more than $30 billion.[27] In fact Nigeria has already emerged as India's second largest supplier of oil, with 15 percent of the market. But it needs more African oil.

In 2008, Reliance Industries, a privately owned Indian energy company began negotiating for refining rights with several African countries including Angola and Nigeria. In the summer of 2010, the Indian Oil Corporation announced plans to acquire oil fields in Africa with $1 billion allocated to overseas investments.

India doesn't have the cash reserves that China has, so its deals are smaller in size and scope. In fact, although the two countries have said they are not competing with one another for African oil, China's large cash coffers impact future deals. India has lost several key energy deals to China. Bloomberg reports that India has lost at least $12.5 billion worth of oil contracts. China spent a record $32 billion acquiring energy and resources assets overseas versus India's single $2.1 billion investment by the Oil and Natural Gas Corporation (ONGC). Of the money China has to throw around for oil deals, R.S. Sharma, chairman and managing director of ONGC says, "The Chinese are different with their big cash. We can't invest just for the sake of it."[28]

But the countries are in deep. As the United States tries to wean itself from Middle East oil, and turns to Africa, it could wind up trading one dependency for another. China is shadowing the United States in its need for oil. As automobiles become more prevalent, China will need to continue to buy up and into foreign oil assets. And as India's middle class grows, so too will its need for oil. The showdown could be fierce. Billions of dollars will be spent. And the oil barbarians couldn't be happier.

Part Six

WHERE TO INVEST NOW AND WHY

Chapter 21

Achieving Energy Independence

The Story of Samsø Island

I t's 8:10 P.M. Samsø Time, Thursday, February 23, 2006, when the ferry pulls into dock at Kolby Kas after a two-hour trip from Kalundborg. It's dark . . . and dusty. And cold.

There are no streetlights between cities, and one has to follow the car ahead to the center of the 20-mile-by-6-mile island, to Tranebjerg and Flinch's Hotel—one of the few hotels open during the off season.

The island feels deserted, and it is in a way. February is Denmark's coldest month, and many of Samsø's 4,300 residents are burrowed snugly in their warm homes—a stark contrast to when an influx of several tens of thousands visit the island during the tourist season. Many come in July for the popular music festival, the beautiful beaches, and sailing. But of late, Samsø has been invaded by a different kind of tourist; an eco-tourist.

In 1997, Denmark held a national competition. The selected winner would be home to a one-of-a-kind experiment: The winner would be expected to convert all its energy supply to 100 percent renewable energy (RE) within 10 years. The small island of Samsø was given the nod. Because it is an island that has no conventional energy resources of its own, Samsø was an ideal choice for such a controlled experiment. In 1998, Samsø began converting its energy into renewable energy, and has been so successful that 100 percent of its electricity comes from wind power, and 100 percent of its heat comes from solar power and biomass energy.

That's a massive eco-revolution. But it gets better. Here's how they did it. . . .

Wind Power: The New Danish Currency

Think of how long wind turbines have been around, and multiply that by 40. Wind turbines and windmills have been a part of the northern European landscape for centuries. Now, wind power makes up approximately 25 percent of Denmark's power consumption, and that figure will grow to 30 percent before 2012 and possibly to 50 percent by 2025, according to the Danish Wind Industry Association.[1]

But Denmark's wind industry isn't just big—and growing—at home. Denmark is globally renowned for its wind power technology and innovations. That's helped Danish manufacturers maintain 30 percent of the world market for wind turbines.[2] This percentage equates to over DKK34.9 billion, or more than $6.54 billion—about 6.5 percent of Denmark's total exports. That's 10 times what it was in 1997![3] With power like that, wind is like Denmark's new currency.

Beautiful, enormous wind turbines provide the island of Samsø with more than enough electricity to power residences and businesses. These wind farms generate so much electricity that sometimes, the island can't use it all.[4] So they sell it back to the mainland. Individuals, cooperatives, and the Samsø municipality have all invested in wind power. A land turbine costs just over a million dollars, but through subsidies, guaranteed rates, and the absolute efficiency of the technology, a turbine can pay back that amount in approximately 10 years.[5]

Samsø wanted to use whatever technology was currently available on a worldwide scale, and as wind power has been pioneered by the Danes, they had the best to choose from. The island's turbines were manufactured by a company named Bonus Energy A/S, which was acquired by Siemens A/G on December 1, 2004, thereby becoming a strong competitor in the wind energy market. Vestas Wind Systems (VWS:Copenhagen) is the main wind turbine producer in Denmark, and the world.[6] It holds the lion's share of the world market.

The most interesting part of the story involves the offshore wind turbines. There are 10 of them off the southern tip of the island, and they are even bigger than their land-bound brothers. That means they cost more—around $1.95 million each.[7] Over 1,500 people invested in this offshore wind farm,[8] one of them Samsø Energy and Environment Office Director Søren Hermansen.

What Samsø's done with wind power is extraordinary, and the communities around the island have embraced the turbines with a strong sense of pride in their independence and ownership. This community support was desirable. Samsø didn't want large companies or corporations coming in just for the business and the profits. The island wanted wind power to not only provide a better environment through renewable energy, but also to save the island's economy, introduce jobs, and prove to the world that they could do this themselves.[9]

And they have. Samsø has picked up the torch and has shown the world what wind power can do. With the completion of an offshore wind farm comprised of 10 beautiful turbines, Samsø has become carbon neutral. The energy produced by these wind turbines compensates for the island's transportation emissions, including the ferries, and all other non-renewable energy sources.[10]

But wind power isn't the only thing that's super-charging Samsø's eco-revolution.

Solar and Biomass Power: The Market's Heating Up

On Samsø, it's much more effective to use solar power for heating rather than electricity. Because of the expense of solar modules, the island has put them to use in a "collective" environment. Instead of installing solar arrays on individual homes for electricity, Samsø uses solar power for heat at its district heating plants.

District heating plants pump hot water to nearby homes for individual heating purposes. The water is heated using a combination of solar panels and renewable wood pellet or straw-furnaces. When we visited, about 250 homes had installed solar cells for heating their water tanks, and these were in instances in which the homes were too far from the district heating plant to use the central source.

By combining solar power with local, renewable biofuel, Samsø has custom-tailored a renewable energy program that is simple and highly effective. Solar panels are so efficient that on a cloudy winter day, they can heat the water to 25 degrees Fahrenheit above freezing on their own.

One of the most difficult steps is heating your home or business while respecting the environment. Samsø has found a unique way of solving this problem that is both cheaper than conventional heating means, and more productive for this island. On Samsø, a large number of homes and businesses get their heat from a district heating plant. There are four on the island: Nordby-Mårup in the north, Onsbjerg in the west, Ballen Brundby in the southeast, and Tranebjerg in the middle of the bottom half of the island.[11]

The heating plants consist of the following:

- A large water tank
- Arrays of solar panels
- A secondary heating source—wood pellets or straw

Water is pumped through pipes attached to the solar panels, and water travels through them becoming hotter and hotter, the more cells it passes through. If the water needs to be heated further, it makes its way into the plant to be heated by a wood pellet or straw furnace. Once the water is hot enough, it is pumped via pipes to individual homes and businesses.

The heating plant in Nordby had 2,500 square meters of solar panels that can heat water sufficiently without the help of the furnaces in warmer months, and then in the winter, the furnaces have to lend a hand. The Nordby plant had 800 cubic meters of chip capacity, and was so fully automated that only a regular check-up was required to keep the plant running.

This is probably the most interesting thing about the heating plants, though: Individuals who don't live close to the district heating plant have their own system. These systems are like mini-district plants. Individuals have a water tank on their property, and solar panels and wood pellet furnaces to heat the water before it's pumped to the home for heat.

That's an important point—the heated water is not consumed. Instead it's used to heat the home by running through pipes below the floor, or to heat water by heating an internal tank. It was interesting to visit a toasty home and be able to take off one's shoes in the middle of February, Denmark's coldest month of the year.

Because all their sources are renewable, this heating process is effective, and now, all heating is generated in this renewable fashion. Not only that, this manner of heating has provided Samsø with two harvestable crops: straw and wood.

There's only one sector left to tackle, and it might prove to be the most difficult.

The Transformation of Transportation

Transportation was by far the biggest impediment to Samsø's quest for 100 percent renewable status. It will probably be the biggest impediment for any country or city wanting to go totally carbon free. But here again, Samsø has shown remarkable ingenuity and self-reliance.

To this day, the largest amount of oil on Samsø goes to transportation. The folks at the Samsø Energy and Environment Office admit it's a huge hurdle to jump, but they want to eventually ban all traditional combustion engines from the island once alternative fuels are in place. And they've got a plan—several plans, actually.

Currently, the 10 offshore wind turbines compensate for all the fossil energy used by the vehicles on the island, and the ferries to and from the island. Effectively, Samsø is carbon neutral. But that's not good enough, and some interesting things have happened to rectify the situation.

One major project that could be in Samsø's future is hydrogen power plants. Using the excess electricity from the wind farms, the island would generate hydrogen to fuel vehicles on the island.[12]

The island's Energy Academy has a hydrogen filling station and hydrogen-powered truck on display. These were provided by H2 Logic in mid-May, 2007.[13] H2 Logic is a Danish company that's making strides in the international market. In fact, in early 2010, the company inaugurated Greenland's first hydrogen plant for renewable energy storage.[14] The truck is available for demonstrations to the community in order to promote its technology at Samsø's new Energy Academy. But in the meantime, another big project to reduce conventional vehicle fuel is taking root: rapeseed oil.

Rapeseed oil is a biofuel made from rapeseeds. The seeds are cold-pressed, not unlike olives for olive oil. Oil is extracted from the seeds and is filtered and stored for use in vehicles and tractors. The remaining pressed seeds are then fed to cows as a source of protein. Samsø can support approximately 600 hectares of rapeseed a year. That's not enough to totally eliminate the demand for gasoline or diesel, but it is an attractive notion for this island's farmers.

Tractors use an astounding amount of diesel, and by replacing their diesel with homemade fuel, farmers can save a lot of money—and sell another crop. For about $1,000, a mechanic can add two small parts to a tractor's engine (for a car, raise the price to $2,000). What's being added is a small heater, and a small pump. Once that update is made, your tractor is ready for rapeseed.

Because this fuel relies on a number of components within the community to contribute to its "harvesting," the community backs projects like these. But there's a kink in the system. Rapeseed is subject to the same taxes as diesel fuel. This made it hard for large-scale production. One company, DLG Samsø, a feed company, had the capacity to press and produce rapeseed oil for the local market, with the rapeseed "cake" going to feed for cows. But every attempt to remove that fuel tax for rapeseed oil met with disappointment, so rapeseed is only produced by individual farmers for their own personal use.[15]

Even though this project has not gotten off the ground in a commercial way, the community strongly supports it, and that says a lot for the whole Samsø project. Generating community interest has been a key way of developing projects and increasing investors. Samsø's Energy and Environment Office was successful because it offered more than just a great chance at a return on investments.

The True Eco-Revolution

In order for the renewable energy project to survive, the Samsø project needed strong backing from the community. In that way, Samsø's success goes way beyond the "greening" of energy consumption. This eco-revolution was not only an environmental change.

Samsø's residents embraced a way to save their economy and improve their way of life. Through investing in co-ops that financed wind power and district heating plants, islanders took personal control over their quality of life. By introducing these renewable energy projects, Samsø has created new, better-paying jobs, increased tourism, and improved its economy.[16] "The community is more inclined to support the project because they see it as something that is done locally by local people. As such, people participate not because they are forced by the authorities but because they want to," says Søren Hermansen, director of the Samsø Energy and Environment Office.[17]

Community commitment is necessary for the advancement of any project, which is why Samsø uses many local resources like straw and wood pellets for the district heating plants. Soon rapeseed could be added to that list.

Residents want to see Samsø succeed, and understand that by participating in the island's renewable energy projects the whole island benefits. Some might argue that the only reason Samsø's renewable energy projects are succeeding is because of government subsidies. We would argue that the island's eco-revolution is flourishing because its participants believe in what they're doing. Monetary gain is only half the incentive.

Samsø is a unique place. This renewable energy project wasn't initiated just to prove that it could be done; it saved the island. The renewable energy project has created higher-paying jobs, and used local resources that have boosted the standard of living for its residents. Approximately 100 people in Samsø had been unemployed due to the closure of a slaughterhouse on the island, so Hermansen has gotten whole communities involved.[18]

Samsø also has a new breed of tourists: eco-tourists. Experts from around the world have visited the island to study its renewable energy success. New eco-tourists have been visiting the island to take back ideas for their own eco-revolutions. Industry experts from Thailand, Japan, Nepal, Indonesia, to name a few, are all interested in Samsø. "The first year, 400 to 500 Japanese visited the RE–island project," noted the 10-year evaluation of the island's progress, titled "Samsø: A Renewable Energy Island." "In the next couple of years Samsø entered several EU initiatives and joined the organization ISLENET. Europeans began to visit the island. Since then, visitors have come from almost everywhere."[19]

When we visited him, Jesper Kjems of the Energy and Environment Office gave this advice on how to get your community involved:

Well, a general "how to" would be great, but it's hard to come up with. I would rather give you some of our advice from experiences with building up this 100 percent renewable energy society. Public projects and public engagement:

1. Hold open meetings
2. Establish co-operatives
3. Get local business involved in building and maintaining
4. Work in cooperation with municipality

Use known technology—let universities do the research. Keep it a good deal for the consumers. It's easier to be good to the environment, when you also save money. Convince the local companies and workmen to sell RE-solutions—they are often asked what to choose. See if you can get guaranties from government, municipality, or others to minimize the risk when local farmers, businesses, or consumers must invest lots of money in a new RE-project.

These tips are just as useful today as they were 12 years ago when Samsø started this project. Major western countries are just starting to catch on but the investment community is certainly offering your portfolio ways to take on an eco-revolution.

Eco-Revolution: The New Danish Currency Investment Solutions

By far, wind power is the foremost renewable source of energy in Denmark and on Samsø. According to the Danish Wind Industry Association, "growth expectations for the wind industry are greater than growth expectations for the Chinese economy." A Reuters article published March 7, 2006 ran with the following headline: "Global Wind Energy Capacity Seen Tripling by 2014."[20] And guess who will be leading the charge? The United States.

Companies are scrambling to get in on this untouched market, and those already involved have already seen massive gains! And they're all coming here, to the United States, to reap billions of dollars in profits from our wind market. For as rich as we are, for as advanced as our technology is, the United States is one of the worst countries when it comes to this industry. In fact, countries like New Zealand, Morocco, and India all trump the United States. But that's about to change.

Nine different companies have entered this massive market here in the United States, and their contracts are worth billions. The U.S. government has just given the green light to boost this industry by 513 percent by 2030!

That figure is not a typo, and it's not an exaggeration. Now, this industry has a measly 3.26 percent market penetration. The market is nearly untouched—pristine. But thanks to this government green light, the industry could grow to 20 percent by 2030.[21] That's 25.8 percent growth a year for the next 20 years.

It's going to take some serious cash. More than $15 billion has already been shelled out, and that's just the beginning. Over the next decade that figure could soar 10 times as high, and certain companies could climb 1,000 percent as massive contracts roll in.

Don't think it can happen? Guess again. As we said, the United States is in bad shape compared to the rest of the world. Some of the world's leaders in wind power, like Spain, Denmark, and Germany, generate a significant percentage of electricity from wind. But the whole of the European Union generates a larger percentage of electricity from wind than the United States.

All 27 members of the Union's electrical capacity see 4.2 percent of its power from wind. The United States gets 3.26 percent from wind,[22] and that's after a $15 billion upgrade. It's no wonder that the talking heads are drumming up support for a tenfold increase in that investment.

In 2008, the United States had 25,000 megawatt wind (MW) in operation.[23] Turbines stand in more than two-thirds of all the states in the nation, and a record 8,358 MW of capacity was installed, more than in any other country in the world. Those 8,358 MW were a $15 billion investment.[24] And get this: At the end of 2009, after one of the roughest economic recessions in generations, installed capacity reached 35,000 MW of wind power![25] That's a fantastic leap considering the economic conditions.

Now imagine a $150 billion investment. That's the future of energy here in the U.S. President Barack Obama is calling for a $150 billion investment[26] in new energy over the next 10 years. On May 12, 2008, the Department of Energy released a 248-page report showing that the United States could generate 20 percent of its electricity from wind power by 2030.[27] That's an increase of 513 percent from current wind generation and means that thousands of additional turbines a year will need to be installed.

We're already seeing demand spike here in the States. . . .

So, wind power is the next emerging market right here in our own backyard. To prove it, consider this: Western Wind Energy, a Canadian small-cap company, turned down the development rights to a project called the Windstar.[28] This contract would have given Western Wind royalties for the next 30 years. Why in the world would a small-cap company turn down easy money? Well, $228 million pales in comparison to the $1.7 billion it can make going with the Windstar Project alone.[29] That's a huge difference, and it's just a drop in the bucket when it comes to wind energy investments in the United States.

The Next U.S. Market Leader

One company, Iberdrola Renewables (IBR:Madrid), is ready and willing to jump into the U.S. wind energy market. In fact, it's already completed projects and has several new projects under construction here in the States. This company could easily become the next U.S. market leader:

> Since the [American Recovery and Reinvestment Act's] reimbursement program was enacted in February 2009, thirteen Iberdrola Renewables projects received funding, creating or supporting 9,000 jobs. These projects are capable of generating 1,795 MW of clean renewable wind energy. By repackaging the long-standing tax credit, the Recovery Act allowed Iberdrola Renewables to leverage $975 million worth of grant money into as much as $6 billion worth of investment in U.S. renewable energy projects through 2012.[30]

As of the third quarter of 2010, Iberdrola Renewables has another 1,200 MW of wind power under construction in the United States.[31] Indeed, the first nine months of 2010 saw this company increase its operating capacity by nearly 53 percent year-over-year in the United States.[32] The company already has 41 percent of its wind production in the United States.[33]

This company is a must-buy for wind energy investors. Scratch that—it's a must-buy for any investor. In the first nine months of 2010, IBR increased its operating capacity by 16.1 percent to 11,434 MW, and its production by 20.2 percent to 18,091 GWh (gigawatt hours). These are outstanding numbers considering the world was just starting to recover from the Great Recession![34] And the United States accounted for 52.8 percent of those increases![35] More than any other market, the United States has the most market growth potential in IBR's basket of projects. The company also showed a 29.6 percent jump in U.S. production and a 27 percent jump in projects in the pipeline over that timeframe.[36]

IBR has operations in over 20 countries and is expanding rapidly to places major investors have targeted for growth: Brazil, Morocco, and China, just to name a few.[37] But this is the reason to focus on IBR's presence here in the United States:

> Iberdrola Renewables plans to invest €9 billion over the 2010–2012 period to bolster its position as the global leader in wind power and drive international expansion, focusing on more profitable markets.

The company's growth in this three-year period will come mainly from the US, where it will invest €4.9 billion, 55 percent of its total investment.[38]

That means the world leader in wind power is gobbling up U.S. market share, and that the company's investments are paying off, big time. Such potential doesn't come around that often in today's financial situation. It's the perfect storm of high energy prices, high demand for alternative energy, and a brand-new investment opportunity.

The gales of this storm could blow IBR as high as 23 euros. That's what happened to Denmark's Vestas Wind Systems (VWS:Copenhagen). On December 6, 2004, VWS was worth 62.25 Danish kroner (US$13.13). By July 7, 2008, VWS was trading for 627 Danish kroner (US$132.27).[39]

Will IBR reach 23 euros, a gain of nearly 1,000 percent? To be honest, it's not guaranteed. It may only climb to 15 euros when all is said and done. Or it could climb to 40 or 45 euros, as when REPower Systems (RPW:XETRA) jumped from 12.08 euros on December 14, 2004 to 211 euros on July 7, 2008.[40]

Now is your best chance to grab an energy company that could climb tenfold in the next couple years. To be blunt, it may be your only chance.

Chapter 22

The Need for Alternative Energy Sources

We've been a country addicted to oil for so long, we forget there are alternative sources of energy available. They include solar, wind, geothermal, tides, and hydroelectric. The important benefit of alternative energy sources is they are usually renewable and have limited to no undesirable side effects, unlike fossil fuels.

The truth is alternative energy sources have been around for thousands of years. Take wind. The first known use of wind as an energy source was about 5,000 B.C. Wind was used on sailboats so that people could travel up and down the Nile River. Windmills were even used in countries such as Persia and China. Around 500 A.D., and Persians constructed windmills for pumping water. The sails were hung vertically, and the entire structure was generally made of wood or bundles of reed. That early design of the windmill was later refined by the Dutch, who created a tower-like structure. The windmills were used mainly for pumping water. But the Europeans began experimenting with windmills and found they could be used to run saw mills and other types of industrial manufacturing plants.

About 1890, the Dutch further refined the windmill so that it could create electricity. By the end of the nineteenth century, there were over 30,000 windmills in use in Europe.[1] As Dutch immigrants came to the United States, they brought with them their windmill technology, however, the Dutch-designed windmill couldn't stand up to the heavy winds that blew across the mid-west states.

Daniel Halladay is credited with creating a windmill that could stand up to the strong winds. A directional tail was added and the blades were made of wood. Almost all windmills in use were made specifically to supply water to homesteads and livestock spread across the midwest. However, over time, the heavy wooden blades were abandoned in favor of lighter and faster steel blades.

The first windmill to produce electricity was the "American multi-blade design," which was designed and built in 1888 by Charles Brush.[2] This new design produced 12 kilowatts of power but was later superseded by the modern-day 70–100 kilowatt wind turbine. Between 1850 and 1970, over 6 million windmills were used in the United States.[3] As oil was discovered and then refined for heating and lighting homes, use of windmills declined.

But in the early 1970s when the Arab oil embargo began, interest in wind-generated energy soared. In fact the U.S. Federal Wind Energy Program was established in 1974. A federally backed wind-power test center was set up in Colorado near Rocky Flats. At the test center, at least 25 different wind turbine systems, mainly of small commercial scale, were tested including residential, commercial and agricultural designs.

But no large-scale systems were developed and tested. The government seemed to concentrate its efforts on small-scale systems. From there, about forty small commercial wind systems were installed in selected areas throughout the United States. They ranged in size from 1.5 kilowatts to 40 kilowatts. They were connected to local utility lines. Surveys were then sent out asking respondents to rate the performance of the wind turbine system. Unfortunately most of the respondents rated the system as poor. The system seemed to have its share of problems. Wind energy advocates criticized the government for telling respondents that the systems could be used to generate electricity at rates cheaper than they were previously paying.

James Schmidt, a noted wind energy expert was puzzled that the testing centers had encountered so many problems. Schmidt asserted that if the government had not stopped building windmills so many years ago, these problems would not have occurred. Andrew Trenka, manager of the Rock Flats test center, commented: "We tended to be blinded because windmills had been used for more than 1,000 years . . . we thought the technology was there and all we had to do was bring it into the 20th century."[4]

Some countries are showing us that wind energy is a worthy source of energy. China is building new wind farms three times faster than the United States. With a president committed to clean energy, the United States installed a paltry 1,634 megawatts of wind generating systems during the first nine months of 2010.

The American Wind Energy Association (AWEA) says the reason that United States hasn't stepped up its hunt for alternative energy rests with Congress. The AWEA says:

> The failure of Congress to support a nationwide Renewable Electricity Standard, requiring all utilities to source a certain proportion of their power supplies from clean sources, was hindering investment in new wind projects.[5]

The Wind Mill That Could

It may not come as a surprise that the government ran into problems developing large-scale, commercially viable windmill systems. After all, let's be honest, what has the government done that has been successful? But just because the government failed, doesn't mean that wind-powered energy isn't an acceptable alternative to fossil fuel backed energy.

Others are succeeding. In Chapter 21, you learned how the small island of Samsø achieved energy independence. Let me tell you the story about a handful of people right here in New York that showed the country it was possible to use alternative energy, such as wind as a power source. And they had plenty of obstacles to overcome, mainly fighting a multimillion-dollar energy company.

In the early days of developing wind-driven power programs, advocates had to get the "buy-in" from utility companies. In the early 1970s, utility companies were a major force in the nation's economy. Utility companies relied on traditional energy sources such as coal, oil or nuclear power-driven plants. Basically utility companies had a monopoly on energy production, including the ways in which it was produced.

That monopoly was challenged in 1976 by a group of New York tenants who wanted to power the building they were living in by wind driven turbines. In order to do so, they would have to connect their wind turbine to Consolidated Edison's power grid, the utility company that provides New York with its electric service. The tenants calculated that using the wind turbine, which was installed on the top of their building, would generate $32,356 worth of electricity over 20 years.[6]

There was one problem with the group's desire to use wind power. Under law, customer-owned generating equipment could not legally connect to utility lines. So Consolidated Edison denied the group access to its lines. Without access to Consolidated Edison's grid, the wind turbine was useless, so the tenants decided to plead their case to the public. The fight caught the attention of the local media. New Yorkers living in the area sided with the tenants. It was an easy decision, because most New Yorkers weren't happy with Consolidated Edison's 300 percent increase in utility rates.

The tenants' fight to hook up to Consolidated Edison's utility lines caught the attention of New York politicians as well as the state's Public Utility Commission. Yielding to pressure, Consolidated Edison agreed to allow the tenants to hook up their wind turbine to their grid lines, but they did so with a few caveats. They charged what was considered excessive liability costs to the group for the venture, along with unusually high minimum charges for electricity.

Not willing to give up the fight to power their building by wind, the tenants appealed to the New York Public Utility Commission. The Commission sided with the tenants, and Consolidated Edison had to withdraw its excessive fees and allow the tenants to hook up to the grid. Senator Edward Kennedy called the wind turbine on top the building, "the little windmill that could."[7]

The tenants' victory was a win for the ordinary citizens standing up against a major monopoly. But it also shows that when it comes to energy, Americans do want choices including alternative sources.

Breaking the Addiction

In 2004, the Rocky Mountain Institute, a non-profit organization dedicated to helping the United States break its oil addiction, released a critical report, *Winning the Oil Endgame.* In the report, the Institute showed how it is possible for the U.S. to become less dependent on fossil fuels and rely more on clean, renewable energy sources.

But the Institute also proved that many of the current prejudices that exist toward other energy sources are biased and in many instances, built on falsehoods. For example biofuels, that is liquid fuels from farming, forestry waste products, and energy crops such as corn, are often considered not worth the effort because their energy potential is small, yet the costs associated are high.

In their report, the Institute cites a study done in 1999 by the National Academies National Research Council (NANRC) that found that biofuels could profitably provide 1.6 million barrels (of crude-oil equivalent) per day by 2020.[8] That's because new methods can convert cellulose and lignin-rich materials into liquid fuels using genetically engineered bacteria and enzymes. The NANRC also says that by 2025, those same biofuels could yield as much as 4.3 million barrels per day at under $35 a barrel. The Institute's report also says that a third or more of road transportation fuels worldwide could be displaced by biofuels from 2050 to 2100.

Many other countries are transitioning to biofuels, leaving the United States in the back of the line. Brazil is the leader in biofuels, especially ethanol. Brazil's use of cheap sugar cane enables it to provide a 22 percent ethanol blend used nationwide, plus 100 percent hydrous ethanol for 4 million cars. The Brazilian ethanol program provided nearly 700,000 jobs in 2003, and cut 1975–2002 oil imports by a cumulative undiscounted total of $50 billion.[9]

In 2003 Europe produced 17 times as much biodiesel as the United States, and the EU is demonstrating that a transition to biodiesel is feasible.

The Rocky Mountain Institute concludes that in short, many of the fuel-system, commercial, vehicle-technology, and production developments that the United States would need for a large-scale biofuel program have already succeeded elsewhere.[10]

The Little Town That Could

Rolling hills surrounds the little Italian town of Larderello, located in Tuscany. Its beauty is spectacular. Romans used the town's natural hot water springs for bathing as well as a treatment for eye and skin diseases. They also used the area's naturally occurring boron salt as a medicine.

The area is also home to sulphur springs, and the odor is so strong the area is often referred to as Valle del Diavolo, or "the Devil's Valley." Historians say Francisco Hoefer, a German chemist working for the Grand Duke of Tuscany in 1777 first discovered the boric acid in Larderello. However, others say the Etruscans knew of its existence and used the boric acid that naturally seeped up on the edges of hot wells, or "lagoni natural" as a medical treatment.

But it was Francois de Lardarel, a Frenchman, who in 1818 figured out how to commercially mine the boric acid. Lardarel extracted boric acid from the volcanic mud by using steam to separate the ingredients.[11] For his efforts, Leopold II, the Grand Duke, rewarded Lardarel with the title of Count of Montecerboli, and eventually the town was renamed in his honor.

Because the town also had natural geothermal reservoirs, where temperatures reached 180 degrees Celsius it was the perfect place to experiment with geothermal energy. In 1904, Italian scientist, Prince Piero Ginori Conti vented the steam coming out of the ground into a pipe connected to a steam-driven turbine engine. He collected enough steam to turn on five light bulbs.[12]

Some people saw the experiment as a failure, but Conti didn't give up, because he knew this energy source was capable of much more. So he kept experimenting, and those efforts paid off. One year later, he produced enough power to light up his entire house, and the townspeople were converted. By 1908, Conti was using his geothermal steam-driven engine to light up entire buildings in Larderello.

In 1913, construction of the first geothermal plant in the world began in Larderello. The plant produced enough energy to provide lighting for most of the power plants surrounding the town. Conti proved to the world that geothermal energy could be used to generate electricity.

Geothermal energy is heat created by the earth's core, which reaches temperatures of over 9,000 degrees Fahrenheit.[13] The heat continuously flows outward toward the mantle, the layer of rock that surrounds the core. The heat melts the mantle turning it into magma, and that magma rises up toward the earth's crust, where we see it as lava. But not all lava reaches the surface. The magma that remains trapped below the surface holds enormous heat, sometimes as much as 700 degrees Fahrenheit.[14] The heat that is trapped below the surface heats up any water or rock nearby. Sometimes that water flows through faults and cracks, forming natural hot springs or geysers, and the rest of the heat remains trapped in porous rock.

This trapped heat and hot water provide the power for geothermal power plants. Steam is piped directly into a turbine, which spins the generator. Water that doesn't produce steam hot enough to power the turbine is still used. However, it is passed through a heat exchanger, where a secondary liquid with a low boiling point is used.

Like other renewable energy sources, geothermal energy is a clean source of energy. It doesn't produce the types of environmentally dangerous emissions that fossil fuel sources do. In fact, geothermal fields produce only about one-sixth of the carbon dioxide that a relatively clean natural-gas-fueled power plant produces, and very little if any, of the nitrous oxide or sulfur-bearing gases. What's more, geothermal energy is vastly abundant. The availability of geothermal energy is 50,000 times the energy of all oil and gas resources in the world.

Geothermal energy can be harnessed just about anywhere. Hydrothermal energy, a form of geothermal energy, is found in steam or hot water reservoirs, like those in Larderello. But it's also available to us in oceans as the sun's heat warms up the surface of the water. Through a process known as ocean thermal energy conversion (OTEC), the heat stored in oceans can be converted into electricity.

Currently there are two ways to convert heat in water into electricity. In open-style OTEC, warm surface water is turned into vapor by decompressing it. The pressure of the expanding vapor is then used to run a turbine and produce electricity. The second way is closed-style and uses a low-boiling-point fluid such as freon or ammonia which is evaporated in a heat exchanger. The expanding vapor is connected to a turbine in much the same way as the open-style system.

Already, small-sized ocean-based test plants have been able to produce a few hundred kilowatts of electric power. One of those plants is the Keahole Plant in Hawaii.[15]

Right now, about 21 countries use geothermal energy. In the United States, nine states have geothermal plants including California, Nevada, Utah, Hawaii, Indiana, Arkansas, Oregon, Wyoming, and New Mexico. A plant producing 2700 megawatts of electricity from geothermal energy sources is equal to burning 60 million barrels of oil each year.[16] By increasing the number of geothermal energy sources, the United States can help kick its addiction to oil.

The Little Engine That Could

In 1860, a Frenchman named Auguste Mouchout thought it might be possible to use the sun's heat to make steam, so he sat down and drew up designs for a solar-powered motor.

But Mouchout wasn't just an ordinary French citizen; he was a celebrated inventor and taught mathematics at the Lyce de Tours. Using the basic materials available to him at the time, Mouchout's engine was a water-filled pot set inside a glass frame. Mouchout designed the engine so that sunlight passed through the glass and then was converted into heat. The iron pot absorbed the heat, which boiled the water sitting inside, and the boiled water then produced steam, which would serve as the power source.

Mouchout tested his design. Unfortunately the boiling water inside the pot didn't produce enough steam, so Mouchout modified his "water-pot" engine by adding a dish-shaped reflector that concentrated the sun's rays. This simple modification turned his design into a working steam-driven engine. Napoleon was impressed with Mouchout's solar powered engine, so much so that he provided Mouchout financial aid to develop and build an industrial-sized solar engine.

Since Mouchout already had a working prototype, he decided the best way to satisfy Napoleon's request was to simply modify his basic design. He made the reflector larger so that the sun's rays could be even more concentrated and added a tracking device so that the reflector could follow the sun's direction. This provided a consistent flow of the sun's rays to the pot.

The improved design worked, and Napoleon was thrilled but wanted more. So he sent Mouchout to the French colony of Algeria to build an even bigger model. Napoleon picked Algeria because of its tropical location and many sunny days.

Mouchout worked diligently on building a large model of his solar power-driven engine. When the work was completed, he returned to Paris to present his idea to Napoleon. To demonstrate the engine's ability, he connected it to a refrigeration-type device and successfully powered it. Napoleon awarded Mouchout a medal for his work, and the French government continued to fund Mouchout's work. But in 1880, Mouchout's fame and funding came to a grinding halt. Coal was now available to the French in large quantities and at low prices.[17] However, Mouchout's ingenuity had shown the world that the sun's rays could be turned into a viable energy source.

Today, as it did in 1880, solar energy has the potential to help wean Americans from their oil addiction. Unfortunately we haven't tapped this readily available, non-depletable source of energy as much as we could. The United States uses solar electricity for only 0.1 percent of its energy needs.[18]

Other countries have beaten us in the race for alternative energy sources, especially solar. China now produces over 18 percent of the world's photovoltaic products. There are 400 companies in China producing solar-related modules, and in 2007, China produced 1,700 megawatts of solar electricity.

Europe isn't far behind. It produces about 3.4 gigawatts of solar electricity. Portugal has already built a solar power plant which produces about 11-megawatts. Germany has a 40-megawatt power plant.

A Matter of Choice

These other countries are showing us *that it is possible* to use alternative sources of energy. According to an article in *Scientific American*, a switch from coal, oil, natural gas, and nuclear power plants to solar power plants could supply 69 percent of U.S. electricity needs and 35 percent of its total energy by 2050.[19]

Right now the United States ranks as the world's most oil-consuming country at 19.8 million barrels a day. China is number two with consumption at 7.8 million barrels. But look how much more oil we use than the Chinese: almost 12 million barrels per day more! We can free ourselves from this horrific oil addiction. The Rocky Mountain Institute says, "America's shift from oil can be led profitably by business at a net savings to the economy of $70 billion a year by 2025.[20]

The sad truth about our lackluster push for alternative energy sources is that it is mostly by choice. It isn't because we don't have the technology or the resources. It's because the barbaric oil mongers want us to stay addicted to oil. After all, the more oil we use, the more money they make. Consider that for the third quarter of 2010, ExxonMobil's income increased 55 percent to $7.35 billion. For the same period last year, the company reported $4.73 billion in income. Shell reported similar returns. It earned $4.9 billion in the third quarter of 2010. In the same period in 2009, it reported $2.6 billion in income.[21]

As oil prices climb, the oil companies are getting richer. The *Los Angeles Times* reports that oil companies have seen profits jump as crude prices increased 12 percent year-over-year.[22] Maggie Fox, president and CEO of Alliance for Climate Protection, says, "The need for legislation has never been more urgent. We must heed the lessons learned from the tragedy in the Gulf, and move forward this year on clean energy policies that will create new jobs, reduce pollution and reduce our dependence on oil."[23]

The oil mongers want to stay rich—at our expense. But we don't have to let these barbarians control our future. As Michael Levi, senior fellow for Energy and the Environment, Council on Foreign Relations says, "The United States could substantially reduce its oil consumption in the next two decades *if it chose to do so.*"[24]

Levi is right. It is a matter of choice.

Chapter 23

The Hybrid Future

At one point in its 100 years of existence, General Motors was the most successful company in the world. Too big to fail, analysts said. . . . Well, we've heard that line before, and we've seen it proved wrong. On June 1, 2009, General Motors filed for bankruptcy.[1] Chrysler had also filed on April 30,[2] and both companies shut down dealerships across the nation. That left a vacuum, and foreign automakers are sure to gain surprising market share on the back side of the global recession.

In January 2010, only 43 percent of all cars sold in the United States were made by GM, Chrysler, and Ford. And for some perspective, these three are believed to have produced 80 percent of the cars here in the United States in 1985.[3]

But production is only half of the equation; let's talk about dealerships. Just before bankruptcy for both GM and Chrysler, the two announced plans to close thousands of dealerships around the country, putting many people on unemployment. *MarketWatch* reported that 3,000 dealerships would be closed over the next couple years, and the news services estimated that 150,000 people would be out of work because of these closures.[4]

Interestingly, those dealerships closed by Chrysler accounted for only 14 percent of the company's sales.[5] That means that these companies had so many dealerships the amount of sales each dealership produced was limited. Customers looking to buy a Chevy Malibu could go, in some cases, right down the road to a competing GM dealership and haggle for a lower price. Foreign competitor Toyota, on the other hand, was able to produce more sales with only a quarter of the dealerships.

Now, you might be thinking that GM and Chrysler are just the unfortunate victims of the current global economic crisis. You'd only be half right. The crisis has certainly brought about these companies' demise in quick fashion, but American automakers have been losing ground for the past thirty years and more.

And what is the appeal of these foreign automakers? Two things: fuel efficiency and quality. For the past 30 years, American automakers have been lagging behind Toyota and Honda and the like. In fact, in 2009 the top five cars sold in the United States were all from foreign manufacturers.[6] We've seen gasoline prices spike above $4 a gallon, and oil prices top $147 a barrel. Investors have to ask themselves: What's the next step for the auto industry? The trend leaves you only one choice: to buy hybrid technology.

Investing in Battery Technology

If tomorrow's cars are trending toward fuel efficiency and hybrid technology, then automakers across the board will be implementing technology—that means battery technology, particularly for the nickel metal hydride and lithium ion batteries.

EV World and Freedonia Group estimate that battery demand will jump to $22.8 billion a year by 2012.[7] The main components of batteries are metals, chemicals and polymers. And while nickel metal hydride batteries currently hold the lion's share of the market, lithium ion batteries are proving to be the more efficient and powerful type of battery.

In mid-December 2008, the Department of Energy and the Department of Defense began supporting the National Alliance for Advanced Transportation Battery Cell Manufacture, an alliance of more than 14 companies, in order to pursue the commercial production of lithium ion batteries for auto manufacturing.[8] The alliance expects to need between $1 billion and $2 billion in funding through 2013, much of which will come from the government.

But some companies have already made great strides in the hybrid battery arena. You may have heard of Energy Conversion Devices (ENER:Nasdaq). This well-known battery maker licenses nickel metal-hydride batteries to companies like Panasonic EV and Ovonics, who make batteries for GM and Toyota. ENER's powerful battery division is sure to treat it well in the hybrid-loving future.

Another possible battery producer is Sanyo (1614:Taiwan) (SANYY.PK). Sanyo (1614:Taiwan) (SANYY.PK) is based in Taiwan, provides nickel metal-hydride batteries to Honda and Ford, and recently signed a deal with VW and Audi to provide lithium ion batteries.[9] Sanyo is planning to up production of both technologies.

Kyocera (KYO:NYSE) has also been selected to provide solar panels for the U.K. release of the new Prius.[10] This technology will power cooling fans to help eliminate gas-guzzling air conditioning.

These battery makers, among others, are going to benefit as more and more manufacturers begin making hybrid and electric vehicles. Consider this: As recently as 2004, news wires were comparing the appeal of the Hummer to the Prius. Between July and November 2002, Hummer sales of H1 and H2 doubled from 1,922 to 3,933. And politicians were saying that driving these types of giant vehicles was engrained in the American way of life.[11] But by mid-2004, as gasoline prices topped $2.00 a gallon for the first time ever, Hummer sales were falling off a cliff. Between December 2003, and January 2004, sales fell nearly 50 percent, and GM slashed its full year forecast by 25 percent.[12] On the other hand, Prius was gaining in popularity. In fact, according to *Autodata*, in 2004, Prius was outselling Hummer by 2 to 1. And Toyota was boosting 2004 production by 50 percent.[13] Do you know what that did to Toyota's share price—between January 2004 and January 2007, Toyota stock climbed 98.5 percent![14]

Electric Cars Become a Reality

Currently, we're seeing additional innovations in the auto industry. Two manufacturers have released fully electric vehicle (EV) models for 2011: GM's Volt and Nissan's Leaf. These two EVs are huge steps forward for the auto industry, and new battery technology is right in the heart of it. Literally.

The new Chevy Volt will have a line of lithium-ion batteries running down the middle of the car, much like a heart pumping power. These batteries will be made by South Korean company, LG Chem.[15]

The Nissan Leaf will also be powered by lithium-ion batteries, and the company is producing them itself with the help of NEC Corp. (NIPNF.PK).[16] This pack is made with lithium-manganese gel, and is on the cutting edge of new battery technology.

Let me give you some more stats for these two new electric vehicles. According to GM, it would cost about $1.50 to "fill up" the new Chevy Volt every night.[17] The Volt can run on battery power for up to 40 miles. Now that may sound like a short distance, but here's the thing—and the main difference between the Volt and the Leaf: The Volt has a small gasoline engine that can recharge the battery so that you can get another 300 miles before you need to recharge and refill your tank.

The Nissan Leaf, on the other hand, is all electric, foregoing the weight of the extra engine. That means the Leaf can drive up to 100 miles on a single charge, 2.5 times more than the Volt's battery capacity, but much less than what you'd get with both Volt's power sources. The company estimates that it would cost about $400 a year to drive the Leaf, using an average driving distance of 15,000 miles and an average cost of $0.11 per kWh.[18]

Of course, GM and Nissan aren't the only companies with new battery technology. In 2010 and 2011, Ford, Toyota, Fisker Automotive, and Coda Automotive will be releasing either plug-in hybrids or all electric vehicles, or both. And let's not forget the previous innovations from Smart Car and the Tesla Roadster. These guys broke the mold on electric vehicles because they saw a huge change coming down the pipeline.

You could say you saw this coming a decade ago, or more, but now the automotive industry has reached a tipping point, and we're about to see a seismic shift in how the auto sector makes cars and meets consumer demand. Two of the "Big Three" automakers in the United States filed for bankruptcy in 2009. GM and Chrysler both threw in the towel, as they couldn't compete with massive amounts of debt weighing them down against the influx of more efficient foreign manufacturers. But these two companies are once again venturing out into the market. They've had a chance to remake themselves into smarter, more adaptable companies. The next decade will be a key chapter for them, but will also test the strength of the rest of the auto industry. The public is demanding cheaper and more efficient cars and trucks, and automakers are responding. Ford's newest line of Explorers will boost fuel economy by 30 percent by using a "car-like" unibody instead of an SUV unibody. The 2011 Explorer will also use the new EcoBoost turbocharged four-cylinder engine that will pump fuel economy above 20 miles per gallon.[19]

The Hybrid Future

But besides evolving into what consumers want these days, auto makers are going to have to change due to political winds. President Obama has said he wants one million rechargeable vehicles on the road by 2015, and that spells change in the auto industry. And there's more: In May 2009, President Obama announced new fuel efficiency standards for all new cars sold in the United States beginning in 2012 and lasting through 2016. The new standards will do the following:

- Raise the current average mileage standard from 25 miles per gallon for all vehicles to 39 miles per gallon for cars and 30 miles per gallon for trucks by 2016.
- Regulate the amount of CO_2 from tailpipe emissions for the first time.
- Are expected to reduce CO_2 emissions from tailpipes by 900 million metric tons, the equivalent of taking 177 million cars off the road.
- Are expected to save 1.8 billion barrels of oil over the life of all new vehicles sold between 2012 and 2016.[20]

This last point is key (particularly when this year saw the worst oil spill in U.S. history): 1.8 billion barrels of oil is more than the United States imported from Saudi Arabia, Venezuela, Libya, and Nigeria combined in 2008.[21] It's a massive amount of oil. In fact, it's about 367 times the size of the BP Gulf Oil Spill from April 2010.[22] And get this: the whole Macondo Prospect (the site of the explosion) was estimated to hold about 50 million barrels of producible oil reserves.[23]

The new CAFE standards would have wiped out the need for that prospect to have been drilled in the first place, 36 times over.

Risky deepwater drilling is a profitable business when the United States is importing 2 billion barrels of oil a year from OPEC nations alone. But it may be more profitable to curb oil consumption through the implementation of efficiency standards, and that's just what the auto industry is starting to do.

With manufactures just starting to get off the "juice," this is a prime opportunity for investors of the hybrid future. "Moto Metals" have been around since the Earth was made. They make up significant portions of our Earth's crust, and are well-known names on the periodic table. You've read about them in science class, and you're using them in your home, in your computer, and the car you're already driving. But new technological innovations are making these metals stars in today's energy market, and the next generation of vehicles will use Moto Metals in unprecedented amounts.

Motor-Driven Metals

So what are Moto Metals and how are they used? Here are just a few names: lithium, nickel, platinum, cobalt, manganese, and silver. These metals are essential components of hybrid batteries and catalytic converters, among other complex auto parts. They play key roles in power generation and efficiency, and as the automotive market trends toward higher fuel efficiency standards and new power options, like plug-in hybrid technology, these Moto Metals are going to be in high demand.

Interestingly, lithium is a difficult element to pin down, and its uses are so varied that it's hard to get specific production and usage data. There is one thing though: the U.S. Geological Survey from January 2008 says that only two companies produced a large array of downstream lithium compounds in the United States from domestic or South American lithium carbonate.[24]

One of those companies is FMC Corp. (FMC:NYSE). We recommended it at one of Taipan Publishing Group's annual summit conferences. FMC has a whole division dedicated to lithium production that has been in existence for more than 60 years.[25] It is a worldwide leading developer and supplier of lithium-based materials for primary and rechargeable batteries.

But aside from battery technology, Moto Metals play a significant role in making traditional internal combustion engines more efficient and clean. ON Semiconductor (ONNN:Nasdaq) is involved in making sensor interfaces, which can help reuse power and decrease pollution. They're also involved in many other power and digital solutions for the auto sector, not to mention, of course, personal computing, telecommunications, and industrial sectors, just to name a few. These "tech" solutions contain Moto Metals like nickel, silver, lead, and palladium.

There are a number of different ways to invest in Moto Metals, from new hybrid battery technology to microchip sensors. Let's dig a little deeper into some specific investment areas, starting with battery technology.

There are a number of battery makers out there, and they range in type from a semiconductor company that also specializes in other green technologies like solar power, to industrial equipment makers that also dabble in nanotechnology.

In addition to Energy Conversion Devices, Kyocera, and Sanyo, battery makers like Ener1, Inc. (HEV:Nasdaq), Valance Technology, Inc. (VLNC:Nasdaq), China BAK Battery, Inc. (CBAK:Nasdaq), and A123 Systems, Inc. (AONE:Nasdaq) might be viable investment ideas. These are just a few, and other battery makers that specialize in electronics batteries are starting to dabble in the auto industry, so the list keeps growing.

Battery demand is expected to climb to $22.8 billion by 2012.[26] And lithium-ion technology is going to gain market share quickly, as they are more efficient than the nickel metal-hydride batteries that the hybrid car market started out with.

And speaking of efficiency, there are a couple other companies that we might want to add to the list of Moto Metal investment ideas. Johnson Controls, Inc. (JCI:NYSE) and Lear Corp. (LEA:NYSE) are two companies to consider. JCI offers a number of automotive efficiency solutions, like electronic power distribution modules and battery management systems. These solutions are also available to the hybrid market. In essence, JCI's centrally integrated systems control how much power is needed where. This means fewer command components, less weight in the car, and lower costs to the consumer.

Lear makes and wires traditional power management systems, and hybrid electrical systems for cars and light trucks. The company has an array of solutions that cut weight and complexity in power management systems. Lear also makes high-voltage power distribution boxes and inverters, among other technologies that are key components to new hybrid and electric vehicles, and every little bit of power saving boosts efficiency.

Neither of these companies, however, is a pure play on Moto Metals. For that, you have to go to the source, and buy the metals themselves or the companies that mine them, such as FMC Corp. (FMC:NYSE), Freeport-McMoRan Copper and Gold, Inc. (FCX:NYSE), Chemical and Mining Company of Chile, Inc. (SQM:NYSE), Vale S.A. (VALE:NYSE), Stillwater Mining Co. (SWC:NYSE), North American Palladium Ltd. (PAL:NYSE), ETFS Physical Palladium Shares (PALL:NYSE), Platinum Group Metals Ltd. (PLG:AMEX), and ETFS Physical Platinum Shares (PPLT:NYSE)

These companies and investment securities are just the tip of the iceberg when it comes to metals and metal mining companies. Moto Metals have many applications outside the auto industry, too, such as the tech sector. No surprise there, since technological advances are revolutionizing the auto industry.

From these three ways to invest in Moto Metals, you can strategically position yourself based on what's already in your portfolio. You may already be holding some metal exchange-traded funds (ETFs) or mining companies in your portfolio as a hedge against inflation, so you might want to consider one of the other Moto Metal opportunities. Buying one of the new electric or hybrid vehicles coming to market wouldn't be a bad move. These new choices are generating substantial interest—and interest, not to mention demand, for Moto Metals will also grow. Remember, the Chevy Volt and the Nissan Leaf are just two of the first electric vehicles to hit the market, but there are more coming down the pipeline, and substantial political and financial backing to go with them.

Investing in the first wave of Moto Metals gets you in on the ground floor of this auto revolution, and the potential is astounding.

Chapter 24

Investment Strategies to Protect (and Grow) Your Wealth

In May 2008 an analyst predicted that we'd see oil climb as high as $200 a barrel, but it never reached that number. In the summer of that same year, oil peaked at $147 a barrel, and then by the following summer, it plunged to $35 a barrel. But that coincides with the height of the Great Recession when oil demand, on a global scale slowed.

Is it possible to believe that oil could go higher? The answer is *yes*. Already in the last quarter of 2010, as the Federal Reserve announced plans to dump more money into the U.S. economy under Quantitative Easing 2 (QE2), oil climbed to $84 a barrel.

Jared Levy, co-editor of *Smart Investing Daily,* likening the Fed's QE2 to playing Monopoly, writes:

With the billions of dollars already having being printed and $500 billion to $1 trillion expected in QE2, that puts severe downward pressure on the U.S. dollar. In Monopoly, this can be equated to every player owning property with hotels on it and going around the board just one time.[It] winds up costing you $5,000 or more. No more $4 rent on Baltic Ave.

In this example (or severe inflation), the dollar bills you have are basically worthless and you MUST have real estate to survive the game.

This is the simplest form of inflation; dollars become worth less and less, which equates to everything costing more and your "nest egg" of $100,000 cash may only get you around "life's Monopoly board" for a short time before you're broke from expenses.

So what happens when the dollar declines? As more money is created by the Fed, the United States, the dollar will weaken. Since commodities like oil are priced in U.S. dollars, a weaker dollar makes them more attractive to buyers who use foreign currencies. A weaker dollar will continue to drive higher gold, silver, and most all other dollar-denominated commodities. So, one of the best protective strategies is to have money in those types of investments including gold and even numismatics (collectible coins).

REITs Opportunities

There's another asset that will benefit as much as gold as the dollar declines, and that's real estate. I'm talking about real estate and hard assets such as raw land. Real estate and land will benefit from inflationary pressures that might come down the pike as the dollar continues to decline.

Even most of the stock market loves a weak dollar. Speaking of the market, one type of overlooked real estate–related investment is REITs (real estate investment trusts). REITs are organizations that combine the capital of many investors to either buy or finance real estate. That real estate could be in the form of office space, hotels, shopping centers, or apartments.

Think of a REIT as a mutual fund—a pool of money that a mutual fund manager oversees, buying and selling stocks that benefit the mutual fund. A REIT is required to invest at least 75 percent of its assets in real estate and pay out 95 percent of their income in the form of dividends. One of the advantages of investing in REITS is that they aren't as subject to volatility as, say, the S&P 500. That's because REITS move independent of the index. In fact the correlation between REITS and the S&P 500 is extremely low at .16 percent.[1]

But you have to pick the REIT that is best for you. REITS can be parceled off by sections of the country. You also need to know what kind of retail estate the REIT is holding. Is money invested in holding strip malls and grocery stores, or apartment buildings and hotels? For example, office-based REIT SL Green Realty Corporation (SLG) focuses on office space in New York. SLG has been aggressively buying high quality buildings because square footage leased in the first six months of 2010 has picked up in New York, where it was previously predicted to be on a decline. As more space is leased, the value of the REIT will increase. The REIT has been trading in the range of $66 to $67. See Figure 24.1 for its chart as of November, 2010.

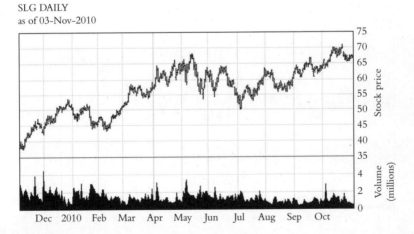

Figure 24.1   SLG Trades in the $66 to $67 Range
Data Source: © BigCharts.com.

Another type of REIT to consider is an investment in student housing. Even with the ebbs and flows of economic strength, young adults generally continue to head off to college to begin their journey into the work force and adulthood. Though the economy may dictate whether their parents send them to Princeton or a state college, these students need a place to live. If you travel to almost any major college campus around the U.S., you are sure to find student-focused housing, either in the form of individual properties (houses) that have been broken up into multi-unit apartments or larger buildings especially constructed to house students.

Being a landlord of student housing may be inherently less risky from a default perspective than being a regular landlord because the parents usually co-sign the lease, offering investors an extra layer of protection. Two REITs to choose from are: American Campus Communities Inc. (ACC), which is up 10 percent in November 2010, and EDR, mentioned next. See Figure 24.2.

The other student housing-related REIT is Education Realty Trust Inc., (EDR), which was up about 52 percent from December 2010 to November 2010. See Figure 24.3.

Both of these REITs (the ACC and the EDR) trade like stocks, and you can buy and sell as you see fit. By the way, both significantly outperformed the S&P in 2010. See Figure 24.4.

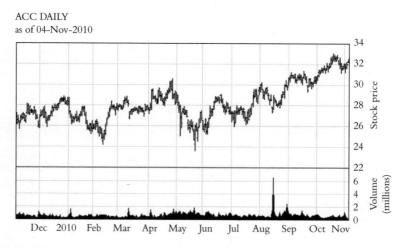

Figure 24.2   ACC was Up 10 Percent in November 2010
DATA Source: © BigCharts.com.

EDR DAILY
as of 04–Nov–2010

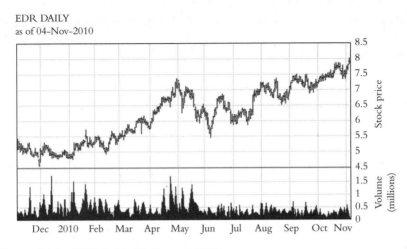

Figure 24.3   EDR is Up 52 Percent YTD
DATA Source: © BigCharts.com.

EDR DAILY
as of 04–Nov–2010

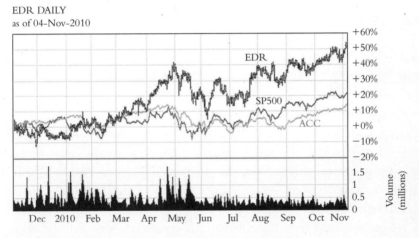

Figure 24.4   EDR and ACC Outperform the S&P 500
DATA Source: © BigCharts.com.

You can find more about REITs, listed by category at DividendDetective.com. (Note: The information is free on the Dividend Detective website and should be used as a starting point for your research.)

Another investment strategy we strongly recommend is alternative energy sources. In earlier chapters (21 through 23) we reviewed the different types of alternatives sources including wind, geothermal, solar, and hybrid technology. In this chapter, we're going to highlight Green Power Metals, a driving force in the hybrid technology.

Cash In on the Clean Energy Future

As mentioned in Chapter 23, Green Power Metals ("Moto Metals") are metals such as lithium, nickel, platinum, cobalt, manganese, and silver. Consumer demand and new technological innovations in the auto industry are making these metals stars in today's renewable energy market, and the next generation of vehicles will use Green Power Metals in unprecedented amounts.

The past two years have seen a seismic shift in how the auto industry runs its business, manufactures cars, and adjusts to changing consumer and political clean energy demands. Now with the development of new clean power technology within the audio industry, investors can cash in on the hybrid future.

Green Power Metals are revolutionizing new clean power technology within the auto industry, and pure metals are an excellent way to cash in on the clean energy future. These metals are essential components of hybrid batteries and catalytic converters, among other complex auto parts. They play key roles in power generation and efficiency, and as consumer demand and the automotive market move toward higher fuel efficiency standards and new power options, such as plug-in hybrid technology, the demand for Green Power Metals is going to increase. And you can cash in on this hybrid future by investing in hybrid battery technology.

You already know that hybrid battery technology will be taking over the auto industry with all-electric vehicles and plug-in hybrids, like the Chevy Volt and the Nissan Leaf. You may have even seen that cute commercial with the polar bear hugging the new Nissan Leaf owner. Major auto-manufacturers are being joined by smaller companies looking to cash in on the trend for more efficient and hybrid vehicles with a number of new makes and models hitting the sales floor in the next couple years.

We're also seeing popular models getting an energy makeover, as we showed you in Chapter 23 with Ford's new Explorer that uses a lighter-weight unibody and new "EcoBoost" engine. These changes will help increase fuel economy by 30 percent. And the combination of new technologies, and more efficient older technologies, can offer investors new ways to profit from demand for more efficient vehicles.

Two Companies Leading the Way

Two companies will benefit from this trend. One, which we briefly mentioned in Chapter 23, is Lear Corporation (LEA). Lear Corp. has a global presence with operations in North and South America, Europe, and Asia. Its Electrical Power Management Systems division is geared up and ready for the hybrid future. According to the company, in 2012, 40 percent of a vehicle's cost will come from electronics. And Lear is ready with high-power systems that will be key technologies for hybrid batteries and alternative fuel vehicles. Lear focuses on everything, from the smallest high-voltage wiring to the most complex battery monitoring system, to help support fuel efficiency.

As an aside, Lear Corp. also makes seats for cars and trucks, and will be supplying the new Ford Explorer just mentioned with Soyfoam Seating Technology. Let's look at some numbers for Lear Corp:

- Price/Earnings: 3.34
- Price/Book: 1.94
- Debt/Equity: 1.49
- Free Cash Flow: $290.4 million
- PEG Ratio: 0.79

This P/E ratio seems low. We're using this company's trailing P/E ratio, which is calculated by dividing Lear's current share price by the past 12 months' earnings per share. One of the reasons this company's trailing P/E ratio is so low is because the company's earnings over the past 12 months have soared. In June 2009, the company lost $1.86 per share, but in December 2009, the company gained $1.01 per share, beating estimates of $0.73. This happened again in March 2010. Lear was expected to earn $0.86 per share, and actually earned $1.23 per share.

LEA DAILY
as of 4-Nov-2010

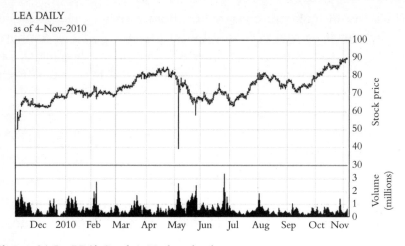

Figure 24.5   LEA's Stock is Undervalued
DATA Source: © BigCharts.com.

Now here's the big one: June 2010, earnings estimate were at $1.31—a huge boost over the previous quarter's estimates, and Lear posted earnings of $2.94! Sales growth is expected to be 16.8 percent this year and 13.2 percent next year. And on average, Lear has a P/E ratio of 13.70. Lear is undervalued, and with the hybrid future looming on the horizon, Lear could once again beat estimates. See Figure 24.5.

The second company worth considering is Rockwood Holdings Corporation (ROC). ROC's Chemetall is the leading producer of lithium compounds. Its Salar de Atacama resource has 31.5 million metric tons of lithium, enough to last more than 215 years! Last year, Chemetall was awarded $28.4 million by the U.S. Department of Energy to expand and upgrade production of lithium for its use in advance transportation batteries.[2] This was part of a $2.4 billion DoE program under the Recovery and Reinvestment Act.

Over the past year, ROC has climbed 77 percent, and second quarterly revenue grew 19.7 percent. This year, analysts estimate that ROC will pull in $2.01 in earnings per share. Next year, analysts expect $2.24. And over the last year, ROC has beaten estimates each of the last four quarters, by as little as 11.1 percent to as much as 123.8 percent. See Figure 24.6.

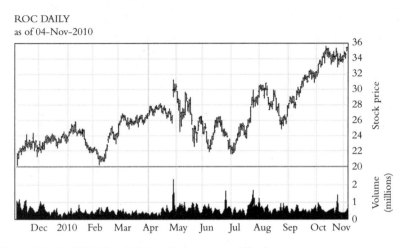

ROC DAILY
as of 04-Nov-2010

Figure 24.6 ROC Stock Price Continues to Climb
DATA Source: © BigCharts.com.

Market researcher Freedonia Group estimates that battery demand will jump to $22.8 billion a year by 2012.[3] The main components of batteries are metals, chemicals, and polymers.

And while nickel metal-hydride batteries currently hold the lion's share of the market, lithium ion batteries are proving to be more efficient and powerful. This Green Power Metal technology is expected to gain market share quickly. In fact, by 2012, it is estimated that nearly 2.5 million cars will be hybrid cars, and more than 1 million will be powered by lithium ion batteries. By 2014, more than 2 million hybrids will be powered by lithium ion batteries.

Lithium demand is expected to double by 2020, and battery makers and auto-manufacturers are buying stakes in mines. That makes Green Power Metals a long-term investment trend—one that will help you cash in on the hybrid future.

Pushing Back

The investment recommendations in this chapter as well as the companies mentioned in previous chapters are not only solid investments, but they offer you the opportunity to "push back" against the Barbarians of Oil.

Although the story of Samsø Island is encouraging, it would be unwise to believe that the United States could ever replicate the island's success. The truth is we probably will never become 100 percent energy independent, especially relying 100 percent on renewable energy sources.

But Samsø's story demonstrates what is possible. The residents of the island achieved 100 percent renewable energy independence because it had no conventional sources of energy to dictate its future. Being free of conventional energy sources allowed island residents to be unconventional in their thinking and in solving their energy problems. They also had the luxury of not being bound by the decisions of power-hungry politicians and greed-driven barbarians of the oil industry.

If there is anything to learn from Samsø, it's that becoming energy independent is a matter of choice. As American citizens, the choices we make now and over the next several years will determine what energy story we write for our future generations. And it is our hope in writing this book that we can help citizens make the right choices.

Notes

Chapter 1

1. Grant Smith, "OPEC Raises Its Forecast for Worldwide Oil Demand for This Year and Next," Bloomberg, August 13, 2010, www.bloomberg.com/news/2010-08-13/opec-raises-its-forecasts-for-worldwide-oil-demand-for-this-year-and-next.html.

2. A. Norman Tate, *Petroleum and Its Products: An Account of the History, Composition, Properties, Uses and Chemical Value* (London: John Davies, 1863), 1.

3. Colorado Geological Society, "Oil, Petroleum, Hydrocarbons: Words That Have Become Popular, But What Do They Mean?" *Rock Talk* 7, no. 2. Accessed September 2010.

4. Tate, *Petroleum and Its Products.*

5. Sir Boverton Redwood, *Petroleum: A Treatise on the Geographical Distribution,* 2nd ed. (London: Charles Griffon and Company, 1901), 2.

6. Pharmaceutical Society of Great Britain, "Petroleum and Its Products: Their Pharmaceutical Uses," *Pharmaceutical Journal: A Weekly Record of Pharmacy and Allied Sciences* (May 1856), 410.

7. *Encyclopedia Americana: A Library of Universal Knowledge,* vol. 21, "Petroleum," 687–688.

8. Pharmaceutical Society of Great Britain, "Petroleum and Its Products," 410.

9. Dr. Steve Sjuggerud, "Investment U, History of Oil," August 2004, www.investmentu.com/2004/August/20040811.html.

10. James H. Gary and Glenn E. Handwerk, *Petroleum Refining: Technology and Economics*, 4th ed. (New York: Marcel Dekker, 2001), 5.

11. Library of Congress, "Business Reference Services, Oil & Gas Refining," Spring 2006.

12. "Number and Capacity of Oil Refineries," U.S. Energy Information Administration, www.eia.doe.gov/dnav/pet/pet_pnp_cap1_dcu_nus_a.htm. Accessed June 2010.

13. Katrina Arade, "Industry Market Trends, How Oil Refining Transformed U.S. History and Way of Life," Thomas Net News, January 2003, http://news.thomasnet.com/IMT/archives/2003/01/how_oil_refinin.html.

14. Gretchen Krueger, *Opportunities in Petroleum Careers* (New York: McGraw-Hill), 2008.

15. Dr. Jean-Paul Rodrique, *The Geography of Transport Systems* (New York: Routledge, 2006), chap. 5.

16. Akweli Parker, "How Oil Tankers Work," http://science.howstuffworks.com/transport/engines-equipment/oil-tanker.htm. Accessed April 2009.

17. Rodrique, *The Geography of Transport Systems*.

18. U.S. Energy Administration, "Number and Capacity of Oil Refineries."

19. "Largest Oil Companies in the World," www.quoteoil.com/oil-companies.html Accessed September 2010.

20. "World's Largest Oil and Gas Companies," PetroStrategies, Inc., www.petrostrategies.org/Links/Worlds_Largest_Oil_and_Gas_Companies_Sites.htm. Accessed December 2010.

21. "Major Disruptions of World Oil Supply," Energy Information Administration, www.eia.doe.gov/emeu/25opec/sld001.htm.

22. Dr. Steve Sjuggerud, "Investment U, History of Oil."

23. "U.S. Petroleum Reserves," U.S. Department of Energy, www.fe.doe.gov/programs/reserves/index.html.

24. Richard Gibson, "What's the Deal with Oil?" Gibson Consulting online, 2005, www.gravmag.com/oilessay.shtml.

25. "Major Disruptions of World Oil Supply."

26. Ibid.

27. Ibid.

28. Gibson, "What's the Deal with Oil?"

29. Jennifer Horton, "Is the United States Addicted to Gasoline?" http://science.howstuffworks.com/environmental/green-science/us-gas-addiction.htm. Accessed August 2008.

30. "Showroom of Automotive History: The Model T," www.hfmgv.org/exhibits/showroom/1908/model.t.html. Accessed September 2010.

31. Arade, "Industry Market Trends."

32. Krueger, *Opportunities in Petroleum Careers*, 10.

33. "Gasoline Service Stations," www.manta.com/mb_34_B121D_000/gasoline_service_stations. Accessed September 2010.

34. "History of Gasoline," American Auto Shipping, www.americanautoshipping.com/history-of-gasoline.asp.

35. "U.S. Retail Gasoline Prices," U.S. Energy Information Administration, www.eia.doe.gov/petroleum/data_publications/wrgp/mogas_home_page.html. Accessed September 2010.

36. Horton, "Is the United States Addicted to Gasoline?"

37. Ibid.

38. *OPEC Monthly Oil Market Report*, August 2010, www.opec.org/opec_web/en/.

39. Anthony Simpson, "The Seven Sisters: The Great Oil Companies and the World They Made," Hodder and Stoughton, 1975, http://journeytoforever.org/biofuel_library/sevensisters/7sistersToC.html.

Chapter 2

1. Abraham Gesner, "Famous Americans, Virtual American Biographies," www.famousamericans.net/abrahamgesner/.

2. Katherine McLean Brevard, *The Story of Oil: How It Changed the World* (Mankato, MN: Compass Point Books, 2010).

3. William Moore and Joshua Sherretts, *Oil Boom Architecture: Titusville, Pithole and Petroleum Center* (Charleston, SC: Arcadia Publishing, 2008).

4. *The Encyclopedia of Americana: A Library of Universal Knowledge*, vol. 21, 685.

5. David Weber, *Around Titusville* (Charleston, SC: Arcadia Publishing, 2004).

6. "Petroleum Education: Oil in Your Backyard," Paleontological Research Institute, www.priweb.org/ed/pgws/backyard/sections/northeast/northeast1.html.

7. *The Derrick's Hand-Book of Petroleum*, vol. 2 (Derrick Publishing Company, 1900).

8. "Petroleum Education: Oil in Your Backyard."

9. Ruth Knowles, *Greatest Gamblers: The Epic of American Oil Exploration* (Norman: University of Oklahoma Press, 1959.

10. Dr. William Brice, "Myth Legend Reality—Edwin Drake and the Early Oil Industry," August 2008, www.oil150.com/essays/2008/04/_edwin-laurentine-drake-1819-1880_-by-dr-william-r-brice.

11. "Biography: Anthony Lucas," Spindletop-Gladys City Boomtown Museum, www.spindletop.org/history/lucas.htm. Accessed September 2010.

12. Ibid.

13. Neil McElwee, "Guffey and Galey—Some People Get Around," 2007, www.oil150.com/essays/2007/12/guffey-and-galey-some-people-get-around.

14. "Spindletop: Great Texas Oil Gusher Is Painted for Life," *Life*, February 10, 1941, 41.

15. Ibid.

16. "Oil and Gas Production, History in California," http://docs.google.com/viewer?a=v&q=cache:sA2DM2X4S7wJ:ftp://ftp.consrv.ca.gov/pub/oil/history/History_of_Calif.pdf+Humboldt+Times+reports+oil+seeps+in+1859&hl=en&gl=us&pid=bl&srcid=ADGEESgpfOmAR_khk6SU1QG6uQi4cBmymP6EddSwFilQ9C3sz7kvifq6M7sAZXaXY5DOyIlIs3Tohf5usay_rBhPhijlq-zAThwIs5_EtflSxnIA5YXCYQHY6rd5cBKZ7bl_qteq8rmy&sig=AHIEtbRKHVAvpB-q5VYFpfSG8yd7ljoj5Q.Accessed September 2010.

17. Lionel Redpath, *Petroleum in California: A Concise and Reliable History of the Oil Industry* (Los Angeles: Lionel Redpath, 1900), 10.

18. Margaret L. Davis, *Dark Side of Fortune: Triumph and Scandal in the Life of Oil Tycoon Edward L. Doheny* (Berkeley, CA: University of California Press, 1998), 9.

19. Ibid., 10.

20. Ibid., 23.

21. Ibid., 29.

22. John Thompson, *Political Scandal: Power and Visibility in the Media Age* (Cambridge, UK: Polity Press, 2000), 181.

23. Lanny Davis, *Scandal: How "Gotcha" Politics Is Destroying America* (New York: Palgrave MacMillan, 2006), 35.

24. David H. Stratton, *Tempest Over Teapot Dome: The Story of Albert B. Fall* (Norman, OK: University of Oklahoma Press, 1998), xiv.

Chapter 3

1. Charles Whiteshot, *The Oil-Well Driller: A History of the World's Greatest Enterprise, The Oil Industry* (Mannington, VA: Charles A. Whiteshot, 1905), 50.

2. John Ingham, *Biographical Dictionary of American Business Leaders* (Westport, CT: Greenwood Press, 1983), 77.

3. "The Story of Oil in Pennsylvania," Petroleum Education, History of Pennsylvania, www.priweb.org/ed/pgws/history/pennsylvania/pennsylvania.html. Accessed September 2010.

4. "Chemical Report of Seep Oil," Petroleum History.org, Oil History, www.petroleumhistory.org/OilHistory/pages/drake/chemical.html. Accessed September 2010.

5. Whiteshot, *The Oil-Well Driller*, 895.

6. Ibid, 118.

7. Brian Black, "Oil Creek As an Industrial Apparatus: Re-creating the Industrial Process Through the Landscape of Pennsylvania's Oil Boom," The Forest History Society, http://webcache.googleusercontent.com/search?q=cache:F-rXEql89joJ:isites.harvard.edu/fs/docs/icb.topic667366.files/Oil%2520Creek%2520as%2520Industrial%2520Apparatus.pdf1terrain1of1oil1creek&hl=en&gl=us. Accessed September 2010.

8. Whiteshot, *The Oil-Well Driller*, 378.

9. "The History of Crude Oil," Live Oil Prices, www.liveoilprices.co.uk/crude_oil/the_history_of_crude_oil.html. Accessed September 2010.

10. "Early Oil Transportation, A Brief History," http://webcache.googleusercontent.com/search?q=cache:_XlzKoJNbrwJ:www.oil150.com/assets/early-oil-transportation-a-brief-history.pdf1transporting1oil1in1titusville&hl=en&gl=us. Accessed September 2010.

11. Ibid.

12. Black, "Oil Creek As an Industrial Apparatus."

13. Whiteshot, *The Oil-Well Driller*, 143.

14. Ibid.

15. John Schmidt, *Growing Up in the Oil Patch* (Toronto: Natural Heritage Books, 1989), 9.

16. "History of Pipelines," www.pipeline101.com/history/timeline.html.

17. "Early Oil Transportation, A Brief History," http://webcache.googleusercontent.com/search?q=cache:_XlzKoJNbrwJ:www.oil150.com/assets/early-oil-transportation-a-brief-history.pdf1transporting1oil1in1titusville&hl=en&gl=us. Accessed September 2010.

18. Jesse Jarnow, *Oil, Steel and Railroads: America's Big Businesses in the Late 1800s* (New York: Rosen Publishing Group, 2004), 4.

19. "Coryville, 1879: Tidewater Pipe Company-World's 1st Successful Pipeline," Smethporthistory.com, www.smethporthistory.org/coryville/oilarticle.html. Accessed September 2010.

20. "Historical Markers," http://explorepahistory.com/hmarker.php?markerId=663. Accessed September 2010.

21. Ibid.

22. Ibid.

23. Schmidt, *Growing Up in the Oil Patch* (Toronto: Dundurn Press, LTD, 1989), 8.

24. Whiteshot, *The Oil-Well Driller*, 24.

25. Thomas Baynes, ed., *The Encyclopedia Britannica: A Dictionary of Arts, Sciences and General Literature*, vol. 10, 191.

26. Ibid.

27. William Brannt, Hans Hofer, and Alexander Veith, *Petroleum: Its History, Origin, Occurrence, Production, Physical and Chemical Constitution* (Philadelphia: Henry Carey Baird), 221.

Chapter 4

1. *The Derrick's Hand-Book of Petroleum: A Complete Chronological and Statistical Review* (Derrick Publishing Company, 1898), 951.

2. Alfred N. Mann, "Some Petroleum Pioneers of Pittsburgh," http://webcache .googleusercontent.com/search?q=cache:Hx0aBgM51PYJ:www.heinzhistory center.org/secondary.aspx?id%3D234%26contentID%3D4171samuel1kier1di stilling1method&hl=en&gl=us. Accessed September 2010.

3. *The Derrick's Handbook of Petroleum*, 947.

4. Mann, "Some Petroleum Pioneers of Pittsburgh."

5. Ibid.

6. David Rosenbaum, ed., *Market Dominance, How Firms Gain, Hold, or Lose It and the Impact on Economic Performance*, (Westport, CT: Praeger Publishers, 1998), 12.

7. "Chicago History, Refining," *Encyclopedia of Chicago*, http://encyclopedia .chicagohistory.org/pages/1052.html. Accessed September 2010.

8. Frank Moore Colby, *The New International Yearbook*, vol. 1914 (New York: Dodd, Mead and Company), 553.

9. "Petroleum Industry," Gale Encyclopedia of U.S. History: Petroleum, www .answers.com/topic/petroleum-industry. Accessed September 2010.

10. "Oil, Demand," U.S. Energy Information Administration, www.eia.doe .gov/pub/oil_gas/petroleum/analysis_publications/oil_market_basics/ demand_text.htm. Accessed September 2010.

11. William Bottorff, "What Was the First Car? A Quick History of the Automobile for Young People," www.ausbcomp.com/~bbott/cars/carhist. htm. Accessed September 2010.

12. Bulletin, United States National Museum, Bibliolife, 144–145.

13. Manfred Weissenbacher, *Sources of Power: How Energy Forges Human History*, vols. 1 & 2 (Santa Barbara, CA: Greenwood Publishing, 2009), 377.

14. Peter D'Epiro, *The Book of Firsts: 150 World Changing People and Events from Caesar Augustus to the Internet* (New York: Anchor Books, 2010), 544.

15. "The Origin of the Automobile," Motorera.com, Automobile History, www.motorera.com/history/history.htm. Accessed September 2010.

16. D'Epiro, *The Book of Firsts*, 544.

17. Ibid.

18. "Henry Ford," www.spartacus.schoolnet.co.uk/USAford.htm. Accessed September 2010.

19. Ibid.

20. William Leffler, *Petroleum Refining in Nontechnical Language*, 4th ed. (Tulsa, OK: PenWell Corporation, 2008), 3.

21. Sebastian Blanco, "Number of Cars in the U.S. Dropped by 4 Million," Autobloggreen.com, January 4, 2010, http://green.autoblog.com/2010/01/04/report-number-of-cars-in-the-u-s-dropped-by-four-million-in-20/.

22. "National Average Prices," AAA's Daily Fuel Gauge Report, www.fuelgaugereport.com/. Accessed September 2010.

23. Institute for Energy Research, www.instituteforenergyresearch.org/energy-overview/petroleum-oil, February 25, 2010. Accessed February 2010.

24. Ibid.

25. Robert Crandall, Barry Felrice, Sam Kazman, and W. Montgomery, "Fuel Economy Standards: Do They Work? Do They Kill?," The Heritage Foundation, March 8, 2002, www.heritage.org/research/reports/2002/03/fuel-economy-standards.

26. "From the Battlefield to the Soccer Field," *TSC Newsletter*, vol. 2, no. 4 (Summer 2005), www.tsc.berkeley.edu/newsletter/Summer05-SUVs/history.html.

Chapter 5

1. Ida M. Tarbell, "History of the Standard Oil Company," Chapter 1, www.history.rochester.edu/fuels/tarbell/UPTO37.HTM. Accessed October 2010.

2. "People & Events: John D. Rockefeller," *The Rockefellers*, PBS.org, American Experience, www.pbs.org/wgbh/amex/rockefellers/peopleevents/p_rock_jsr.html. Accessed October 2010.

3. Tarbell, "History of the Standard Oil Company," Chapter 2 .

4. "People & Events: John D. Rockefeller."

5. Tarbell, "History of the Standard Oil Company," Chapter 2.

6. "People & Events: John D. Rockefeller."

7. Tarbell, "History of the Standard Oil Company," Chapter 2.

8. Silas Hubbard, *John D. Rockefeller and His Career*, vol. 3 (New York: Silas Hubbard, 1914), 23.

9. Ibid.

10. "John D. Rockefeller," Ancestory.com message boards, posted September 14, 2008, http://boards.ancestry.com/topics.obits2/16944/mb.ashx?pnt=1.

11. Burton Folson, "John D. Rockefeller and The Oil Industry," *The Freeman Ideas on Liberty* 38 (October 1988), www.thefreemanonline.org/columns/john-d-rockefeller-and-the-oil-industry/#.

12. Grant Segall, *John D. Rockefeller: Anointed with Oil* (New York: Oxford University Press, 2001), 36.

13. Ron Chernow, *Titan: The Life of John D. Rockefeller*, 2nd ed. (New York: Vintage Books, 2004), 27.

14. "The Rockefeller Monopoly," www.hermes-press.com/rocky1.htm. Accessed October 2010.

15. Londonlady, "John D. Rockefeller: A Robber Baron?," http://hubpages.com/hub/John-D-Rockefeller-A-robber-baron. Accessed October 2010.

16. "People & Events: Ida Tarbell," PBS.org, *The Rockefellers*, www.pbs.org/wgbh/amex/rockefellers/peopleevents/p_tarbell.html. Accessed October 2010.

17. Gilbert Montague, *The Rise and Progress of the Standard Oil Company* (Batoche Books, Kitchener, 2003), socserv.mcmaster.ca/~econ/ugcm/3ll3/montague/standardoil.pdf.

18. Ibid.

19. "History of the Lake Shore and Michigan Railroad Company," www.s363.com/dkny/lsms.html.

20. Hubbard, *John D. Rockefeller and His Career*, 24–28.

21. Ibid.

22. Whiteshot, *The Oil-Well Driller*, 597.

23. Ibid.

24. "Rockefeller," www.spartacus.schoolnet.co.uk/USArockefeller.htm.

25. Michael Reksulak and William Shughart II, "Of Rebates and Drawbacks: The Standard Oil (N.J.) Company and the Railroads," School of Economic Development, Georgia Southern University, http://docs.google.com/viewer?a=v&q=cache:4zzTLyuiSZgJ:home.olemiss.edu/~shughart/Standard_Oil.pdf1standard1oil%27s1secret1rebates&hl=en&gl=us&pid=bl&srcid=ADGEEShuCIT5cg2HkwG2LliBfgYbwZBmdA2LcdkkbYIvJNASPPixamwQJqytZY-9nIsq_3lS9W7_G43fAlMMei58clI-wcRVUFcJOmzC5zcoDOLEmr4rc43rnMYkWBCcYG0uALmqNFzg&sig=AHIEtbQg8t4LVBEiABfiu0oWZuI-6xZbLw. Accessed October 2010.

26. Hubbard, *John D. Rockefeller and His Career*, 24–28.

27. Bnet, "The Return of Big Oil—Exxon-Mobil Merger Represents Dangerous Thinking," *The Progressive*, January 1999, http://findarticles.com/p/articles/mi_m1295/is_1_63/ai_53531051/.

28. "Company Histories, Exxon Mobil Corporation," www.fundinguniverse. com/company-histories/Exxon-Mobil-Corporation-Company-History. html. Accessed October 2010.

29. Cutler Cleveland, "*Exxon Valdez* Oil Spill," June 9, 2010, www.eoearth. org/article/Exxon_Valdez_oil_spill?topic=58075.

30. "Oil: Exxon's Chairman's $400 Million Parachute," *ABC News*, April 4, 2006, http://abcnews.go.com/GMA/story?id=1841989&page=1&gma=tru e&gma=true.

Chapter 6

1. "Murex," Shipwrecks of Egypt, www.shipwrecksofegypt.com/images/ shippages/murex.html. Accessed October 2010.

2. Ibid.

3. Ibid.

4. Ron Chernow, *Titan: The Life of John Rockefeller, Sr.*, 2nd ed. (New York: Vintage Books, 2004, original copyright Ron Chernow, 1998), 248.

5. James Dodd Henry, *Thirty-Five Years of Oil Transport: The Evolution of the Tank Steamer* (London: Bradbury, Agnew, 1907), 33.

6. Ibid.

7. "Indonesia," Encyclopedia of the Nations, www.nationsencyclopedia.com/ Asia-and-Oceania/Indonesia-LOCATION-SIZE-AND-EXTENT.html. Accessed October 2010.

8. "Indonesia: History, Geography, Government, and Culture," www.infoplease. com/ipa/A0107634.html#ixzz111oLMK00. Accessed October 2010.

9. "Indonesia, Oil," Energy Information Administration, Independent Statistics and Analysis, www.eia.doe.gov/cabs/Indonesia/Oil.html. Accessed October 2010.

10. J. P. Poley, *Eroica: The Quest for Oil in Indonesia* (Norwell, MA: Kluwer Academic Publishers, 2000), 81.

11. Daniel Yergin, *The Prize: The Epic Quest for Oil* (New York: Free Press, Simon & Schuster, 1991, 1992, 2008), 57.

12. Poley, *Eroica*, 82.

13. A. Beeby Thompson, *Oil Field Development and Petroleum Mining: A Practical Guide to the Exploration of Petroleum Lands* (London: D. Van Nostrand & Company, 1916), 42.

14. Yergin, *The Prize*, 57.

15. Ibid.

16. A. J. Barber, Michael Crow, and John Milsom, *Sumatra: Geology, Resources and Tectonic Revolution*, Memoir No.# 31, 131 (Geology Society of London, 2005).

17. F. C. Gerretson, *History of the Royal Dutch*, vol. 1 (Royal Dutch Petroleum Company, 1958), 127.

18. Stephen Pelletiere, *Iraq and the International Oil System: Why America Went to War in the Gulf* (Westport, CT: Praeger Publishers, 2001), 16.

19. Yergin, *The Prize*, 60.

20. Paul Frankel, *Essentials of Petroleum: A Key to Oil Economics* (New York: Frank Cass and Company Limited, 1946, 1969, 1973, 1976, 1983, 2005), 92.

21. Marcy Gordon, "SEC Fines Royal Dutch/Shell $120," The Associated Press, 2004, www.law.com/jsp/article.jsp?id=900005413749. Accessed October 2010.

22. Justin Blum, "U.S., Britain Fine Shell $150 Million For Lying On Oil Reserves," *Washington Post*, August 2004, www.corpwatch.org/article .php?id=11507. Accessed October 2010.

23. "Compliance Reporter," Royal Dutch Shell Group, November 1, 2004, www.shellnews.net/2004%20Documents/codds/compliance_reporter 1nov04.htm.

24. Chip Cummins, "Shell Trader, Unit Are Fined Over Bogus Oil Trades," *Wall Street Journal*, January 5, 2006, www.corpwatch.org/article. php?id=13039.

25. John Donovan, "Shell's Shocking Track Record of Unethical Trading in the U.S.," April 12, 2008, Blogger News Network, www.bloggernews .net/115102.

26. John Vidal, "Nigeria's Agony Dwarfs the Gulf Oil Spill. The U.S. and Europe Ignore It," *The Observer*, May 30, 2010, www.guardian.co.uk/ world/2010/may/30/oil-spills-nigeria-niger-delta-shell.

27. "UNEP Investigation into Shell Oil Spills in Nigeria Ongoing," www .suite101.com/content/unep-investigation-into-shell-oil-spills-in-nigeria-ongoing-a278514#ixzz112HArCWg. Accessed October 2010.

28. Daniel Howden, "Report Blames Shell Over Cover-Up of Nigeria Oil Spills," *The Independent*, July 1, 2009, www.independent.co.uk/news/world/ africa/report-blames-shell-over-coverup-of-nigerias-oil-spills-1726207.html.

29. Caroline Duffield, "Nigeria: World Oil Pollution Capital," BBC News, June 15, 2010, www.bbc.co.uk/news/10313107.

30. Kerry Sheridan, "Environment Group Warns of Artic Oil Drilling Risks," Yahoo! News, November 10, 2010, http://news.yahoo.com/s/ afp/20101110/ts_alt_afp/environmentusarcticoil.

31. "90 Billion Barrels of Oil and 1,760 Trillion Cubic Feet of Natural Gas Assessed in the Arctic," USGS Newsroom, July 23, 2008, www.usgs.gov/ newsroom/article.asp?ID=1980&from=rss_home.

Chapter 7

1. Wah Keung Chan, "The Voice of Caruso," *La Scena Musicale* 7, no. 7 (April 1, 2002), www.scena.org/lsm/sm7-7/caruso-en.html.

2. "William Knox D'Arcy," Academic Dictionary and Encyclopedias, http://en.academic.ru/dic.nsf/enwiki/122710. Accessed October 2010.

3. "Knox D'Arcy—The First Great Oil Tycoon," www.turtlebunbury.com/history/history_heroes/hist_hero_knoxdarcy.html. Accessed October 2010.

4. Zvi Yehuda Hershlag and E.J. Brill, *Introduction to Modern Economic History in the Middle East* (Leiden, The Netherlands, 1980), 359.

5. Ibid.

6. Nathan Aaseng, *Business Builders in Oil* (Minneapolis: Oliver Press, 2001), 81.

7. "Knox D'Arcy—The First Great Oil Tycoon."

8. Ibid.

9. "Francis Hopwood, 1st Baron Southborough," *Wikipedia*, www.ask.com/wiki/Francis_Hopwood,_1st_Baron_Southborough.

10. *The World's Work*, vol. 40 (Doubleday, Page & Company, 1920), 49.

11. Clarence Walton and Ronald Duska, *Education, Leadership and Business Ethics* (Norwell, MA: Kluwer Academic Publishers, 1998), 241.

12. "Ango-Iranian Oil Company," www.answers.com/topic/anglo-iranian-oil-company.

13. James Bill, *The Eagle and the Lion: The Tragedy of American-Iranian Relations*, (New Haven, CT: Yale University Press, 1988), 58.

14. Lewis Kaplan, *God Bless You Joe Stalin: The Man Who Saved Capitalism* (New York: Algora Publishing, 2006), 123.

15. Walton and Duska, *Education, Leadership and Business Ethics*, 241.

16. James O'Rourke, *The Businesss Communication Casebook: A Notre Dame Collection* (Soldotna, AK: Thomson-South-Western, 2004, 2007), 10.

17. "BP America," *Encyclopedia of Cleveland*, http://ech.cwru.edu/ech-cgi/article.pl?id=BA. Accessed October 2010.

18. David Dayen, "BP Spilled 4.4 Million Barrels into Gulf, According to New Estimates," September 25, 2010, http://news.firedoglake.com/2010/09/25/bp-spilled-4-4-million-barrels-into-gulf-according-to-new-estimate/.

19. Wade Goodwyn. "Previous BP Accidents Blamed on Safety Lapses," May 6, 2010, www.npr.org/templates/story/story.php?storyId=126564739&ft=1&f=2&utm_source=feedburner&utm_medium=feed&utm_campaign=Feed%3A1NprProgramsATC1%28NPR1Programs%3A1All1Things1Considered%29.

20. Ibid.

21. Craig Welch, "BP's Trail of Accidents, Scandals Stretches to Alaska," *Seattle Times*, May 5, 2010, http://seattletimes.nwsource.com/html/localnews/2011791796_bpalaska06m.html?syndication=rss.

22. Ibid.

23. "BP Profit Plunges on Another Spill Charge," *E&P News*, November 2, 2010, www.rigzone.com/news/article.asp?a_id=100843.

24. Steven Mufson, "BP Facing a Wave of Pressure, But Not from Its Balance Sheet," *Washington Post*, May 11, 2010, www.washingtonpost.com/wp-dyn/content/article/2010/05/10/AR2010051004664.html.

Chapter 8

1. Hubert Bancroft, *Chronicles of the Builders of the Commonwealth: Historical Character Study*, vol. 4 (The Historical Publishers, 1892), 360.

2. Ibid.

3. Ibid., 366–370.

4. Ibid.

5. Ibid.

6. "About Us," Conoco Company History, www.conocophillips.com/EN/about/who_we_are/history/conoco/Pages/index.aspx#1875. Accessed October 2010.

7. "ConocoPhillips Profit Tops $1 Billion," Tulsa World-McClatchy-Tribune Information Services, January 28, 2010, www.tradingmarkets.com/news/stock-alert/cop_conoco-phillips-profit-tops-1-billion-fourth-quarter-results-reflect-higher-production-and-a-lowe-735044.html.

8. Sarah Ives and Robynne Boyd, "Pick Your Poison," ConocoPhillips, January/February 2007, www.sierraclub.org/sierra/pickyourpoison/#conoco.

9. Nicholas Gerainos, "Plans to Haul Big Oil Refinery Loads Spark Battle," *News Tribune*, September 26, 2010, www.thenewstribune.com/2010/09/26/1357310/big-oil-refinery-loads-spark-big.html#storylink=mirelated.

10. Ives and Boyd, "Pick Your Poison."

11. David Sneed, "ConocoPhillips to Clean Oil Spill," *The Tribune*, September 5, 2010, www.sanluisobispo.com/2010/09/04/1276393/conocophillips-to-clean-oil-spill.html.

12. "Brief History of Oil Development in Pico Canyon," www.elsmerecanyon.com/picocanyon/history/history.htm.

13. "Oil," www.californiabusinesshistory.com/page31/oil.html. Accessed October 2010.

14. "Development of the Oil Business in California," *Standard Oil Bulletin* 1 (May 1913), 11.

15. "Leading the Way, 1876–1911: The Quest for Black Gold," Chevron, www
.chevron.com/about/leadership/history/1876/. Accessed October 2010.

16. Ibid.

17. Ibid.

18. "Chevron Revenue Tops Views, but Profit Misses Forecast," *Fox Business News*, Matt Egan, October 20, 2010, www.foxbusiness.com/markets/2010/10/29/chevron-revenue-beats-profit-misses-forecast/.

19. Ben Casselman, "Chevron Expects to Fight Ecuador lawsuit in U.S.," *Wall Street Journal*, July 20, 2009, http://finance.yahoo.com/insurance/article/107364/chevron-expects-to-fight-ecuador-lawsuit-in-us.html.

20. Ibid.

Chapter 9

1. "Cartel," *Merriam-Webster Online Dictionary*, August 10, 2010, www.merriam-webster.com/dictionary/cartel.

2. Nathan J. Citino, *From Arab Nationalism to OPEC: Eisenhower, King Sa'ūd, and the Making of U.S-Saudi Relations* (Bloomington: Indiana University Press, 2002), 1.

3. Ibid.

4. Francisco Parra, *Oil Politics: A Modern History of Petroleum* (London, New York: I.B. Tauris & Co. Ltd., 2004), 11.

5. Ibid., 6.

6. Ibid., 9.

7. Douglas Little, *American Orientalism: The United States and the Middle East Since 1945*, 3rd ed. (Chapel Hill, NC: University of North Carolina Press, 2008), 60.

8. Ibid.

9. Shireen Hunter, *OPEC and the Third World: The Politics of Aid*, (Sydney: Croom Helm Ltd., 1984), 11.

10. "OPEC: Brief History, Organization of the Petroleum Exporting Countries," August 12, 2010, www.opec.org/opec_web/en/about_us/24.htm.

11. Citino, *From Arab Nationalism to OPEC*, 40.

12. Hunter, *OPEC and the Third World*, 15.

13. Ian Skeet, *OPEC: Twenty-Five Years of Prices and Politics* (Cambridge, UK: Press Syndicate of the University of Cambridge, 1988), 22.

14. Ibid., 16.

15. Ibid., 22.

16. Ibid., 29.

17. Ibid., 6.

18. Margaret McQuaile, "The Parallel Worlds of OPEC Quotas and Actual Production," *The Barrel*, November 11, 2009, www.platts.com/weblog/oilblog/2009/11/11/the_parallel_wo.html.

19. Ibid.

20. Maher Chmaytelli and Margot Habiby, "OPEC Agrees to Cut Production Quotas as Price Slumps (Update3)," Bloomberg.com, October 24, 2008, www.bloomberg.com/apps/news?pid=newsarchive&sid=azg0in03PRLk&refer=energy.

21. Helen Chapin Metz, ed. "Oil Industry," in *Saudi Arabia: A Country Study* (Washington, DC: GPO for the Library of Congress, 1992), http://countrystudies.us/saudi-arabia/40.htm.

22. Skeet, *OPEC: Twenty-Five Years of Prices and Politics*, 29.

23. Helen Chapin Metz, ed. "Post-World War II Through the 1970s," in *Iraq: A Country Study* (Washington, DC: GPO for the Library of Congress, 1988), http://countrystudies.us/iraq/54.htm.

24. "Iraq Petroleum Company," *Encyclopedia of the Modern Middle East and North Africa* (The Gale Group, Inc.). www.answers.com/topic/iraq-petroleum-company. Accessed August 2010.

25. Helen Chapin Metz, ed. "The Reigns of Saud and Faisal," in *Saudi Arabia: A Country Study* (Washington: GPO for the Library of Congress, 1992) http://countrystudies.us/saudi-arabia/11.htm.

26. Ibid.

27. Ibid.

28. Ibid.

29. Skeet, *OPEC: Twenty-Five Years of Prices and Politics*, 26.

30. Metz, "Oil Industry."

Chapter 10

1. Michael Kramer, "What's Happening in the Middle East—This Time," *New York Magazine*, June 1, 1981, 19.

2. John F. Murphy, *The United Nations and the Control of International Violence: A Legal and Political Analysis* (Manchester, NY: Manchester University Press, 1983), 44.

3. Raymond A. Hinnebusch, *The International Politics of the Middle East* (Manchester, NY: Manchester University Press), 174.

4. Kramer, "What's Happening in the Middle East—This Time," 19.

5. James E. Dougherty, "The Aswan Decision in Perspective," *Political Science Quarterly* 74, no. 1 (March 1959): 22.

6. Pierre Tristam, "What Is Egypt's Suez Canal?," About.com Guide, http://middleeast.about.com/od/egypt/f/me080803c.htm. Accessed October 2010.

7. "Consideration of the Provisions of Article 25 of the Charter," Chapter XII in Repertoire of the Practice of the Security Council, Supplement 19524955, United Nations Department of Political and Security Council Affairs (New York, 1957), www.un.org/en/sc/repertoire/52-55/52-55_12.pdf.

8. Michael B. Oren, *Six Days of War: June 1967 and the Making of the Modern Middle East* (New York: Presidio Press Books and Random House Ballantine Publishing Group, 2003), 10.

9. Thomas Risse-Kappen, *Cooperation among Democracies: The European Influence on U.S. Foreign Policy.* (Princeton, NJ: Princeton University Press, 1995), 94.

10. Isaac Alteras, *Eisenhower and Israel: U.S.–Israeli Relations, 1953–1960* (Gainesville, FL: University Press of Florida, 1993), 246.

11. Ibid., 252.

12. Ibid., 259.

13. Ibid., 261.

14. Isabella Ginor and Gideon Remez, *Foxbats over Dimona: The Soviets' Nuclear Gamble in the Six-Day War* (New Haven, CT: Yale University Press, 2007), 2.

15. Oren, *Six Days of War*, 23.

16. Chaim Herzog and Shlomo Gazit, *The Arab-Israeli Wars: War and Peace in the Middle East*, 2nd ed. (New York: Vintage Books, 2005),154.

17. Yaacov Ro'i and Boris Morozov, *The Soviet Union and the June 1967 Six-Day War* (Washington, DC: Woodrow Wilson Center Press, 2008), 43–44.

18. Herzog and Gazit, *The Arab-Israeli Wars*, 148.

19. Ginor and Remez, *Foxbats over Dimona*, 22.

20. Indar Jit Rikhye, *The Sinai Blunder: Withdrawal of the United Nations Emergency Force Leading to the Six-Day War of June 1967* (London: Frank Cass and Company Limited, 1980), 74.

21. Ibid.

22. Richard W. Bulliet, Pamela Kyle Crossley, Daniel R. Headrick, Steven W. Hirsch, and Lyman L. Johnson, *The Earth and Its Peoples: A Global History, Volume 2—Since 1500*, 4th ed. (Boston: Cengage Learning, 2008), 783.

23. Hinnebusch, *The International Politics of the Middle East*, 168.

24. Rikhye, *The Sinai Blunder*, 100.

25. Herzog and Gazit, *The Arab-Israeli Wars*, 161.

26. Oren, *Six Days of War*, 156.

27. Ibid., 212.

28. Herzog and Gazit, *The Arab-Israeli Wars*, 162.

29. Richard Bordeaux Parker, *The Six-Day War: A Retrospective* (Gainesville, FL: The University Press of Florida, 1996), 154.

30. Ibid., xix.

31. Herzog and Gazit, *The Arab-Israeli Wars*, 169–170.

32. Benny Morris, *Righteous Victims: A History of the Zionist-Arab Conflict, 1881–2001* (New York: Vintage Books, Random House, 2001), 318.

33. Ibid., 324.

34. "The Mideast: A Century of Conflict, Part 4: The 1967 Six-Day War," *Morning Edition*, October 3, 2002, National Public Radio, www.npr.org/news/specials/mideast/history/transcripts/6day-p4.100302.html.

35. Ibid.

36. Herzog and Gazit, *The Arab-Israeli Wars*, 185.

37. Nadav Safran, *From War to War: The Arab-Israeli Confrontation, 1948–1967* (New York: Pegasus, 1969), 375.

38. Oren, *Six Days of War*, 212.

39. Rikhye, *The Sinai Blunder*, 120.

40. Ibid., 133.

41. Hinnebusch, *The International Politics of the Middle East*, 174.

42. "Egyptians Report Poor Communication Services on Day of Anger," Almasry Alyoum, January 25, 2011. www.almasryalyoum.com/en/news/egyptians-report-poor-communication-services-day-anger-1.

43. David D. Kirkpatrick, "Egypt Erupts in Jubilation as Mubarak Steps Down," *New York Times*, February 11, 2011, www.nytimes.com/2011/02/12/world/middleeast/12egypt.html.

44. "Egypt crisis: President Hosni Mubarak Resigns as Leader," BBC News, February 12, 2011, www.bbc.co.uk/news/world-middle-east-12433045.

45. "Country Comparison: Oil, CIA—The World Factbook," www.cia.gov/library/publications/the-world-factbook/rankorder/2173rank.html?countryName=Egypt&countryCode=eg&regionCode=af&rank=29#eg

46. "U.S. Imports by Country of Origin," U.S. Energy Information Administration, January 28, 2011, www.eia.doe.gov/dnav/pet/pet_move_impcus_a2_nus_ep00_im0_mbbl_m.htm. (572,000 barrels a month / 30 days = 19,067 barrel a day; 19,067 / 681,000 = 2.799%).

47. "Jordan's King Fires Government, West Bank to Hold Local Vote," MSNBC.com, February 1, 2011, www.msnbc.msn.com/id/41366134/ns/world_news-mideast/n_africa/

48. Toyin Falola and Ann Genova, *The Politics of the Global Oil Industry: An Introduction* (Westport, CT: Praeger Publishers, 2005), 68–69.

49. Ibid., 70.

Chapter 11

1. Stewart Ross, *The Arab-Israeli Conflict, Volume 5* (Chicago: Discovery Books, Ltd., 2004), 32.

2. Simon Dunstan, *The Yom Kippur War: The Arab-Israeli War of 1973* (Oxford: Osprey Publishing, 2007), 8.

3. Benny Morris, *Righteous Victims: A History of the Zionist-Arab Conflict, 1881–2001* (New York: Vintage Books, Random House, 2001), 347.

4. Michael B. Oren, *Six Days of War: June 1967 and the Making of the Modern Middle East* (New York: Presidio Press Books, Random House Ballantine Publishing Group, 2002), 172.

5. Dunstan, *The Yom Kippur War*, 8.

6. Morris, *Righteous Victims*, 347.

7. Ibid., 348.

8. Dunstan, *The Yom Kippur War*, 8.

9. Said K. Aburish, *Nasser, the Last Arab* (New York: St. Martin's Press, 2004), 309–310.

10. Dunstan, *The Yom Kippur War*, 17–18.

11. Ibid., 19.

12. Morris, *Righteous Victims*, 392.

13. Chaim Herzog and Shlomo Gazit, *The Arab-Israeli Wars: War and Peace in the Middle East*, 2nd ed. (New York: Vintage Books, 2005), 228–229.

14. Morris, *Righteous Victims*, 396.

15. Herzog and Gazit, *The Arab-Israeli Wars*, 230.

16. Morris, *Righteous Victims*, 394.

17. Abraham Rabinovich, *The Yom Kippur War: The Epic Encounter That Transformed the Middle East* (New York: Schoken Books, Random House, 2004), 3.

18. Ibid.

19. Walter J. Boyne, *The Yom Kippur War: And the Airlift Strike That Saved Israel* (New York: Thomas Dunne Books, 2002), 23.

20. Aaron Rosenberg, *The Yom Kippur War* (New York: The Rosen Group, Inc., 2004), 10.

21. Boyne, *The Yom Kippur War*, 25.

22. Ibid., 31–32.

23. Ibid., 34.

24. Morris, *Righteous Victims*, 404.

25. Warner D. Farr, "The Third Temple's Holy of Holies: Israel's Nuclear Weapons," Counterproliferation Paper No. 2 (Alabama: USAF Counterproliferation Center, 1999, www.fas.org/nuke/guide/israel/nuke/farr.htm.

26. Ibid.

27. Morris, *Righteous Victims*, 404.

28. Rabinovich, *The Yom Kippur War*, 491.

29. Ibid., 495.

30. Daniel Yergin, *The Prize: The Epic Quest for Oil, Money & Power* (New York: Free Press, Simon & Schuster, 2008), 587.

31. Daniel Ammann, *The King of Oil: The Secret Lives of Marc Rich* (New York: St. Martin's Press, 2009), 72.

32. Arshad Khan, *Islam, Muslims, and America: Understanding the Basis of Their Conflict* (New York: Algora Publishing, 2003), 36.

33. Herzog and Gazit, *The Arab-Israeli Wars*, 229.

34. Franklin Tugwell, *The Energy Crisis and the American Political Economy: Politics and Markets in the Management of Natural Resources* (Stanford, CA: Stanford University Press, 1988, 97.

35. Ibid.

36. Thomas C. Schelling, "Thinking through the Energy Problem," vol. 42 of Supplementary paper, Committee for Economic Development. Design Committee on Long-Range Energy Policy, Committee for Economic Development (Berkeley: University of California, 1979), 15.

37. Yergin, *The Prize*, 597.

38. David Frum, *How We Got Here: The '70s* (New York: Basic Books, 2000), 320.

39. Ammann, *The King of Oil*, 117.

40. Yergin, *The Prize*, 573.

41. Ibid., 580.

42. Ibid., 581.

43. Toyin Falola and Ann Genova, *The Politics of the Global Oil Industry: An Introduction* (Westport, CT: Praeger Publishers, 2005), 76.

44. Yergin, *The Prize*, 580.

45. Falola and Genova, *Politics of the Global Oil Industry*, 77.

46. Bat Ye'or, *Eurabia: The Euro-Arab Axis* (Cranbury, NJ: Associated University Presses, 2005), 48.

47. Rachel Bronson, *Thicker than Oil: America's Uneasy Partnership with Saudi Arabia* (New York: Oxford University Press, 2006), 112.

48. Ibid.

49. Yergin, *The Prize*, 599.

50. Ibid., 601.

51. Ross, *The Arab-Israeli Conflict*, 33.

52. Ammann, *The King of Oil*, 58.

Chapter 12

1. Sharon Otterman, "Saudi Arabia: Withdrawal of U.S. Forces," Council on Foreign Relations, May 2, 2003, www.cfr.org/publication/7739/saudi_arabia.html#p3.

2. Patrick Martin, "U.S. Firms Lose Out in Bidding for Iraq Oil Fields," December 14, 2009, *World Socialist*, www.wsws.org/articles/2009/dec2009/iraq-d14.shtml.

3. David Hammes and Douglas Wills, "Black Gold: The End of Bretton Woods and the Oil-Price Shocks of the 1970s," *The Independent Review* IX, no. 4 (Spring 2005): 501, www.independent.org/pdf/tir/tir_09_4_2_hammes.pdf.

4. Ibid., 507.

5. Anthony Sampson, "Who's to Blame for the High Price of Oil," *New York Magazine*, July 9–16, 1979, 64.

6. "1970s Oil Crisis," http://recession.org/history/1970s-oil-crisis. Accessed November 2010.

7. Gawdat Bahgat, "U.S. Oil Outlook," *Middle East Economic Survey* XLIX, no. 9, February 27, 2006, www.mees.com/postedarticles/oped/v49n09 5OD01.htm.

8. Ibid.

9. "Safe, Strong and Secure: Reducing America's Oil Dependence," Natural Resource Defence Council, 2004, www.nrdc.org/air/transportation/aoilpolicy2.asp. Accessed November 2010.

10. Daniel Yergin, *The Prize: The Epic Quest for Oil, Money & Power* (New York: Free Press, Simon & Schuster, 2008), 615.

11. Helen Chapin Metz, ed., "Relations with the United States," in *Saudi Arabia: A Country Study* (Washington, DC: GPO for the Library of Congress, 1992). http://countrystudies.us/saudi-arabia/59.htm.

12. Ibid.

13. Robert Vitalis, *America's Kingdom: Mythmaking on the Saudi Oil Frontier* (Stanford: Stanford University Press, 2007), 229.

14. Robert Owen Freedman, *Moscow and the Middle East: Soviet Policy Since the Invasion of Afghanistan* (Cambridge, UK: Cambridge University Press, 1991), 15.

15. Vitalis, *America's Kingdom*, 247.

16. William R. Clark, *Petrodollar Warfare: Oil, Iraq and the Future of the Dollar* (Gabriola Island, BC, Canada: New Society Publishers, 2005), 43.

17. Francisco Parra, *Oil Politics: A Modern History of Petroleum* (New York: I.B. Tauris & Co. Ltd., 2004), 11.

18. William B. Quandt, *Saudi Arabia in the 1980s: Foreign Policy, Security, and Oil* (Washington, DC: The Brookings Institution, 1981), 139.

19. Metz, ed., "Relations with the United States."

20. Sharon Otterman, "Saudi Arabia: Withdrawal of U.S. Forces."

21. Kathlyn Gay and Martin Gay, *Persian Gulf War* (Brookfield, CT: Twenty-First Century Books, a division of The Millbrook Press, 1996), 22.

22. "Saudi Arabia: Oil," U.S. Energy Information Administration, November 2009. www.eia.doe.gov/emeu/cabs/Saudi_Arabia/Oil.html. Accessed November 2010.

23. Rodney Carlisle and John Stewart Bowman, *Persian Gulf War* (New York: Facts On File, Infobase Publishing, 2003), 45–46.

24. Ibid., 52.

25. Ibid., 63.

26. Ibid., 66.

27. Ibid., 68.

28. "Conversion Table: USD to EUR (Interbank rate), Time period: 03/20/02 to 03/20/03," www.oanda.com/currency/historical-rates?date_fmt=us&date=02/20/03&date1=02/20/03&exch=USD&expr=EUR&format=HTML&margin_fixed=0.

29. Richard Benson, "Oil, the Dollar, and U.S. Prosperity," SFGroup, August 8, 2003, www.gold-eagle.com/editorials_03/benson080903.html.

30. Ibid.

31. "Conversion Table: USD to EUR (Interbank rate)."

32. "Weekly OPEC Countries Spot Price FOB Weighted by Estimated Export Volume (Dollars per Barrel)," U.S. Energy Information Administration, www.eia.gov/dnav/pet/hist/LeafHandler.ashx?n=PET&s=WTOTOPEC&f=W. Accessed November 2010.

33. http://motherjones.com/politics/2003/03/thirty-year-itch.

34. Craig Unger, *House of Bush, House of Saud: The Secret Relationship Between the World's Two Most Powerful Dynasties* (New York: Scribner, 2004), 2.

35. Ibid., 9.

36. Leonardo Maugeri, *The Age of Oil: The Mythology, History, and Future of the World's Most Controversial Resource* (Westport, CT: Praeger Publishers, 2006), 72.

37. Glenn Minnis, "Halliburton: $61M Overcharge?," CBS News, Dec. 12, 2003, www.cbsnews.com/stories/2003/12/12/politics/main588216.shtml.

38. "Halliburton Unit Faces Pentagon Inquiry," *CNN/Money*, March 15, 2005, http://money.cnn.com/2005/03/15/news/fortune500/halliburton/.

Chapter 13

1. Antonia Juhasz, *The Bush Agenda: Invading the World, One Economy at a Time* (New York: HarperCollins Publishers, 2006), 102.

2. Robert Bryce, *Cronies: Oil, the Bushes, and the Rise of Texas, America's Superstate* (New York: PublicAffairs, a member of the Perseus Books Group, 2004), 67.

3. Erik Eckholm, "Army Contract Official Critical of Halliburton Pact Is Demoted," *New York Times*, August 29, 2005, www.nytimes.com/2005/08/29/international/middleeast/29halliburton.html?_r=1.

4. Jane Mayer, "Contract Sport: What Did the Vice-President do for Halliburton?," *The New Yorker*, February 16, 2004, www.newyorker.com/archive/2004/02/16/040216fa_fact.

5. John Steele Gordon, *An Empire of Wealth: The Epic History of American Economic Power* (New York: HarperCollins, 2004), 217.

6. Ibid., 217–218.

7. Ibid., 218.

8. *The Encyclopedia Americana: A Library of Universal Knowledge*, vol. 8 (New York: The Encyclopedia Americana Corporation, 1918), 173.

9. John Steele Gordon, *An Empire of Wealth*, 219.

10. *The Encyclopedia Americana: A Library of Universal Knowledge*, 173.

11. Jane Mayer, "Contract Sport."

12. Lou Dubose and Jake Bernstein, "Secretary of War," chap. 5 in *Vice: Dick Cheney and the Hijacking of the American Presidency* (New York: Random House, 2006), 87.

13. Ibid., 91.

14. Ibid., 98.

15. Donald E. Schmidt, *The Folly of War: American Foreign Policy, 1898–2005* (New York: Algora Publishing, 2005), 297.

16. Ibid., 299.

17. Ibid., 298.

18. George H. W. Bush's Address to Congress on the Persian Gulf Crisis, Milestone Documents, September 11, 1990, www.milestonedocuments.com/documents/full-text/george-h-w-bushs-address-to-congress-on-the-persian-gulf-crisis/.

19. George H. W. Bush's Address to Congress on the Persian Gulf Crisis.

20. Queen Noor, *Leap of Faith: Memoirs of an Unexpected Life* (New York: Miramax Books, 2005), 310.

21. Schmidt, *The Folly of War*, 307.

22. Homer Duncan, *Bush and Cheney's War: A War without Justification* (Victoria, BC: Trafford Publishing, 2005), 81.

23. Ibid.

24. Duncan, *Bush and Cheney's War*, 82.

25. Ibid.

26. Ibid., 83.

27. Antonia Juhasz, *The Bush Agenda*, 102.

28. Bryce, *Cronies*, 189.

29. Antonia Juhasz, *The Bush Agenda*, 122.

30. Dan Briody, *The Halliburton Agenda: The Politics of Oil and Money* (Hoboken, NJ: John Wiley & Sons, 2004), 213.

31. Ibid.

32. Ibid.

33. Ibid., 221.

34. Antonia Juhasz, *The Bush Agenda*, 147.

35. Richard B. Cheney, "Defending Liberty in a Global Economy," Collateral Damage Conference, Cato Institute, June 23, 1998, www.cato.org/speeches/sp-dc062398.html.

36. Briody, *The Halliburton Agenda*, 208.

37. Duncan, *Bush and Cheney's War*, 84.

38. Bryce, *Cronies*, 190.

39. "Locations," Halliburton, www.halliburton.com/locations/. Accessed November 2010.

Chapter 14

1. Leonardo Maugeri, *The Age of Oil: What They Don't Want You to Know About the World's Most Controversial Resource* (Guilford, CT: Lyons Press, 2008), 25.

2. Douglas Little, *American Orientalism: The United States and the Middle East Since 1945*, 3rd ed. (Chapel Hill: The University of North Carolina Press, 2008), 60.

3. Daniel Yergin, *The Prize: The Epic Quest for Oil, Money & Power* (New York: Free Press, Simon & Schuster, 2008), 216.

4. Ibid., 216–217.

5. Gregory Wilpert, "The Economics, Culture, and Politics of Oil in Venezuela," August 30, 2003, http://venezuelanalysis.com/analysis/74.

6. Franklin Tugwell, *The Politics of Oil in Venezuela* (Stanford: Stanford University Press, 1975), 182.

7. Ibid., 2.

8. Wilpert, "The Economics, Culture, and Politics of Oil in Venezuela."

9. Yergin, *The Prize*, 494.

10. Tugwell, *The Politics of Oil in Venezuela*, 150.

11. Wilpert, "The Economics, Culture, and Politics of Oil in Venezuela."

12. Miguel Tinker-Salas, "Fueling Concern: The Role of Oil in Venezuela," *Harvard International Review*, Harvard International Relations Council, Inc., January 1, 2005, www.thefreelibrary.com/Fueling1concern%3a1the1role1of 1oil1in1Venezuela.-a0129463344.

13. Cesar J. Alvarez and Stephanie Hanson, "Venezuela's Oil-Based Economy," Council on Foreign Relations, February 9, 2009, www.cfr.org/publication/ 12089/venezuelas_oilbased_economy.html.

14. Wilpert, "The Economics, Culture, and Politics of Oil in Venezuela."

15. Tinker-Salas, "Fueling Concern."

16. Alvarez and Hanson, "Venezuela's Oil-Based Economy."

17. Wilpert, "The Economics, Culture, and Politics of Oil in Venezuela."

18. "Venezuela's Economy Shows Strong Signs of Recovery after Lock-out/ Strike," September 27, 2003, http://venezuelanalysis.com/news/127.

19. Tinker-Salas, "Fueling Concern."

20. Alvarez and Hanson, "Venezuela's Oil-Based Economy."

21. Ibid.

22. Ibid.

23. Maugeri, *The Age of Oil*, 23.

24. Ibid.

25. Yergin, *The Prize*, 131.

26. Maugeri, *The Age of Oil*, 22.

27. Yergin, *The Prize*, 132.

28. Ibid., 144.

29. Thomas R. Mattair, *Global Security Watch—Iran: A Reference Handbook* (Westport, CT: Greenwood Publishing Group, 2008), 7.

30. Ibid.

31. Ibid., 8.

32. Ibid.

33. Ibid.

34. Maugeri, *The Age of Oil*, 63.

35. Ibid., 65.

36. Edward Jay Epstein, "The Secret Deals of the Oil Cartel: An Illustrated History, Part I: How Seven Companies Carved Up the World," *New York Magazine*, June 23, 1975, 57.

37. Ibid.

38. Ibid.

39. Maugeri, *The Age of Oil*, 66.

40. Ian Skeet, *OPEC: Twenty-Five Years of Prices and Politics* (Cambridge, UK: Press Syndicate of the University of Cambridge, 1988), 20.

41. Mattair, *Global Security Watch—Iran*, 14.

42. Ibid., 18.

43. Skeet, *OPEC: Twenty-Five Years of Prices and Politics*, 100.

44. Ibid., 90.

45. Mattair, *Global Security Watch—Iran*, 19.

46. Ibid.

47. Ibid.

48. Saeed Alizadeh, Alireza Pahlavani, and Ali Sadrnia, *Iran: A Chronological History* (Iran: Published by the Authors, 2002), 205.

49. Maugeri, *The Age of Oil*, 124.

50. Ibid., 125.

51. Ibid.

52. Ali Gheissari and Seyyed Vali Reza Nasr, *Democracy in Iran: History and the Quest for Liberty* (New York: Oxford University Press, 2006), 87.

53. Scott MacLeod, "Can Iran Be Forgiven?" *Time*, August 3, 1998, www.time.com/time/magazine/article/0,9171,988829,00.html#ixzz15OmhzI95.

54. Ibid.

55. Herman Franssen and Elaine Morton, "A Review of U.S. Unilateral Sanctions Against Iran," *Middle East Economic Survey* XLV, no. 34 (August 26, 2002), www.mafhoum.com/press3/108E16.htm.

56. Adam Tarock, *The Superpowers' Involvement in the Iran-Iraq War* (Commack, New York: Nova Science Publishers, Inc., 1998), 21.

57. Franssen and Morton, "A Review of U.S. Unilateral Sanctions Against Iran."

58. Ibid.

59. "Iran: Economy," *The World Factbook*, Central Intelligence Agency, www.cia.gov/library/publications/the-world-factbook/geos/ir.html. Accessed November 2010.

60. "Iran Oil Stabilisation Fund," SWF Institute, www.swfinstitute.org/swfs/iran-oil-stabilisation-fund/. Accessed November 2010.

61. Parra, *Oil Politics*, 258.

62. N. A. Krylov, A. A. Bokserman, and EvgeniRomanovich Stavrovski, *The Oil Industry of the Former Soviet Union: Reserves and Prospects, Extraction, Transportation* (Amsterdam: Overseas Publishers Association, 1998), 3.

63. Maugeri, *The Age of Oil*, 23.

64. Yergin, *The Prize*, 116.

65. Maugeri, *The Age of Oil*, 23.

66. Simon Bromley, *American Hegemony and World Oil: The Industry, the State System and the World Economy* (University Park: The Pennsylvania State University Press, 1991), 190.

67. Ibid., 190–191.

68. Walter Moss, *A History of Russia: Since 1855* (London: Anthem Press, 2005), 432.

69. Steven R. Weisman, "Bitter Outburst by Putin a Sign U.S.-Russian Relations Cooling," *New York Times*, September 12, 2004, http://seattletimes.nwsource.com/html/nationworld/2002033535_usrussia12.html.

70. Vladimir Gusinsky, "Putin's Reign of Fear," *Moscow Times*, November 10, 2003, www.eng.yabloko.ru/Publ/2003/PAPERS/11/031110_mt.html.

71. Edward Lucas, "Putin: The Brutal Despot Who Is Dragging the West into a New Cold War," *The Daily Mail*, January 18, 2008, www.dailymail.co.uk/pages/live/articles/news/worldnews.html?in_article_id=509177&in_page_id=1811.

72. Gary Peach, "Putin Warns of Outside Forces that Wish to Split Russia and Take Over Its Natural Resources," AP Worldstream, November 4, 2007, www.highbeam.com/doc/1A1-D8SMVBA80.html.

73. Parra, *Oil Politics*, 84.

74. Robert Service, *A History of Modern Russia: From Tsarism to the Twenty-First Century*, 3rd ed. (Cambridge, MA: Harvard University Press, 2009), 561.

75. Ibid.

76. Steve LeVine, *Putin's Labyrinth: Spies, Murder, and the Dark Heart of the New Russia* (New York: Random House, 2009), xx–xxi.

77. Ariel Cohen, "Putin's Legacy and United Russia's New Ideology," The Heritage Foundation, June 1, 2006, www.heritage.org/Research/Reports/2006/06/Putins-Legacy-and-United-Russias-New-Ideology.

78. Max Hastings, "Corruption, Violence and Vice Have Triumphed in Putin's Russia," *The Guardian*, November 27, 2006, www.guardian.co.uk/commentisfree/2006/nov/27/comment.russia.

Chapter 15

1. Siobhan Hughes, "Steele Gives GOP Delegates New Cheer: 'Drill, Baby, Drill!,' *Wall Street Journal*, September 3, 2008, http://blogs.wsj.com/washwire/2008/09/03/steele-gives-gop-delegates-new-cheer-drill-baby-drill/?mod=googlenews_wsj.

2. Thomas L. Friedman, "Palin's Kind of Patriotism," *New York Times*, October 8, 2008, www.nytimes.com/2008/10/08/opinion/08iht-edfriedman .1.16784160.html?_r=1.

3. Permanent Fund Dividend Division, Department of Revenue, State of Alaska Website, www.pfd.alaska.gov/. Accessed November 2010.

4. Erik A. Bruun, *Our Nation's Archive: The History of the United States in Documents* (New York: Black Dog & Leventhal Publishers, 1999), 387.

5. Claus-M Naske and Herman E. Slotnick, *Alaska: A History of the 49th State*, 2nd ed. (Norman: University of Oklahoma Press, 1987), 64.

6. Erik A. Bruun, *Our Nation's Archive*, 387.

7. Naske and Slotnick, *Alaska: A History of the 49th State*, 66.

8. Ibid., 69.

9. "Modern Alaska: Oil Discovery and Development in Alaska," Alaska History & Cultural Studies, www.akhistorycourse.org/articles/article. php?artID=140. Accessed November 2010.

10. Ibid.

11. Bryan Cooper, *Alaska: The Last Frontier* (New York: William Morrow & Company, 1972), 119.

12. Jack Roderick, *Crude Dreams: A Personal History of Oil & Politics in Alaska* (Fairbanks, AK: Epicenter Press, 1997), 123.

13. "Modern Alaska: Oil Discovery and Development in Alaska."

14. Joe Clyde Truett and Stephen R. Johnson, *The Natural History of an Arctic Oil Field: Development and the Biota* (San Diego, CA: Academic Press, 2000), 18.

15. Roderick, *Crude Dreams*, 126.

16. Ibid.

17. Truett and Johnson, *The Natural History of an Arctic Oil Field*, 18.

18. "History of Northern Alaska Petroleum Development," American Petroleum Institute, March 10, 2009, www.api.org/aboutoilgas/sectors/explore/history ofnorthalaska.cfm.

19. Truett and Johnson, *The Natural History of an Arctic Oil Field*, 18.

20. "Trans-Alaska Pipeline System Renewal Environmental Impact Statement," TAPS History, http://tapseis.anl.gov/guide/history.cfm. Accessed November 2010.

21. Ibid.

22. Truett and Johnson, *The Natural History of an Arctic Oil Field*, 18.

23. "History of Northern Alaska Petroleum Development."

24. "ANWR Oil," http://anwroil.com/. Accessed November 2010.

25. Elizabeth Shogren, "For 30 Years, a Political Battle Over Oil and ANWR," National Public Radio, November 10, 2005, www.npr.org/templates/story/story.php?storyId=5007819.

26. Ibid.

27. Ibid.

28. Ibid.

29. Ibid.

30. Mary Lynne Corn, et al., *Arctic National Wildlife Refuge: Background and Issues* (New York: Nova Science Publishers, 2003), 71.

31. Ibid.

32. "10 Years to TAPS Shutdown?—America's Rejected Oil," Arctic Power, www.anwr.org/Headlines/10-Years-to-TAPS-Shutdown---America's-Rejected-Oil.php. Accessed November 2010.

33. "ANWR Oil," Arctic Power, http://anwroil.com/. Accessed November 2010.

34. "Petroleum Statistics," U.S. Energy Information Administration, October 28, 2010, www.eia.doe.gov/energyexplained/index.cfm?page=oil_home#tab2.

35. Elizabeth Shogren, "For 30 Years, a Political Battle Over Oil and ANWR."

36. Brandon Keim, "The *Exxon Valdez* Spill Is All Around Us," *Wired Science*, March 24, 2009, www.wired.com/wiredscience/2009/03/valdezlegacy/.

37. Jere Beasley, "Exxon Pays First *Valdez* Oil Spill Payments," Jere Beasley Report, January 6, 2009, www.jerebeasleyreport.com/2009/01/exxon-pays-first-valdez-oil-spill-payments/.

38. "The *Exxon Valdez* Oil Spill Disaster," *Explore North*, March 24, 1999, www.explorenorth.com/library/weekly/aa032499.htm.

39. Keim, "The *Exxon Valdez* Spill Is All Around Us."

40. Corn, et al., *Arctic National Wildlife Refuge*, 81.

41. Ibid., 71.

42. Ibid., 81.

43. Ibid., 85.

44. Ibid., 89.

45. "ANWR Oil," http://anwroil.com/. Accessed November 2010.

Chapter 16

1. "Dirty Money: Big Oil and Corporate Polluters Spent over $500 Million to Kill Climate Bill, Push Offshore Drilling," September 27, 2010, Climate Progress, www.eenews.net/assets/2010/09/15/document_gw_01.pdf.

2. Ibid.

3. "About API, Join Us," American Petroleum Institute, www.api.org/aboutapi/joinus/.

4. "Dirty Money."

5. Anne Mulkern, "Oil and Gas Interests Set Spending Record for Lobbying in 2009," *New York Times*, February 2, 2010, www.nytimes.com/gwire/2010/02/02/02greenwire-oil-and-gas-interests-set-spending-record-for-l-1504.html?pagewanted=print.

6. Lindsay Mayer, "Big Oil, Big Influence," Public Broadcasting Service, August 1, 2008, www.pbs.org/now/shows/347/oil-politics.html.

7. Ibid.

8. "Killing the Climate, from API to Tom Donohue," PolluterWatch blog, January 11, 2010, www.polluterwatch.com/blog/killing-climate-api-tom-donohue.

9. "H.R. 2454—American Clean Energy and Security Act of 2009," http://maplight.org/us-congress/bill/111-hr-2454/371786/contributions by vote?sort=asc&order=%24+From+Interest+Groups%3Cbr+%2F%3EThat+Oppose&interests-support=&interests-oppose=E1100. Accessed November 2010.

10. Dana Milbank and Justin Blum, "Document Says Oil Chiefs Met with Cheney Task Force," *Washington Post*, November 16, 2005, www.washingtonpost.com/wp-dyn/content/article/2005/11/15/AR2005111501842_pf.html.

11. "AMIN Highlights, Washington," *The American Independent*, May 10–16, 2010, http://tainews.org/impact/may-2010/may-20-update/.

12. Gina-Marie Cheeseman, "How BP Money Spent on Lobbying and Campaign Contributions Pays Off," Triple Pundit, May 13, 2010, www.triplepundit.com/2010/05/how-bp-money-spends-on-lobbying-and-campaign-contributions-pays-off/.

13. Mike Lillis, "Some Gulf Lawmakers with Ties to Oil Industry Downplay Spill in Their Own Backyard," *Washington Independent*, May 5, 2010, http://washingtonindependent.com/83945/some-gulf-lawmakers-with-ties-to-the-industry-downplay-spill-in-their-own-backyard.

14. David Dayen, "Giant Oil Spill Threatens Alternative Energy Legislation," May 5, 2010, http://news.firedoglake.com/2010/05/05/giant-oil-spill-threatens-alternative-energy-legislation-wait-what/.

15. Jim Hightower, "The GOP's Genetic Link to Big Oil," June 30, 2010, www.commondreams.org/view/2010/06/30-1.

16. Ibid.

17. Ibid.

18. "Obama Wants Reform on 'Cozy Relationship' Between Oil Companies, Regulators," PBS Newshour, May 14, 2010 www.pbs.org/newshour/bb/environment/jan-june10/oil_05-14.html.

19. Kent Garber, "Obama, Congress Question Cozy Relationship with Oil Companies," U.S. News & World Report, May 25, 2010, http://politics.usnews.com/news/energy/articles/2010/05/25/obama-congress-question-cozy-relationship-with-oil-companies.html.

20. Evan Thomas and Daniel Stone, "Black Water Rising," Newsweek, May 29, 2010, www.newsweek.com/2010/05/29/black-water-rising.html.

21. Cassandra LaRussa, "Solar, Wind Power Groups Becoming Prominent in Washington Lobbying Forces After Years of Relative Obscurity," Open Secrets blog, August 25, 2010, www.opensecrets.org/news/2010/08/solar-wind-power-groups-becoming-pr.html.

22. Adam Liptak, "Justices, 5–4, Reject Corporate Spending Limit," New York Times, January 21, 2010, www.nytimes.com/2010/01/22/us/politics/22scotus.html?_r=1.

23. "BP Client Profile: Summary 2009," Open Secrets blog, www.opensecrets.org/lobby/clientsum.php?year=2009&lname=BP&id=. Accessed November 2010.

24. Erika Lovley, "Obama Biggest Recipient of BP Cash," May 5, 2010, http://dyn.politico.com/printstory.cfm?uuid=6584A5A0-18FE-70B2-A838E6437FBEC75D.

25. "ConocoPhillips Spent $5.5 Million on Lobbyists in 2Q," October 4, 2009, Associated Press, News Center, http://articles.moneycentral.msn.com/news/article.aspx?feed=AP&date=20101004&id=12110728.

26. "Dirty Money: Oil Companies and Special Interests Spend Millions to Oppose Climate Legislation," Center for American Progress, September, 2010, http://zedc4test.techprogress.org/issues/2010/09/dirty_money.html.

27. A.C. Thompson and Sonya Hubbard, "Oil Slick," Center for Investigative Reporting, Waking to Warming, April 24, 2007, www.centerforinvestigativereporting.org/articles/oilslick.

28. "Shell Spent $4M lobbying in 2Q," Bloomberg Businessweek, October 4, 2010, http://royaldutchshellplc.com/2010/10/04/shell-oil-spent-4m-lobbying-in-2q/.

29. Ralph Nader, www.brainyquote.com/quotes/quotes/r/ralphnader127641.html.

Chapter 17

1. CBS News, "Blowout: The *Deepwater Horizon*," *60 Minutes*, May 16, 2010, www.cbsnews.com/stories/2010/05/16/60minutes/main6490197_page3.sht ml?tag=contentMain;contentBody.

2. English News, "4.4 Million Barrels of Oil Leaked into Gulf of Mexico: U.S. Researchers," September 24, 2010, http://news.xinhuanet.com/ english2010/world/2010-09/24/c_13526710.htm.

3. Frank Jordans and Garance Burke, "*Deepwater Horizon* Rig Had History of Spills, Fires before Big Gulf of Mexico Oil Spill," April 30, 2010, www.nola.com/ news/gulf-oil-spill/index.ssf/2010/04/deepwater_horizon_rig_had_hist.html.

4. Ibid.

5. Lisa Myers and Rich Gardella, "*Deepwater Horizon* Rig: What Went Wrong?," MSNBC, May 21, 2010, www.msnbc.msn.com/id/37279113/.

6. "Transocean: BP Probe Self-Serving and Misleading," MSNBC, staff and news service reports, September 8, 2010, www.msnbc.msn.com/ id/39046088/ns/us_news-environment/.

7. Robert Stewart, "Oil Spills," Department of Oceanography, Texas A&M University, http://oceanworld.tamu.edu/resources/oceanography-book/oilspills .htm. Accessed November 2010.

8. Glen Garvin, "Ixtoc: The Gulf's Other Massive Oil Spill No Longer Apparent," McClatchy Newspapers, June 12, 2010, www.mcclatchydc. com/2010/06/12/95793/ixtoc-the-gulfs-other-massive.html.

9. "PEMEX Expects Oil Depletion in Seven Years," August 6, 2007, http:// seekingalpha.com/article/43634-pemex-expects-oil-depletion-in- seven-years.

10. Glen Garvin, "Ixtoc: The Gulf's Other Massive Oil Spill No Longer Apparent."

11. Amy Barnett, "The Coast Is Clear . . . Or Is It?," Sam Houston State University, September 16, 2010, www.shsu.edu/~pin_www/ T@S/2010/ bpimplications.html.

12. "Ekofisk Bravo," Oil Rig Disasters, http://home.versatel.nl/the_sims/rig/ ekofiskb.htm

13. Ibid.

14. Jim Redden, "Drilling Advances, U.S. Could Find Some Answers at Ekofisk," *World Oil* 231, no. 9 (September 2010), www.worldoil.com/drilling- advances-September-2010.html.

15. Ibid.

16. Oklahoma Historical Society, "Phillips Petroleum Company," *Encyclopedia of Oklahoma History & Culture*, http://digital.library.okstate.edu/encyclopedia/ entries/P/PH004.html. Accessed November 2010.

17. "Ekofisk Field, Norway, Commercial Asset Valuation and Forecast to 2007," Energy and Utilities Report, August 10, 2010, www.companiesandmarkets. com/Market-Report/ekofisk-field,-norway,-commercial-asset-valuation- and-forecast-to-2027-337792.asp.

18. "Country Analysis Briefs, Norway," U.S. Energy Information Administration, www.eia.doe.gov/cabs/Norway/Full.html. Accessed November 2010.

19. "Brief Oil and Gas History of Santa Barbara County," County of Santa Barbara Planning and Development, www.countyofsb.org/energy/information/ history.asp. Accessed November 2010.

20. "Oil and Gas," The Santa Barbara Channel, www.sbck.org/index.php?optio n=content&task=view&id=5. Accessed November 2010.

21. "1969 Oil Spill," UC Santa Barbara Department of Geography, www .geog.ucsb.edu/~jeff/sb_69oilspill/69oilspill_articles2.html.

22. "Regulation Is Necessary to Prevent Oil spills in the Future," May 5, 2010, http://mustangdaily.net/tag/1969-santa-barbara-oil-spill/.

23. George Draffan, "Major Oil Spills," www.endgame.org/oilspills.htm. Accessed November 2010.

24. "The Ixtoc Blowout—31 Years Ago Today," Greenpeace, June 3, 2010, www .greenpeace.org/usa/en/news-and-blogs/campaign-blog/the-ixtoc-blowout- 31-years-ago-today/blog/26044.

25. Dagmar Etkin, "Estimating Cleanup Costs for Oil Spills," International Oil Spill Conference, 1999, Arlington, Massachusetts, http://docs.google.com/ viewer?a=v&q=cache:T0KX0b9D0AgJ:www.environmental-research.com/ publications/pdf/1999-IOSC-Cost.pdf1costs1to1clean1up1campeche1oil1s pill&hl=en&gl=us&pid=bl&srcid=ADGEESgbkWK8wP1y3bGu2unL6Pbls Wy9MgNITvDk-_ctZqnoLcmk74K-cRKq1cKx4Dq_7MepFbJifna9zB_iiY Wt7zhZmCrPcfmKE2BNMYX8ePb9Ag-F-bToyyvMLO45NJ2NAkP5SHI F&sig=AHIEtbTvdFQPC-bjpb69L5tOS1Zq9fpsKw.

26. www.itopf.com/spill-compensation/cost-of-spills/.

27. "BP Says Deepwater Horizon Oil Spill Costs Rise to $11.2 Billion," Associated Press, October 1, 2010, http://blog.al.com/wire/2010/10/bp_ says_deepwater_horizon_oil.html.

28. Mark Guarino and Peter Spotts, "Gulf Oil Spill's Environmental Impact: How Long to Recover," Christian Science Monitor, May 10, 2010, www .csmonitor.com/USA/2010/0510/Gulf-oil-spill-s-environmental- impact-How-long-to-recover.

29. "Oil Production and Environmental Damage," American University research paper #15, www1.american.edu/ted/projects/tedcross/xoilpr15.htm.

30. Ibid.

Chapter 18

1. "Motor Vehicle Fuel Efficiency," Consumer Federation of America, www
   .consumerfed.org/index.php/transportation/motor-vehicle-fuel-efficiency.

2. "America and Its Auto Industry, Need a Tough New Fuel Standard,"
   Portland Press Herald, Opinion, October 2, 2010, www.pressherald.com/
   opinion/America-and-its-auto-industry-need-a-tough-new-fuel-standard.
   html.

3. Joe Spitz, "Story of the U.S. Government's C.A.F.E. Standards," www
   .cars101.com/cafe.html.

4. "Auto Dealers Resist Move to Hybrids and Higher Fuel Efficiency," April
   5, 2010, www.hybridcars.com/news/auto-dealers-resist-move-hybrids-and-
   higher-fuel-efficiency-27688.html.

5. Jacob Gordon, "Will New Fuel Economy Standards Make Cars
   Less Safe?," Editorial, MSN, http://editorial.autos.msn.com/article.
   aspx?cp-documentid=434514.

6. "EPA, DOT Draft Rules to Curb Carbon Emissions from Heavy Trucks,"
   Environmental Leader, August 17, 2010, www.environmentalleader.
   com/2010/08/17/epa-dot-submit-draft-rules-to-curb-carbon-emissions-
   from-heavy-trucks/.

7. "Fueling the Dragon: China's Race into the Oil Market, 2003–2004,"
   Institute for the Analysis of Global Security, www.iags.org/china.htm.

8. Stephanie Hanson, "China, Africa and Oil," Council on Foreign Relations,
   June 6, 2008, www.cfr.org/publication/9557/china_africa_and_oil.html.

9. Christopher DeMorro, "China Will Buy Between 15 and 17
   Million Cars this Year," May 26, 2010, http://gas2.org/2010/05/26/
   china-will-buy-between-15-and-17-million-cars-next-year/.

10. "Auto Sales Expected to Surpass 17 Million," October 12, 2010, http://english
    .sina.com/business/p/2010/1011/343008.html.

11. Keith Bradsher, "China Is Said to Plan Strict Gas Mileage Rules," *New York
    Times*, May 27, 2009, www.nytimes.com/2009/05/28/business/energy
    environment/28fuel.html.

12. "1.6 Turbo Chevrolet Cruz Sighted at Long Last," *China Car
    Times*, October 14, 2010, www.chinacartimes.com/2010/10/14/
    1-6-turbo-chevrolet-cruze-sighted-at-long-last/.

13. Bertel Schmitt, "GM Sells More Cars in China Than Back Home," The
    Truth About Cars Newsblog, October 24, 2009, www.thetruthaboutcars.
    com/2009/10/gm-sells-more-cars-in-china-than-back-home/.

14. "GM: 1.8 Million Cars Sold in China in 2009," CBS News, January 4,
    2010, www.cbsnews.com/stories/2010/01/04/business/main6052403.shtml.

15. Jennifer Horton, "Is the United States Addicted to Gasoline?" http://science.howstuffworks.com/environmental/green-science/us-gas-addiction.htm. Accessed November 2010.

16. "What Gasoline Really Costs Us: The Real Price of Gas," *The Progress Report*, www.progress.org/2003/energy22.htm.

17. Dallas Kachan, "Oil Industry Subsidies for Dummies," Cleantech Group, January 5, 2007, http://cleantech.com/news/node/554.

18. Ibid.

19. "How Much Are We Paying for a Gallon of Gas?," Institute for the Analysis of Global Security, www.iags.org/costofoil.html.

20. National Defense Council Foundation, Testimony of James Martin, Chairman, before the House Committee on Foreign Affairs, July 31, 2008, www.ndcf.org/.

21. Benjamin Jones, "Ethanol Use in U.S. and Brazil Rises Sharply," May 22, 2008, http://gas2.org/2008/05/22/ethanol-use-in-us-and-brazil-rises-sharply/.

22. Emily Winfield, "Ethanol in Brazil," International Finance and Development, UICIFD Briefing No. 6, University of Iowa, May 2008, www.uiowa.edu/ifdebook/briefings/docs/brazil.shtml.

23. "DTN Finds Oil Industry Subsidized Much Higher than Ethanol," October 13, 2010, http://discussions.agweb.com/showthread.php?10652-DTN-Finds-Oil-Industry-Subsidized-Much-Higher-Than-Ethanol.

24. Ibid.

25. Mike Gaworecki, "How We Subsidize a Mega-Rich Industry that Destroys Us," Environment.change.org, June 10, 2010.

26. Kim Geiger and Tom Hamburger, "Oil Companies Have a Rich History of U.S. Subsidies," *Los Angeles Times*, May 25, 2010, http://articles.latimes.com/2010/may/25/nation/la-na-oil-spill-subsidies-20100525.

27. Ibid.

28. Raymond Learsy, *Over a Barrel: Breaking Oil's Grip on Our Future* (New York: Encounter Books, 2007), 49.

29. Ibid., 71.

30. Ibid., 75.

Chapter 19

1. "China's Oil Demand Increase 'Astonishing,' Says IEA," BBC News, March 12, 2010, http://news.bbc.co.uk/2/hi/business/8563985.stm.

2. Christian Bedford, "The View from the West: String of Pearls: China's Maritime Strategy in India's Backyard," *Canadian Naval Review* 4, no. 4 (Winter 2009), http://naval.review.cfps.dal.ca/archive/1928859-6427241/vol4num4art9.pdf.

e3302   NOTES

3. "New Spat Over Bill Increases Stress on US-Chinese Relations," *Deutsche Welle*, January 1, 2010, www.dw-world.de/dw/article/0,,6062640,00 .html.

4. Trevor Johnson, "China Signs $23 Billion Oil Deal with Nigeria, World Socialist Web Site, May 28, 2010, www.wsws.org/articles/2010/may2010/ nige-m28.shtml.

5. "Deal for Oil Fields Extends China's Quest for Energy," *New York Times*, March 15, 2010, http://dealbook.blogs.nytimes.com/2010/03/15/ deal-for-oil-fields-extends-chinas-quest-for-energy/.

6. "About Us: Profile," Petrobras, www.petrobras.com.br/en/about-us/profile/. Accessed November 2010.

7. "China to Buy Oil Reserves," Zacks Investment Research, March 4, 2009, www.zacks.com/stock/news/17917/China1to1Buy1Oil1Reserves.

8. Lynn Herrmann, "China Lands Multi-Billion Dollar Deal in Texas Oil and Gas Fields," *Digital Journal*, October 13, 2010, www.digitaljournal.com/ article/298900#ixzz12vjLcsaP.

9. Richard Spencer, "China Prepares to Buy Up Foreign Oil Companies," *The Telegraph*, February 22, 2009, www.telegraph.co.uk/finance/newsbysector/ energy/4781037/China-prepares-to-buy-up-foreign-oil-companies.html.

10. "China's Billions Buy Up Resources Worldwide," Infinite Unknown, October 3, 2010, www.infiniteunknown.net/2010/10/03/chinas-billions-buy-up-resources-worldwide/.

11. "Iran, Oil," U.S. Energy Information Administration, www.eia.doe.gov/ cabs/Iran/Oil.html.

12. "China Imports More Crude Oil from Iran," Alexander's Gas and Oil Connections 15, no. 8 (June 24, 2010), www.gasandoil.com/GOC/news/ nts102596.htm.

13. BNO news, "Chinese Official Says China Opposes Sanctions against Iran," October 18, 2010, http://wireupdate.com/wires/11406/chinese-official-says-china-opposes-sanctions-against-iran/.

14. Shai Oster and Simon Hall, "China Plans to Keep Iran Oil Projects Moving Ahead," *Wall Street Journal*, May 19, 2010, http://online.wsj.com/article/ SB10001424052748704513104575255971990854254.html.

15. John Pomfret, "Chinese Firms Bypass Sanctions on Iran, U.S. Says," *Washington Post*, October 18, 2010, www.washingtonpost.com/wp-dyn/ content/article/2010/10/17/AR2010101703723.html.

16. Maseh Zarif, "Nuclear, Technology Sources for Iran's Nuclear Program," July 24, 2009, www.irantracker.org/nuclear-program/technology-sources-irans-nuclear-program#china.

17. Ibid.

18. International Assessment and Strategy Center, www.strategycenter.net/research/pubID.117/pub_detail.asp.

19. Richard Fisher, Jr., "China Shows the Whirlwind: Implications of Hezbollah's Iranian-Chinese Weapons," International Assessment and Strategy Center, July 26, 2006, www.strategycenter.net/research/pubID.117/pub_detail.asp.

20. Maseh Zarif, "Nuclear, Technology Sources for Iran's Nuclear Program."

21. Gal Luft, "China's Energy Policy & Its Effects on U.S. Interests," *Progressive Conservative* 7, no. 172 (August 10, 2005), www.proconservative.net/PCVol7Is172LuftChinasEnergyPolicy.shtml.

22. "Group: China Supplies Most Small Arms to Sudan," *USA Today*, March 13, 2008, www.usatoday.com/news/world/2008-03-13-china-sudan_N.htm.

23. Eric Beinhocker, Diana Farrell, and Adil Zainulbhai, "Tracking the Growth of India's Middle Class," *McKinsey Quarterly*, August, 2007, www.mckinsey quarterly.com/Tracking_the_growth_of_Indias_middle_class_2032.

24. "Automobile Industry in India," http://business.mapsofindia.com/automobile/.

25. "Country Analysis Briefs, India," U.S. Energy Information Administration, August 2010, www.eia.doe.gov/cabs/India/Full.html.

26. "Indian Oil Leader Producer ONGC Will Invest $19 Billion in Venezuelan Mega Oil Project," February 22, 2010, www.neftegaz.ru/en/news/view/93036.

27. "Oil Diplomacy," *Security Research Review*, June 29, 2006, www.bharat-rakshak.com/SRR/2006/01/65-Oil%20Diplomacy.html.

28. Press Trust of India, "US Names Indian Oil, Gas Firms Doing Business with Iran," *Hindustan Times*, May 14, 2010, www.hindustantimes.com/US-names-Indian-oil-gas-firms-doing-business-with-Iran/Article1-543661.aspx.

Chapter 20

1. "History of Africa," www.historyworld.net/wrldhis/PlainTextHistories.asp?historyid=ab24. Accessed November 2010.

2. "Rural poverty in Africa," www.ruralpovertyportal.org/web/guest/region/home/tags/africa. Accessed November 2010.

3. Kallie Szczepanski, "Causes of Poverty in Africa," Politics, News & Issues, www.helium.com/items/1003065-causes-of-poverty-in-africa.

4. Thomas Nchinda, "Malaria: A Reemerging Disease in Africa," *Emerging Infectious Diseases* 4, no. 3 (July–September 1998), www.cdc.gov/ncidod/eid/vol4no3/nchinda.htm.

5. Ebiegberi Alagoa, *The Early History of the Niger Delta* (Hamburg: Buske, 1988), 21.

6. Andrew Walker, "The Day Oil Was Discovered in Nigeria," BBC News, March 17, 2009, http://news.bbc.co.uk/2/hi/africa/7840310.stm.

7. Jedrzej Frynas, *Oil in Nigeria: Conflict and Litigation between Oil Companies and Village Communities* (Hamburg: Lit Verlag Münster, 1993), 9.

8. Chika Amanze-Nwachuku and Ejiofor Alike, "Nigeria: FG to Raise Crude Oil Export in December, October 24, 2010, http://allafrica.com/stories/201010251002.html.

9. Paulin Djite, *The Sociolinguistics of Development in Africa* (Great Britain: MPG Books, 2008), 124.

10. "World Proved Reserves of Oil and Gas," U.S. Energy Information Administration, March 3, 2009, www.eia.doe.gov/emeu/international/reserves.html.

11. "New Oil Discoveries in Libya," Afrol News, October 24, 2010, www.afrol.com/articles/17178.

12. Ibid.

13. "Chinese Diplomat Says China-Africa Relations Based on Equality and Mutual Trust," Ghana Business News, October 1, 2010, www.ghanabusinessnews.com/2010/10/01/chinese-diplomat-says-china-africa-relations-based-on-equality-and-mutual-trust/.

14. "Timeline: China's Oil and Mineral Deals in Africa," Reuters, October 22, 2010, http://uk.reuters.com/article/idUKTOE69L03U20101022.

15. Cindy Hurst, "China's Oil Rush in Africa," Institute for the Analysis of Global Security," July 2006, http://docs.google.com/viewer?a=v&q=cache:EHaKVKUVSnUJ:fmso.leavenworth.army.mil/documents/chinainafrica.pdf1china1gets1oil1from1africa&hl=en&gl=us&pid=bl&srcid=ADGEESiiW9zIaowO4cwQa82glNKlI35ML0ZC3wdLQuroR5dOmyK-X-G_98EC_mdlRbnkeAnCGIEzMYYru80ke-lbHnWXlT-GBQFUfYLgGyEXDcjj6f56msjHExR60RLt8QOQeORZGl8V&sig=AHIEtbRX_Jay_uRqmHMHEqTqzPdVKqNEMw.

16. Vince Wade, "The Pentagon Fears Peak Oil and War with China," April 23, 2010, www.vincewadeusa.com/?p=85.

17. Ibid.

18. "Russia, China Sign Strategic Deals as Major Oil Pipeline Set to Pump Oil," September 27, 2010, www.rttnews.com/ArticleView.aspx?Id=1429172.

19. Dr. Cyril Widdershoven, "West African Oil: Hope or Hype?," Institute for the Analysis of Global Security, www.iags.org/africa.html.

20. Barry Schutz, Paul Wihbey, and Robert Heiler, "African Oil: A Priority for US National Security and African Development," African Oil Policy Initiative Group, http://docs.google.com/viewer?a=v&q=cache:MBpEGbfzOp4J:www.iasps.org/strategic/africawhitepaper.pdf1Africa1declared1a1US1national1strategic1interest.&hl=en&gl=us&pid=bl&srcid=ADGEESgM

4yp3e5z2Ab4kKLU2IaAL6HIeYKkTwcsjkrnZVESPdi7fJ1LG64h-0fY04w
iGsRUyZkNr0xW2QQ6IcWsEOV8vYrlnnpTSMnaZhNVgSSFYNyo4
8Dre8c06L13L-lXSaI5Gldd&sig=AHIEtbQEQjKhUUqmD2Iwe0LzzRaw0
oMcIg.

21. Anthony Cordesman and Khalid Al-Rodhan, *The Changing Dynamics of Energy in the Middle East*, vol. 2 (Westport, CT: Praeger International, 2006), 34.

22. "Fact Sheet: United States Africa Command," U.S. Africa Command Public Affairs Office, www.africom.mil/getArticle.asp?art=1644.

23. Jennifer Giroux and Caroline Hilpert, "Relationship between Energy Infrastructure Attacks and Crude Oil Prices," *Journal of Energy Security*, October 27, 2009, www.ensec.org/index.php?option=com_content&view=article&id=216:the-relation ship-between-energy-infrastructure-attacks-and-crude-oil-prices&catid=100:issuec ontent&Itemid=352.

24. Will Conors, "The Nigerian Rebel Who 'Taxes' Your Gasoline," *Time*, May 28, 2008, www.time.com/time/world/article/0,8599,1809979,00. html#ixzz13UL13YbC.

25. "Transport in South Asia, India Transport Sector," World Bank, http://web.worldbank.org/WBSITE/EXTERNAL/COUNTRIES/ SOUTHASIAEXT/EXTSARREGTOPTRANSPORT/0,,contentMDK :20703625~menuPK:868822~pagePK:34004173~piPK:34003707~theSit ePK:579598,00.html.

26. Deloitte, "Transportation Sector per Budget Expectations," World Bank, February 2010, http://docs.google.com/viewer?a=v&q=cache:ym2kjoL2 jSMJ:https://www.deloitte.com/assets/Dcom-India/Local%2520Assets/ Documents/23022010_Transport_GP.pdf1growth1of1india%27s1transportati on1sector12010&hl=en&gl=us&pid=bl&srcid=ADGEESiAvFUhJ_dvGDu1y Fm2OFQU9aLYuRAbdrzCC8Q9H7BMzGhed2y7HiCFRqJYr2DsKOvl_ QymHeYuHkLNHAyEKQQbDYHO78ytfYCSD7ZBlS9_p3GuSNOvH2G oLlKnNWMAOtdA75M1&sig=AHIEtbQjrSOFo28i6-6wyK1Ipl-cyO0vLA.

27. South Asia Monitor, "Africa: Moving beyond Oil," Center for Strategic and International Studies, June 10, 2008, http://docs.google.com/viewer?a=v&q =cache:sHVcN00gjAMJ:csis.org/files/media/csis/pubs/sam119.pdf+india+oi l+deals+in+africa&hl=en&gl=us&pid=bl&srcid=ADGEESgWWhNVT1vAP DL5Ef-7gPOQjxkihtZtfXKtvULFzQiQeV1Kn_ekQlcW72OKYPFClTEiK zOA9CItiQILeQwybqoUwBpfbhvHDgWzWodnwCODrxZMWIOA-d1kS n4wPJlY_5h3Oaa6&sig=AHIEtbTfKZjTEFJZFlp5cVot6q0pncMuaA.

28. Rakteem Katakey and John Duce, "India Loses to China in Africa-to-Kazakhstan-to-Venezuela Oil," Bloomberg, June 29, 2010, www.bloomberg.com/news/2010-06-30/india-losing-to-china-in-africa-to-kazakhstan-to-venezuela-oil-purchases.html.

Chapter 21

1. "Denmark—Wind Power Hub: Profile of the Danish Wind Industry," Danish Wind Industry Association, 2008, 6, www.windpower.org/down load/378/profilbrochure_2008.pdf.

2. Ibid., 4.

3. Ibid., 7.

4. Clemens Höges, "An Ecotopia for Climate Protection: Samsø Island Is Face of Danish Green Revolution," Spiegel Online International, October 22, 2009, www.spiegel.de/international/europe/0,1518,656325,00.html.

5. Peter Jacob Jørgensen, "Samsø: A Renewable Energy Island, 10 Years of Development and Evaluation," PlanEnergi, 21, www.onlinepdf.dk/Books/00964366-c939-4a83-84af-80187135f6af/24054/2chronoOnline PDF.pdf.

6. "No. 1 in Modern Energy," www.vestas.com/en/about-vestas/strategy.aspx. Accessed October 2010.

7. Jørgensen, "Samsø: A Renewable Energy Island," 22.

8. Ibid.

9. Höges, "An Ecotopia for Climate Protection."

10. Jørgensen, "Samsø: A Renewable Energy Island," 22.

11. "Samsø's Renewable Energy," Samsø Flashmap, www.energiakademiet.dk/flashmap_uk.asp. Accessed October 2010.

12. "100% Renewable Energy," Samsø Energy Academy, 2. www.energiakade miet.dk/images/imageupload/file/UK/RE-island/handout_generel.pdf.

13. "H2 Logic Delivers H2 Truck and Refueling Unit for Samsø Energy Academy," May 11, 2007, www.h2logic.com/com/shownews.asp?lang=en&id=141.

14. "Greenland's First Hydrogen Plant for Renewable Energy Storage Inaugurated," March 22, 2010, www.h2logic.com/com/shownews.asp?lang=en&id=307.

15. Jørgensen, "Samsø: A Renewable Energy Island," 26.

16. David Biello, "100 Percent Renewable? One Danish Island Experiments with Clean Power," Scientific American, January 19, 2010, www.scientificamerican.com/article.cfm?id=Samsø-attempts-100-percent-renewable-power&page=4.

17. Giles Brown, "Samsø Island, Denmark," Absolute Magazine, www.abso lutemagazine.co.za/index.php/Samsø-island.html. Accessed November 2010.

18. Ibid.

19. Jørgensen, "Samsø: A Renewable Energy Island," 26.

20. "Global Wind Energy Capacity Seen Tripling by 2014," Reuters, March 8, 2006, www.windaction.org/news/1903.

21. "20% Wind Energy by 2030: Increasing Wind Energy's Contribution to U.S. Electricity Supply," U.S. Department of Energy, Energy Efficiency and Renewable Energy, July 2008, www1.eere.energy.gov/windandhydro/pdfs/41869.pdf.

22. "U.S. Electric Net Summer Capacity," U.S. Energy Information Administration, www.eia.doe.gov/cneaf/solar.renewables/page/table4.html. Accessed November 2010.

23. "Market Update: Record 2009 Leads to Slow Start in 2010," American Wind Energy Association, May 2010, www.awea.org/documents/factsheets/Market_Update_Factsheet.pdf.

24. Brad Kenney, "Wind Turbine Supply Chain Spinning Up," *IndustryWeek*, Dec. 15, 2008, www.industryweek.com/articles/wind_turbine_supply_chain_spinning_up_18042.aspx?SectionID=2.

25. "Market Update: Record 2009 Leads to Slow Start in 2010," American Wind Energy Association, May 2010, www.awea.org/documents/factsheets/Market_Update_Factsheet.pdf.

26. "Recovery Act Fourth Quarterly Report—Provisions of the Recovery Act that Leverage Other Spending," Council of Economic Advisers, July 15, 2010, www.whitehouse.gov/administration/eop/cea/factsheets-reports/economic-impact-arra-4th-quarterly-report/section-5.

27. "20% Wind Energy by 2030."

28. "Western Wind Turns Down US $228 Million Offer for Wind Project," May 22, 2008, www.renewableenergyworld.com/rea/news/article/2008/05/western-wind-turns-down-us-228-million-offer-for-wind-project-52548.

29. Ibid.

30. "Major US Wind Power Installer Hails Recovery Act As Driver of Job Creation, Ongoing Domestic Investment," Iberdrola Renewables, October 14, 2010, http://iberdrolarenewables.us/news/rel_10.10.14.pdf.

31. Ibid.

32. "Results Presentation: Nine Months 2010," Iberdrola Renewables, October 18, 2010, www.iberdrolarenovables.es/wcren/gc/en/comunicacion/hechosrelevantes/101018_HR_01_en.pdf.

33. Ibid.

34. Ibid.

35. Ibid.

36. Ibid.

37. "Global Reach across More than 20 Countries," Iberdrola Renewables, www.iberdrolarenovables.es/wcren/corporativa/iberdrola?IDPAG=ENRENDONDEESTAMOS&codCache=12900109795698141. Accessed November 2010.

38. "World Leader in Wind Energy," Iberdrola Renewables, www.iberdrolaren
ovables.es/wcren/corporativa/iberdrola?IDPAG=ENIBERRENOVAB&cod
Cache=1290010961682791. Accessed November 2010.

39. "VESTAS WIND SYSTEMS (VWS.CO): Historical Prices," Yahoo!
Finance, http://finance.yahoo.com/q/hp?s=VWS.CO1Historical1Prices.

40. "REpower Systems AG (RPW.DE): Historical Prices," Yahoo! Finance, http://
finance.yahoo.com/q/hp?s=RPW.DE1Historical1Prices.

Chapter 22

1. Ali Lorden, Drew Anderson, Luke Donahue and Claire Mullen, "Wind
Energy," www.slideshare.net/kkublbeck/wind-power-point-presentation.

2. Ibid.

3. "Illustrated History of Wind Power Development, Part 1—Early History,
Wind Power's Beginnings," www.telosnet.com/wind/early.html.

4. Robert Righter, *Wind Energy in America, A History* (Norman, OK: University
of Oklahoma, 1996), 172.

5. "US Lags Behind China and Europe in Wind Energy Growth," November
2, 2010, www.yourrenewablenews.com/news_item.php?newsID=55987.

6. Ibid., 185.

7. Righter, *Wind Energy in America*, 188.

8. Rocky Mountain Institute, "Option 2. Substituting Biofuels and Materials,"
Winning the Oil Endgame, 2007, www.oilendgame.com/Substituting.html.

9. Ibid.

10. Ibid.

11. "Larderello: History," www.servinghistory.com/topics/Larderello::sub::History.
Accessed November 2010.

12. Ronald DiPippo, *Geothermal Power Plants: Principles, Applications, Case Studies
and Environment*, 2nd ed. (Oxford, UK: Butterworth-Heinemann, Elsevier
Ltd., 2008), 13.

13. "Geothermal Energy Facts, Introductory Level," http://geothermal.marin.
org/pwrheat.html#Q1. Accessed November 2010.

14. Ibid.

15. Karsh Gupta and Sukanta Roy, *Geothermal Energy: An Alternative Energy Source
for the 21st Century*, 1st ed. (Amsterdam, The Netherlands: Elsevier, 2007), 8.

16. "Geothermal Energy Facts, Introductory Level," http://geothermal.marin.
org/pwrheat.html#Q1. Accessed November 2010.

17. Zachary Alden and Katrina Taylor, *Renewal and Alternative Energy Resources:
A Reference Handbook* (Santa Barbara, CA: ABC-CLIO, Inc., 2008), 173.

18. Jason Chavis, "Which Countries Use Solar Electricity," www.ehow.com/facts_5103982_countries-use-solar-electricity.html. Accessed November 2010.

19. Ken Zweibel, James Mason, andVasilis Fthenakis, "A Solar Grand Plan," *Scientific American*, December 16, 2007, posted January 2008, www.scientific american.com/article.cfm?id=a-solar-grand-plan.

20. Amory Lovins, "How America Can Free Itself of Oil Profitably," *Fortune*, September 20, 2004, www.mutualofamerica.com/articles/Fortune/October04/fortune.asp.

21. Tim Webb, "Shell Profits Flow Faster as Oil Prices Rise and New Ventures Deliver," *The Guardian*, October 29, 2010, www.guardian.co.uk/business/2010/oct/29/shell-profits-oil-sands-deepwater.

22. Chris Kahn, "ExxonMobil 3Q Income Increases 55% to $7.35 Billion on Higher Oil Prices," *Los Angeles Times*, October 28, 2010, www.latimes.com/sns-ap-us-earns-exxon-mobil,0,684209.story.

23. "How Can the U.S. Wean Itself Off Oil?," National Journal Energy & Environment Expert Blogs, May 10, 2010, http://energy.nationaljournal.com/2010/05/how-can-the-us-wean-itself-off.php.

24. "Reducing US Oil Consumption," Council on Foreign Relations Expert roundup, June 11, 2010, www.cfr.org/publication/22413/reducing_us_oil_consumption.html.

Chapter 23

1. Chris Isidore, "GM Bankruptcy: End of an Era," CNNMoney, June 2, 2009, http://money.cnn.com/2009/06/01/news/companies/gm_bankruptcy/index.htm.

2. Associated Press, "Chrysler Files for Bankruptcy Protection," April 30, 2009, www.msnbc.msn.com/id/30489906/.

3. Josh Hakala, "Detroit Three's US Market Share at Record Low," February 4, 2009, www.mlive.com/auto/index.ssf/2009/02/detroit_threes_us_market_share.html.

4. Shawn Langlois, "Chrysler Delivers the Bad News to 789 Dealers," May 14, 2009, www.marketwatch.com/story/chrysler-says-789-dealers-to-close-gms-up-next.

5. Langlois, "Chrysler Delivers the Bad News."

6. "Top-Selling Cars in 2009 Yield Some Surprises," *Consumer Reports*, http://editorial.autos.msn.com/article.aspx?cp-documentid=1115992. Accessed November 2010.

7. "World Demand for Battery Materials Forecast to Hit $22.8 Billion by 2012," Freedonia Group, May 6, 2009, http://evworld.com/news.cfm?newsid=20980.

8. "FMC Lithium Joins Alliance to Manufacture Advanced Automobile Batteries in the United States," FMC Lithium, December 19, 2008, www.fmclithium.com/LinkClick.aspx?link=Content%2fDocs%2fNewsReleases%2f20091FMC1Joins1Battery1Alliance_final.pdf&tabid=2674&mid=7499.

9. John O'Dell, "Audi, Sanyo Enter Hybrid Battery Development Deal," May 6, 2008, Edmunds.com, http://blogs.edmunds.com/greencaradvisor/2008/05/audi-sanyo-enter-hybrid-battery-development-deal.html.

10. Ucilia Wang, "Share Kyocera Brings Solar to Prius Rooftops," May 19, 2009, Greentech Media, www.greentechmedia.com/green-light/post/kyocera-solar-on-prius-rooftop-4732/.

11. Daniel Gross, "Hummer vs. Prius," NPRs Moneybox, www.slate.com/id/2096191/. Accessed November 2010.

12. Ibid.

13. Ibid.

14. "Toyota Motor Corp. (TM)," Yahoo! Finance, http://finance.yahoo.com/echarts?s=TM1Interactive#chart2:symbol=tm;range=my;indicator=volume;charttype=line;crosshair=on;ohlcvalues=0;logscale=on;source=undefined.

15. Sam Abuelsamid, "BREAKING: Detroit 2009—GM Building Volt Battery Packs with LG Chem Cells," AutoBlogGreen, January 12, 2009, http://green.autoblog.com/2009/01/12/breaking-detroit-2009-gm-will-build-volt-battery-packs-with-lg/.

16. "Nissan, NEC Investing $115M in Li-Ion Battery Factory," Autopia, May 19, 2008, www.wired.com/autopia/2008/05/nissan-nec-inve/#ixzz10xdDj9b1.

17. Tom Krisher, "GM's Chevy Volt Electric Car Will Cost $41K," The Huffington Post, July 27, 2010, www.huffingtonpost.com/2010/07/27/gms-chevy-volt-electric-c_n_660872.html.

18. "Nissan Leaf Electric Car Calls, Emails If You Forget to Plug It In," USAToday, September 14, 2010, http://content.usatoday.com/communities/driveon/post/2010/09/nissan-leaf-electric-car-calls-emails-if-you-forget-to-plug-it-in/1.

19. HybridCars, "New Ford Explorer Boosts Fuel Economy by 30 Percent—and It's Not a Hybrid," July 21, 2010, www.matternetwork.com/2010/7/new-ford-explorer-boosts-fuel.cfm.

20. Larry West, "The Obama Administration's CAFE Standards: President Obama's CAFE Standards Require New Cars to Average 35.5 mpg by 2016," http://environment.about.com/od/environmentallawpolicy/a/obama-sets-new-fuel-efficiency-standards.htm. Accessed November 2010.

21. West, "The Obama Administration's CAFE Standards."

22. Bill Chameides, "Putting BP's Oil Spill into Context," Duke University, August 6, 2010, www.nicholas.duke.edu/thegreengrok/bpspillstats.

23. Edward Klump, "Spill May Hit Anadarko Hardest as BP's Silent Partner," Bloomberg, May 13, 2010, www.bloomberg.com/apps/news?pid=20601072&sid=aawwCXDN1UsM.

24. "Lithium," U.S. Geological Survey, Mineral Commodity Summaries, January 2008, http://minerals.usgs.gov/minerals/pubs/commodity/lithium/mcs-2008-lithi.pdf.

25. "About Us: Lithium Today," FMC Corp., www.fmclithium.com/Home/AboutFMCLithium.aspx.

26. "World Demand for Battery Materials Forecast to Hit $22.8 Billion by 2012," Freedonia Group, May 6, 2009, http://evworld.com/news.cfm?newsid=20980.

Chapter 24

1. Matthew Emmert, "REITallocate Your Portfolio," The Motley Fool, Investing Commentary, December 22, 2003, www.fool.com/investing/general/2003/12/22/reitallocate-your-portfolio.aspx.

2. "Rockwood Holdings' Lithium Business Awarded $28.4 Million in Stimulus Funds for the Production of Advanced Materials for Lithium Ion Batteries in the U.S.," August 10, 2009, www.istockanalyst.com/article/viewiStockNews/articleid/3405050.

3. Jossie Garthwaite, "Battery Materials Market to Swell, No Thanks to Lead," GigaOM, May 7, 2009, http://gigaom.com/cleantech/battery-materials-market-to-swell-no-thanks-to-lead/.

Index